Our Dearest Son-in-Law

with our love

Marie & Doric —

Gideon Haigh's

Australian Cricket Anecdotes

Melbourne

OXFORD UNIVERSITY PRESS

Oxford   Auckland   New York

Oxford New York
Athens Auckland Bangkok Bombay
Calcutta Cape Town Dar es Salaam Delhi
Florence Hong Kong Istanbul Karachi
Kuala Lumpur Madras Madrid Melbourne
Mexico City Nairobi Paris Singapore
Taipei Tokyo Toronto

and associated companies in
Berlin Ibadan

OXFORD is a trade mark of Oxford University Press

National Library of Australia
Cataloguing-in-Publication data:

Haigh, Gideon.
Gideon Haigh's Australian cricket anecdotes.

Includes index
ISBN 0 19 553936 2.

1. Cricket – Australia – Anecdotes. I. Title. II. Title:
Australian cricket anecdotes

796.3580994

Cover design by Caroline Laird
Cover illustration by John Spooner
Typeset by Scriptorium Desktop Publishing Pty Ltd
Printed by McPhersons Printing Group, Australia
Published by Oxford University Press,
253 Normanby Road, South Melbourne, Australia

CONTENTS

INTRODUCTION

v

CRICKET ANECDOTES

1

SOURCES AND ACKNOWLEDGMENTS

262

INDEX

267

To Caroline, who won't read a word of this

INTRODUCTION

Of all the games in which Australians indulge, none is richer than cricket in lore and literature.

Probably, in fact, a bit too rich. But better that folk should write too much about cricket than too much about war, crime, angst, politics or the Internet.

Within cricket's corpus, the staff of life is the anecdote: the short, telling, enlightening story that, by either novelty, humour or pathos, communicates character and senses of time and place. Any reasonable exposure to the game as player or spectator will create a fund of moments and musings, cuts and glances. Shake any biography, autobiography, tour book or history and anecdotes seem almost literally to tumble forth.

How, then, to research a survey of all that material when everybody who reads what you come up with will have something better?

I collated and culled by a fairly strict definition of what constituted an anecdote. Nothing qualified simply by dint of being well-written (so you won't find, for instance, Arthur Mailey's oft-quoted reminiscence of bowling to Victor Trumper, lovely as it is). I also excluded anything that was, more accurately, a joke (so no variations on the blind umpire telling the bowler who's just bowled his opponent: 'You nearly had him that time').

My preference has also been for the incidents that either verifiably happened, or at the least could possibly have occurred. Embellishment was admissable, but the obviously apocryphal was to be avoided.

To give an example: I read a charming story about the Catholics Jack Fingleton and Leo O'Brien batting together in the Sydney Test of 1933. O'Brien, so the story went, lost a St Christopher's medal he'd been given by Brisbane's Archbishop Duhig, and Fingleton prevailed on members of Douglas Jardine's team to scramble round on their hands and knees to find it.

The problem? Fingo and Mo didn't play together in either of the Sydney Tests that season. Out it went.

Another priority was a point of embarkation. The earliest identifiable reference to cricket in Australia is a paragraph in the *Sydney Gazette* on 8 January 1804, but I've chosen to commence this collection somewhat later: the instance of Australia's first meeting with cricketers from outside, in the inaugural match played by H. H. Stephenson's pioneering Englishmen against XVIII of Victoria on New Year's Day 1862.

The reason is that Australianness in cricket, I think, did not really begin to define itself until it had some opponent from without. Until that time, the bulk of cricketers here felt themselves to be transplanted Britons engaging in their national pastime. Thereafter the idea of getting together and beating someone else took root, and cricket here diverged to take on a character that makes it unique.

In consequence, the orientation in this book is the Test and first-class game. It's there that we find the characters on whom our cricket heritage is based. If a match or an event is referred to outside that arena, it's because it is in some respect evocative or truly singular: like the game played by William Lane's Utopians in Paraguay, Charles Eady's 566, or what may be cricket's longest hit by Brighton's Gordon Robinson (186 yards, 11 yards longer than that acknowledged in *Wisden Cricketers' Almanack* by the Rev. W. Fellowes).

When commissioned to create this anthology, there were two personal priorities. One was to assemble a collection that, by coherence of narrative, gave a sense of the evolution of cricket in Australia: an informal history of the game, if you like, through personalities and their play.

The other was to enjoy myself on the way. Having misspent my youth reading far too much about cricket for my own good, I felt as if I knew most of the stories or variants on them already. I resolved to find at least some yarns that I hadn't heard many times before.

While you can judge my success in the first respect, I can assure you that in the latter I was kept richly entertained. It was the first occasion, for instance, on which I'd made a concerted effort to read the newspaper writings of Tom Horan: the Australian Test captain who wrote for the *Australasian* under the nom de pad of 'Felix'.

His 'Round the Ground' column was a revelation. Horan's technique was to take a walk round the MCG or a suburban oval and write 5000 words or so about whomever he bumped into (interspersed with quotations from his favourite English verse).

On Horan's side was that he seems to have known everyone in cricket's community at the time, and every meeting precipitated a torrent of quite compulsive reminiscence. He also had a genuine sense of the eccentric, like the interview that Hugh Trumble and Jack Blackham granted a deaf and dumb man on the way home from the 1893 Ashes tour, or the way Prince Ranjitsinhji took care of a stricken sparrow during the 1897 Melbourne Test.

It's always absorbing, of course, to discover that things maybe haven't changed as much as imagined. The very First Test at the MCG in March 1877, for instance, throws up instances of intimidatory fast bowling, gamesmanship and dissent. We find that the Englishman Gilbert Jessop put money on himself before his match-winning Ashes century at the Oval in 1902. That Arthur Mailey tampered freely with the ball for his pacemen Gregory and McDonald in the 1920s.

It was with some delight that I read in J. A. H. Catton's *Wickets and Goals* an account of the 1896 Lord's Test implying that Australian captain Harry Trott stayed put when legitimately caught mid-way through a valiant century, and that one Englishman opined 'no one but a ------ Australian would have stood still'. It's no wonder they say that the only time an Australian 'walks' is when he runs out of petrol!

Pranks might be thought a trapping of more recent, less conservative, times, but they are not. In fact, if anything, the reverse is true: that modern cricketers, under their constant media supervision, have less scope for really extravagant horseplay.

When Fred Spofforth decided to slip down a hawser onto the shore as the SS *Assam* went through the Suez Canal en route to England in 1882, his teammates delighted in shaking him off and dumping him in the drink. Imagine the fuss today!

Compare the maximum security conditions under which Australia recently toured the sub-continent for the World Cup with the experience of Jack Ryder getting lost on the Paris Metro as he and his teammates wended their way to the 1921 Ashes series. And would a current Australian captain be permitted, as Lindsay Hassett did in 1953, to debag in the dining room of the Savoy Hotel? Ponder the headlines now: 'Star Mooning Shock Probe: Pics'.

The best anecdotes don't necessarily arise from the greatest deeds, but some feats demanded inclusion: McCabe's three great Test innings, Macartney's pre-lunch frolic, Bradman's 334 and 304, Victoria's 1107, the lethal overs by Gregory at Trent Bridge in 1921 and by O'Reilly at Old Trafford in 1934.

Some matches were also mandatory: the 1882 Oval Test, the 1894 Sydney Test, Tate's match of 1902, the Leeds Tests of 1938 and 1948, the Tied Tests, the 1972 Oval Test, the 1975 World Cup Final. A few more appeared to merit inclusion for their sheer prodigality: like Victoria's record dismissal for 15 against England in 1903–04 (still our lowest first-class total) and Australia's tie with Gloucestershire in 1930 (the first tie in which an Australian team was involved).

A particular pleasure has been unearthing the unacknowledged individualists in Australian cricket: not just the famous (Bradman, Trumper, Lillee, Chappells and Border etc), or even the famously-irreverent (Miller, Barnes, Fleetwood-Smith, Richardson and Walters), but the likes of Alick Bannerman, George Bonnor, Charlie McLeod, Albert Cotter, Ernie McCormick, John Rutherford, Ken Mackay and Wayne Phillips.

The mental images of the pint-sized Bannerman muttering sotto voce racing tips to umpires to gain their confidence, and of Rutherford and Mackay losing their way on their way to the wicket at Lord's in 1956, are delicious.

A sprinkling of the salty Cec Pepper is also included, although he played and umpired most of his cricket in England, for he is representative of that host of exports who kept an identifiable 'Aussie' spirit even in faraway League and County Cricket (Jack Walsh, Bruce Dooland, Bill Alley, Ken Grieves, Jock Livingston, John McMahon et al.). Pepper's advice to a batsman when a black fast bowler was called into the attack — 'Batsman, change of bowler, same action, different colour' — is a reminder, too, that cricket is a pretty PC-free zone.

No apologies, either, for a few of my personal prejudices coming in selections. Quite a high proportion of the cricket stories one sees recycled these days are thinly-disguised drinking jokes, fart jokes etc. I find them tedious. If you want to read about beer drinking records en route to England, or how so-and-so made a century with a skinful, feel free to look elsewhere. Hilarious as they might be to some, you won't find any jolly japes from commentators in here either. I can't abide them.

I did, incidentally, try to exhume a few good stories about one-day international cricket, especially the 1987 World Cup, but to my disappointment found them thin on the ground. Perhaps everything happens too quickly in the abbreviated game.

It's purely suspicion, too, but the more recent the material I examined about Australians in Test matches, the more 'in' it seemed, and the less universal. Perhaps that sense of exclusivity is also inevitable, given the amount of time cricketers now spend in orbits separate from those of their spectators.

Lastly, a warning. Anthologies of this sort should provoke further reading, not act as a substitute for it. I've had a hoot of a time roving back through all the galaxy of biographies and autobiographies spun off by Australian cricketers past and present, the literature of Fingo, Ray Robinson, Tom Horan, Dick Whitington, Johnny Moyes, Richie Benaud, Phil Derriman, Jack McHarg and sundry others. You would, too.

Gideon Haigh
Melbourne 1996

Colour Transmission

The embryonic colonial game was given valuable inspiration and expert tuition when caterers Spiers and Pond sponsored the first tour by an ensemble of English cricketers in 1861–62. One of the members of H. H. Stephenson's XI was Bill Caffyn, whose account of his team's first match against XVIII of Melbourne at the MCG intimates the excitement provoked by the visit, and demonstrates that coloured clothing has a long antiquity.

There was a great stir in the city at an early hour of the morning. People flocked in from the surrounding country in all directions, in coaches, wagons, cars and conveyances of every description. The trains, too, were filled to overflowing. More than 15 000 people were on the ground when the English XI arrived. We lost the toss and H. H. Stephenson, who had been appointed our captain, led us onto the field.

We had all been supplied with very light hats of a helmet shape. Each of us had a coloured sash and a ribbon round his hat — one man's colour being blue, another green, another crimson, and so on. These colours were printed against each of our names on the scorecard, so that any one provided with one of these could at once identify every member of the team. My own colour was dark blue. The National Anthem was played as we entered the field, amidst the silence of the vast concourse of spectators. When the band stopped playing a tremendous burst of cheering rent the air. The weather was so hot as to burn the skin off our faces. I commenced the bowling, but was obliged to come off after a short time owing to my arm being so painful from mosquito bites, which had again troubled me at Melbourne.

Seventy-one Not Out (Caffyn) pp176–7

The First Australians

The first Australian team to tour England was a group of Aborigines collected and chaperoned by a Surrey emigre called Charles Lawrence (who had remained behind after Stephenson's 1861–62 tour). In addition to playing 47 matches, they provided audiences in Victorian England with a multitude of entertainments.

The most impressive activity was a mock battle, involving six or more men. At Nottingham three Aborigines standing some eighty yards apart from three other spearmen were completely hedged in by accurately thrown spears …

Charley Dumas was the star boomerang thrower but he was ably assisted in this by Mullagh. Sundown must have made the voyage chiefly on his expertise in this field ...

Yet it was a hazardous sport for the spectators. A stray dog was almost cut in two at the Oval and Wood saw a brass spur struck off the heel of an incautious spectator who moved across the boomerang's line of flight. There were windy days when this event was cancelled as a safety precaution. However, one windy day in Bootle, Mullagh's boomerang drifted and struck a spectator, slicing his hat and lacerating his face. Modern cricketers might wish for such an armoury with which to silence persistent barrackers ...

Dick-a-Dick was adept at running backwards and he invariably won the race. But his reputation rested upon his remarkable adaptation of a native practice to a European application. His crowd-pleasing act began when he stood in the arena grasping a narrow wooden parrying shield in his left hand ... He held a curved wooden club, a single-combat weapon termed a leowell or langeel in his right hand.

Dick-a-Dick challenged all comers to stand 15 to 20 yards distant and pelt him with cricket balls. He protected his body and head with the shield and his legs with the club, used baseball fashion to deflect the missiles. Pitt-Rivers saw him ward off balls thrown by three men simultaneously and forcefully, and Wood described 'a positive rain of cricket balls'. On one occasion in Australia, sixty balls had been aimed at him. Many witnesses describe such incidents but not a single source records a hit being scored on Dick-a-Dick's body.

Cricket Walkabout (Mulvaney) pp64–6

Timed Out

Dick-a-Dick's idiosyncrasies were also described in detail by Lawrence's sometime assistant William Shepherd, a young member of the Surrey groundstaff.

His favourite was Dick-a-Dick, a true eccentric with an aristocratic ignorance of the value of money. It was his pleasure to waste his substance on riotous living, as exemplified by the hoop-la stall and wheel of fortune at local fairs and bazaars. Whatever money he had earned, he risked every penny of it with a gambler's passion on the prizes that such side-shows dispense.

These were mainly of the china ornament or pot-dog variety and can have been no less hideous than the rest of their kind. Their aesthetic appeal to Dick-a-Dick, however, was strong. The prize that appealed to him most was a Swiss alarm clock. It cost him anything up to 10 times its value to win it and, once won, he carried it under his arm practically every moment of the tour. Shepherd had to wind it up for him each day.

Once Dick-a-Dick introduced drama into the humdrum routine of travel. The eleven were peacefully assembled in the railway station of a West Riding town. Dick-a-Dick broke away from them and bolted. Lawrence, who thought his protege was about to run amok, made a wild but vain effort to grab him. Dick-a-Dick was the best hurdler in the team and the sight of a tall, lean black man determinedly hurling through the streets of Dewsbury must have given the inhabitants a rare treat. It may even have disturbed one or two of the inhabitants out of their native imperturbability inducing at least one to murmur: 'Ee, you don't see so much of that sort of thing nowadays'.

Dick-a-Dick was seen to dash into the hotel and out again, a happy smile on his face and the precious clock — which he had in a moment of aberration left behind — now safely tucked under his arm. The train was late, so Dick-a-Dick caught it and everyone was happy.

Odd Men In (Thomson) pp77–8

THE CAPTAIN'S BURDEN

Lawrence himself later shared these reminiscences of the trip with Felix of the Australasian *(player-writer Tom Horan).*

Johnny Cuzens fell deeply in love with a young English country girl, who was led by Johnny to believe that he owned a big station in Australia. Johnny afterwards said that he saw no harm in what he had stated, because if the girl came to Australia she would be all right, whether Johnny owned a sheep station or not.

Dick-a-Dick's shield manoeuvering was a great success in England. Many an English cricketer had a shot at him from distances ranging from 12 yards to 18 yards but they never once hit him. On one ground a lot of reporters were lying on the ground watching this interesting feature in the day's programme and the cricket balls thrown passed the reporters and went amongst the spectators who amused themselves by throwing the balls back at the reporters, until the latter were obliged to clear out and seek shelter from the attack.

King Cole died in Guy's Hospital from inflammation of the lungs and 'it is a curious thing,' observes the veteran, 'that not one of his comrades ever mentioned his name or made the slightest reference to him after his death'.

'Twopenny was a bit of a bother, and at times he would turn up at the train just at the last moment, with only one leg of his trousers left, and no one ever could find out what became of the other leg.

'The blacks fell in love with England and were sorry to leave it. Johnny Mullagh's splendid jumping powers pleased the English public, and when Johnny Cuzens used to walk under a bar, turn, and bound clean over it, the applause was tremendous.

'That trip,' the veteran adds, 'resulted in a loss of £2000.'

'Round the Ground' by Felix, the *Australasian*, 13 January 1894

The Doctor Calls

Dr W. G. Grace toured Australia for the first time in 1873–74. Though he commanded a fee in keeping with his imperial cricketing stature, he was unimpressed from the first by the rudimentary nature of the Australian game. The team's nightmarish journey from Stawell to Warrnambool was made especially irritating by an intrusive colonial press.

The trip was completed in two stages, and torrential rain made the second of these a nightmare. The thick dust turned to mud and the first 31 miles took five and a half hours. A number of players got off en route to lighten the load because, as the papers reported, 'the four weedy horses were not equal to carry 14 passengers'. The survivors arrived soaking wet at half past eleven at night, after a journey of nineteen hours. WG called it the most unpleasant of all his travelling experiences.

To add insult to injury, a reporter woke the captain after midnight in the hope of obtaining some quotes. Needless to say, the ones he got, he couldn't print.

W. G. Down Under (Smith & Williams) pp16–17

The Umpire Strikes Back

As much as the standard of play varied, the standard of umpiring varied more. W. G. remembered this eccentric brace of decisions from the match at Castlemaine.

When I was batting I hit a ball high in the air toward the boundary. The fieldsman, in bringing off a good catch, fell over the ropes whereupon I appealed to the umpire who at once gave me 'not out' on grounds that the ball was caught out of bounds.

An ordinary boundary hit was regarded as four but a hit over the ropes counted as five, and the scorers naturally wanted to know with how many runs they should credit me. To our surprise the umpires refused to allow us any more than the single which we had run before the ball was caught. As I had a keen suspicion that I ought to have been given out I did not argue out the point, though I was greatly amused by the inconsistency of the umpire, who happened to be our man.

The Australian umpire, not to be outdone, gave an equally ridiculous decision. One of the batsman who had ventured out of his ground, was plainly stumped by Mr Bush, but much to everyone's astonishment was given 'not out'. This was a decision we could scarcely accept, but in response to our request for an explanation the umpire promptly said: 'Ah Mr Bush, I was watching you then, and when you took the ball the tip of your nose was in front of the wicket, and, as you know, rule 35 says that if any part of the wicketkeeper's person be over or before the wicket the striker shall be not out if he is stumped.' Of course we could not dispute the decision after this ingenious explanation; so the batsman went on with his innings.

'W. G.': Cricketing Reminiscences and Personal Recollections (Grace) pp92–3

THE FIRST TEST

Three years later came a weaker English team captained by James Lillywhite which — by agreeing to play a combination of NSW and Victorian players in an eleven-a-side contest — became Australia's first Test opponents. Charles Bannerman — a Woolwich-born batsman of twenty-five coached by Bill Caffyn — scored an unbeaten 126 on the first day to become Australia's first Test centurion. As ever after, he enjoyed his share of good fortune. The Englishmen had just stepped off a steamer after a stint in New Zealand and, as Alfred Shaw remembered, were badly underprepared for the match.

Not one of us was fit to play cricket. We had arranged the match for a date that should have left us plenty of time for rest, but we were delayed on the voyage, and the accommodation on shipboard was so bad that some of us had to sleep on deck. I was simply spun out myself.

Others of our bowlers were also completely knocked up. Armitage, in trying to bowl C. Bannerman, tossed one ball wide over the batsman's head — a delivery which brought forth the remark that the Australians could not reach Armitage's bowling with a clothes prop! The next ball he bowled along the ground. Another delivery went wide over the heads of both batsman and wicketkeeper and was called a wide by the umpire.

Bannerman, whose 165 was the first three-figure innings scored by an Australian batsman against an English team, was missed by Armitage at mid-off before reaching double figures. I was the bowler and the ball lobbed up in the simplest fashion and struck Armitage in the stomach.

Alfred Shaw: Cricketer (Pullin) pp59–60

Bannerman gave no other chance, and drove with ferocity until his innings was brought to an untimely conclusion.

One ball sent down by Hill was sent back with such force that, after hitting Hill on the wrist, the ball travelled to the boundary for four. In two or three minutes there was a huge contused lump on Allan's left wrist.

'Round the Ground' with Felix, the *Australasian*, 14 January 1911

Bannerman's great innings had reached 165 when he was hit by a short-pitched ball from Ulyett. Unfortunately the india-rubber had disappeared from part of his right-hand glove and Bannerman's middle-finger was unpleasantly split to the bone. The England team waited for 10 minutes, as a doctor tended the wound in the pavilion, and then called for another batsman.

This reasonably chivalrous action was not reciprocated in the second innings when Bannerman bravely batted again. Ulyett continued to bowl short and 'Bannerman showed he now had a wholesome dread of that vigorous bowler's bumpy ones and suffered himself to be clean bowled in consequence'.

Summers in Winter (Meredith) p62

HARD LINES

The day after inflicting the first maiming in Test cricket history, Yorkshireman Ulyett perpetrated the first instance of player dissent.

The first case of a batsman disputing an umpiring decision in a Test match arose when Ulyett, who replaced Charlwood, was given out leg before wicket after a breezy ten to make the score 3-98. He shook his head and left little doubt that he had no wish to leave the wicket. He told friends and listeners that, if they would go with him to the wicket with a tape-line, he could prove that his leg could not possibly have been in the way of the Thomson delivery that had caused his downfall.

Test Eleven (Whimpress & Hart) p18

'LET THEM DROWN'

Twenty-two years would elapse before Federation, and the team representing 'Australia' that toured England in 1878 was riven by parochialism, as Fred Spofforth explained.

I doubt if Englishmen will ever understand the spirit of rivalry that runs high between the colonies of Victoria and New South Wales. The spirit is not limited to the field: it extends to politics, to society, to every side of life, indeed, in which the two are brought into contact one with another. Often enough this rivalry went too far; and in the matter of the selection of the first team, the press and the public were widely at variance. One felt Victoria had been slighted, another NSW; and even on the tour itself the players might be seen separating themselves as far as possible from their compatriots of the other colony.

Let me give one example. While we were coasting along New Zealand we were caught by a terrible storm, and being in a very small steamer were in great danger. Charles Bannerman, who was an expert swimmer, was very frightened. He refused to go into his cabin, and said if he got on dry land again he would never leave it as long as he lived.

'Well,' I said. 'Suppose we are wrecked. What would you do?'

'First,' he said. 'I'll save Alick, then Murdoch, then you.'

'Well, but what about the Victorians?' I asked.

'Let 'em drown,' he replied. 'Let them drown. D'you think I'm going to risk my life for them?'

Australian Cricket and Cricketers: A Retrospect New Review Vol 10, 1894 p515

'THE CHAAPS'

The curiosity that awaited the 1878 tourists was not completely satisfied by the Australians' commonplace appearance, as Charles Bannerman recalled.

Charlie smiles as he recalls the incident at Batley when an old fellow came up to him at the door of the hotel and said: 'Be they coom yet?'

'Who?' said Charlie.

'The chaaps.'

'What chaps?'

'The Australians,' retorted the old man.

'We're the Australians,' replied Charlie.

'Coom, that woan't do; ah mean the craacketers — the black fellows.' Charlie chuckled for days over that.

'Round the Ground' by Felix, the Australasian, 11 January 1898

'Ain't I a Demon?'

At Lord's, 27 May 1878, Australia met an elite MCC side. They murdered them. Spofforth and Boyle dismissed the home team for a paltry 33 then, although Gregory's Australians could only muster 41 in reply, were even more destructive a second time.

When he bowled WG in that match he jumped about two feet in the air, and sang out: 'Bowled! Bowled! Bowled!' And at the finish in the dressing-room he said: 'Ain't I a demon? Ain't I a demon?' gesticulating the while in his well-known demoniac style. Whether or not he christened himself the demon, he certainly was a demon bowler.

Felix on Bowling, the Australasian, 2 October 1897

Mid Goes Missing

Spofforth's match analysis of 10–20, including hat-trick, rumbled MCC for 19 second time round. Partly in retaliation after the tourists' nine-wicket win, Grace held Australia's Gloucester-born, Ballarat-bred Billy Midwinter to an agreement that he play for the county in dramatic circumstances during the tourists' match against Middlesex.

On 20 June, 'Mid' sat padded up at Lord's waiting to open the batting with Bannerman. The Coroner, E. M. Grace, and Bush the huge Gloucester wicketkeeper flanked the Champion as he strode into Lord's and literally hijacked 'Mid' from under the nose of Dave Gregory. They talked him into joining them, pads and all, in their waiting cab, which then transported them to the Oval where Grace had been furious to find his team a man short. Thus was effected what 'Cricket' called Midwinter's 'severance from the colonial players'.

John Conway, the Australian manager, organised a group of vigilantes to recapture 'Mid'. David Gregory accompanied the posse, as did Mid's boyhood friend Harry Boyle. They just managed to overtake the renegade at the Oval Gates and, to the delight of the crowd, a furore took place in which, among other epithets, Grace condemned his opponents as 'a damned lot of sneaks'.

W.G. Grace: His Life and Times (Midwinter) p71

'WE CAN'T STAND THIS!'

Australia's cricket reputation was tarnished by an infamous riot at the SCG on 8 February 1879 when Lord Harris's Englishmen were manhandled in a crowd invasion that followed a run-out decision against NSW's Billy Murdoch. One of the invaders was a boy 'Banjo' Paterson.

I was sitting by the picket fence just below where the scoring board is now, and of course we couldn't tell from there whether he was out or not, but we all started to hoot, and a chap near me said: 'Come on boys, we can't stand this!' And he jumped in over the pickets.

His feet had hardly touched the ground when there were a thousand people over the fence, all running for the centre of the ground. The Englishmen thought they were going to be murdered and some of them got round the umpires and the others pulled the stumps out of the ground to defend their lives. I remember seeing a big Yorkshireman named Ulyett waving a stump at the crowd so I sidestepped him. I was only a boy.

When we got to the wicket we didn't know what to do. Everyone was hooting and shouting and arguing and the people from the members' stand were crowding in to help the English. Nobody really interfered with the English players — we just hooted them off the ground — and then it struck us that if we didn't go back to our seats we wouldn't see any more play.

So we all went back and that was the end of the great Lord Harris riot which gave Australia a bad name for years.

Song of the Pen (Paterson) p569

A Long Spell

An Australian team arrived in England at the start of May 1880, captained for the first time by Billy Murdoch, an opening batsman of exemplary technique and a captain softly-spoken but strict.

On one occasion he was captaining an Australian XI in a match against one of our leading counties, and when play had been in progress a little while, Murdoch, as captain, thought a change of bowling desirable. Addressing one of the bowlers, whose name I need not disclose — he said: 'Mr So-and-so will go on now'.

The bowler objected; said he hadn't been given a fair chance. Murdoch said nothing, and let him keep on bowling unchanged until the end of the day's play. It is needless to say the bowler never again complained he was not given a fair chance.

'W. G.': *Cricketing Reminiscences and Personal Recollections* (Grace) p366–7

Thrown To The Wolves

When the Australians played Scarborough at the North Marine Road Ground in August 1880, defeat by a local XVIII was the least of their worries. Their main concern was local fast bowler Joseph Frank. This is how the correspondent of the Sydney Mail *saw it.*

A gentleman player named Frank was put on, and directly the ball was delivered, it was the general opinion not only by the Australians but by the on-lookers and even by some of the XVIII that it was a throw.

He was put on at the latter end of the Australians' innings. No objection was taken then, as it was thought advisable to wait until the innings had terminated when the captain of the XVIII (Charlwood) was told about it and asked by Murdoch not to put him on in the next innings.

On Charlwood saying that he would bowl him, Frank himself was asked not to go on, and told that if he did an objection might be made and a scene occur. No notice was taken of the objection as the second innings commenced. Frank again went on.

Bannerman, after getting a severe blow on the leg, objected and drew away from the wicket. Murdoch then went out and asked Charlwood to discontinue the unfair proceeding, as it was not fair cricket besides being very dangerous. An appeal was made to the umpire, whose reply was that 'some of the balls were unfair, but it was very difficult to catch them'.

During this time frequent cries were heard of 'another Lord Harris affair' and 'go on' & c. After the reply of the umpire the game proceeded and Frank was allowed to continue and throw in such a way that not only did he get the batsmen out but hit them so frequently and with such force that it caused them to limp about the ground in the most painful manner. This seemed to cause the spectators no end of amusement, judging from the laughter that burst out after each knock.

The 2nd Australian XI's Tour (James) p111

SOVEREIGN STATUS

Spofforth took 12 wickets for 98 in the game but, in the second innings, was hit on the bottom joint of the third finger of his right hand by Frank. When the fracture deprived Australia of Spofforth's services during the first Test match on English soil at the Oval the following month, and allowed W. G. Grace to make a mighty 152 out of 420 on his Test debut, a weighty responsibility fell on Murdoch's shoulders.

Ever optimistic, he bet Grace he would top his huge score. Will was caught for 0 and his side fell for 149 after rain. Told to follow-on they lost 8–187. Defeat by an innings seemed near until the young skipper led one of the great comebacks of Test history. In the first Test on English soil the colonials won the crowd's respect when the last two tailenders stayed with their captain while 140 were added …

When Notts all-rounder William Barnes bowled Moule at 327, Murdoch, 153 not out, had moved one run ahead of the world's champion. This strained credulity even more than it did the muscles of England's bowlers but, as proof, the sovereign he won from Grace hung on Will's watchchain until his dying day.

On Top Down Under (Robinson) p15

A SUEZ CRISIS

When Murdoch's Australians undertook their journey to England in 1882, they shared the SS Assam with the noted dramatist Haddon Chambers and involved him in some of their more dangerous pranks.

One day in the Suez Canal when the vessel was moored to the bank for hours … Mr Chambers and Mr Spofforth went ashore by means of 'swarming' along the steel hawser employed for the purpose of mooring. On the return journey of the adventurous pair, their companions who were lining the side of the vessel wickedly began shaking the heavy hawser and produced so violent a vibration that Spofforth, who was lightly clad, let go his hold and swam to the ship.

But Haddon Chambers ... scorned so base a surrender to the enemy! Hanging onto the steel cable with all his strength and at the risk of severe injury to his hands, he successfully resisted all efforts to dislodge him and finally arrived on board again by this means amid the loud cheering and louder laughter of his fellow-passengers.

Cricket of Today Vol 1 pp38–9

THE AUSTRALIAN HERCULES

George Bonnor of Bathurst was a prodigious hitter, a superb fielder and a supremely confident individual always ready to back his own ability. Manager Charles Beal recalled this vignette of the journey.

Soon after leaving Malta an army officer was talking about throwing a cricket ball 100 yards. Bonnor in his usual grandiloquent way said: '100 yards! 100 yards! Why, I could jerk it!' And so he could.

After a little talk it culminated in a wager of 100 pounds that Bonnor would not throw 115 yards or more with the first throw on the first day he landed on English shores. I remember Bonnor coming down on board ship and telling me he had made the wager. Old Caleb Peacock of Adelaide was stakeholder.

We got to Plymouth and it was a fine day, so Bonnor, Murdoch, Garrett and myself got off the boat, the others going on. We tried to get a 5¼ oz cricket ball but could not get any lighter than 5½ oz. Before finally agreeing to the ground we went to several places including the Hoe, but that was down hill — all right for Bonnor, but it did not suit the other party. Then we went to the racecourse but that was slippery and of course did not suit us, so at last we arrived at the Barracks at Plymouth. As it was gravel and there was no wind we agreed the conditions were fair.

We got hold of the quartermaster — he happened to have a record in the army, he had thrown 107 yards I think. When we told him what the event was he became deeply interested. Bonnor got the quartermaster to put a pile of newspapers down as a target about two feet high at a distance of 120 yards to aim at. He was going to throw without taking his waistcoat off. It showed the cool belief he had in his powers. I insisted on his stripping to his singlet, though he didn't like the idea. He was toying with the ball. 'A man of my inches not being able to throw this little thing 115 yards!'

Well he threw 119 yards 7 inches and won the wager. I remember the quartermaster begged for the ball and we gave it to him. He never dreamt that anyone could throw the ball so far and wanted the ball as a souvenir. You ought to have seen 'Bon', the centre of admiration at Plymouth barracks after that throw. It was a pretty good throw, seeing that Bonnor had been six weeks on board ship.

Charles Beal in The Referee, November 1914

JOOMBO

The Australians were made to feel warmly welcome when they played before a packed house of 20 000 garrulous Yorkshiremen at Sheffield's Bramall Lane ground in June 1882, recorded player-writer Tom Horan.

Every dress was sombre and funereal, but the spectators were far from funereal in their manner. They were indeed, the gayest, jolliest crowd I have ever seen. We had not been out in the field five minutes when each of us had a nickname, and by it we were known right through.

Bonnor's tall form attracted special notice and he was called 'Jumbo', or 'Joombo', as the Yorkshiremen sound it. Everywhere Bonnor went in the field, the cry 'Joombo' would ring in his ears. Alick Bannerman was nicknamed 'Little Joombo' and 'Quicklime', Horan 'Features', Palmer 'Ribs', Blackham 'Darkie', Spofforth 'Spider' and so on.

Australasian, 5 August 1882

TOILET TRAINING

Yorkshire left-armer Ted Peate, who took 7–51 in that match, was an especially dreaded opponent of early Australian sides. George Giffen related a story of the extreme measures to which he drove one (anonymous) teammate.

The Yorkshireman beat him with a clinking leg-break in the first innings. The batsman, determined that such a disaster should not happen again took a bat into his room at the hotel and began to make strokes at imaginary balls. At one he would play back and mutter: 'That's the way to play you Peate'. Then he would play forward, remarking: 'Not this time Peate, my boy'. At last he ventured on a big hit at a leg-ball and swinging round with a 'How do like that Peate?' sent the toilet seat which he had forgotten all about in fragments on the floor. Later on in the day, confident that he would make a score, he faced the real Peate — and was bowled first ball.

Cricket of Today Vol 2 pp46–7

THE DAY OF THE DEMON

Spofforth took 157 wickets at 13 apiece on the 1882 tour, although he remained throughout subject to a curious superstition.

There is truth in the statement of the Hon R. H. Lyttelton that Spoff used to study night after night how to get English batsmen out. He and W. L. Murdoch as a rule chummed together, and Billy used to say: 'Spoff has got a new plan today and says it will come all right provided he does not meet a cross-eyed woman.'

If the plan didn't come off, Spoff would say: 'Well you know, I met a cross-eyed woman and what could I do after that?'

'About Bowling' by Felix, the *Australasian*, 2 October 1897

Spofforth evidently saw no cross-eyed women on 29 August 1882, when England needed but 85 in its second innings to win the Oval Test, for he bowled Australia to an astonishing victory: its first in Tests on English soil.

It sometimes take an irritant to put that extra yard into a bowler's speed. Spofforth and the rest of the Australians were upset at the manner of young Sammy Jones' dismissal towards the end of Australia's second innings. Jones having completed a run left his crease to pat down a bump on the pitch and W. G. Grace having taken the return, strode across and removed the bails. Upon appeal, umpire Thoms had no alternative but to give the batsman out 'run out'. Perhaps Jones ought not to have left his crease, particularly with W. G. in the vicinity; but it was now 'in the book' and the Australians were fuming.

'This thing can be done!' growled Spofforth ...

As W. G. and Ulyett built England's score (to 2 for 51), Spofforth switched to the pavilion end in place of Garrett, the fast medium bowler. The breakthrough came when Ulyett touched a fast one to Blackham, who held the catch low down ...

W. G. went next, caught at mid-off from Harry Boyle's bowling for 32, and a tremor of alarm swept through the English camp, With six wickets remaining, England needed 32 more as the Hon Alfred Lyttelton went out to join A. P. Lucas, the hour-hand of the clock dropping slowly to five, the ground becoming firmer for the bowlers.

Spofforth and Boyle tightened their grip on the situation. There was an eerie silence about the ground; England's waiting batsmen sat huddled, shivering in the cold air. As maiden over followed maiden over the tinkle of hansom cabs could be heard outside.

Stalemate was broken by a tactical ploy. Though England required only 20 to win, the Australians gave a single with a misfield so that the bowlers could have fresh targets. Soon the dividend was delivered. Spofforth charged in on his angled run, eight menacing strides. Over went the arm and the ball crashed through Lyttelton's guard and took the top of the middle stump.

A. G. Steel entered and had to pass Spofforth's baleful glare as he walked to the crease. Within minutes he was on his way back, caught-and-bowled halfway down the pitch by Spofforth, whose slower ball had claimed another victim. His next ball bowled local hero Maurice Read. England 70 for 7: 15 needed.

A yorker first ball to Bill Barnes almost did its work, but the batsman chopped down on it. Then three byes drew everyone's attention to the boldness and magnificent teamwork of Spofforth and his wicketkeeper Blackham throughout the innings in having no long-stop despite the delicate position.

The bearded Boyle, medium pace round the wicket, turning from leg, continued to bowl tightly and Murdoch stuck to this attack, praying that the burly Barnes would not unleash one or two tension-breaking hoicks through mid-wicket. Then Spofforth broke through again, forcing Lucas to play on to one which turned a lot from outside the off. When Barnes was caught at point off his glove off Boyle, England were 75 for nine.

Edmund Peate, Yorkshire's slow left-arm bowler, came in, his captain A. N. Hornby having told him to leave everything to C. T. Studd, one of England's finest batsmen held back to number ten and now stranded at the non-striker's end.

Peate was expected to exercise caution. He had an almighty swing and got two runs. One ball left, then Spofforth could do his worst on Studd. But it never got to that. Peate irresistibly thrashed again … missed … and it was all over. England all out 77. Boyle 3–19 off 20 four-ball overs. Spofforth 7–44 off 28, 14–90 in the match. Australia winners by seven runs.

For the first time Australia had humbled the full might of England and small boys were forgiven for believing that F. R. Spofforth had horns in his head.

The Fast Men (Frith) pp54–6

The Birth Of The Ashes

George Giffen and Tom Horan provided their recollections of the aftermath of the famous victory that inspired the Ashes.

While the tension had lasted the spectators rarely gave vent to their feelings, and when Peate, the last man, was out they seemed unable for a moment or two to realise that England had actually been beaten. The great crowd was like a man stunned.

But they soon forgot their sorrow to applaud us, and we had cheer after cheer from those healthy British lungs. A small coterie of Australians who sat in the pavilion were wild with joy; and I remember Mrs Beal, the mother of our manager, running down the steps and I being the first who came along, although I had contributed as little as any to the victory, found her arms around my neck and a motherly kiss implanted upon my brow.

With Bat and Ball (Giffen) p105–6

The vast concourse rushed the ground and Boyle was fairly carried into the pavilion by several enthusiastic Australians. I am only speaking the truth when I say that we were as heartily cheered as if we had won the match on an Australian ground before an Australian public.

Cries of 'Massie', 'Murdoch', 'Spofforth', 'Boyle' and 'Blackham' were heard again and again from the tremendous throng in front of the pavilion and each of these players had to go out and bow his acknowledgements amidst multitudinous shouts of 'Bravo, Australia', 'Well done boys', and so on.

Never shall I forget the wild excitement of the moment; how, for instance, our manager Charlie Beal in rushing out to congratulate us sent the man at the gate head over heels; how one man dropped dead in the pavilion from over-excitement; how not only the Australians but Englishmen rushed into our dressing room and shook hands with us all around; how they mingled champagne, seltzer, and lemons, and passed the drink round like a loving cup; and how true sportsman that he is

A. N. Hornby came up to Murdoch and said: 'Well old fellow, it would have been the proudest moment of my life to have won, but I cannot help congratulating you sincerely on the splendid uphill game you played and your well-merited success.'

Then when we were leaving the ground how the crowd around our conveyances cheered us to the echo; how they almost took Spofforth off his legs in their desire to pat him on the back and shake hands with him for his really superb efforts with the ball; how the ladies from the windows in Kennington Road waved their handkerchiefs to us, and how all the way back to the Tavistock [Hotel], the passers-by looked at us as if we really had done something to make us famous for all time.

Australasian, 21 October 1882

THE PRINCE OF WICKETKEEPERS

In spartan gauntlets, on often unreliable pitches, John McCarthy Blackham kept wicket for Australia for seventeen years after the first Test.

Once when W. H. Cooper was bowling on the Melbourne ground (in January 1882), George Ulyett jumped out to hit him. He missed the ball and, never looking back, walked straight to the pavilion. On entering the gate, someone said: 'Why didn't you try to get back?; he might have missed it.'

That 'he' was Jack Blackham.

Happy Jack's reply was simply: 'Oi never knowed him to miss one.' Rather a compliment to our prince of wicketkeepers, wasn't it?

'Round the Ground' by Felix, the Australasian, 16 January 1909

Cooper had his own story of Blackham's irreproachable standards of sportsmanship, recalling this incident involving Dr W. G. Grace at Lord's in 1884.

WG stepped out to a ball from me and apparently WG was 6 inches out or probably more. He missed the ball and Blackham had the bails off like a shot. WG waited for the appeal but none was made.

On crossing I asked Blackham why WG was not out. He said: 'I did not appeal'. To the question why, he said: 'I was in such hurry to get WG out that I took the ball a couple of inches in front of the wicket'. I wonder how many wicketkeepers would have left that matter to the umpire?

Cooper to Les Hill 30 July 1935, published in Wisden Cricket Monthly, June 1983 p45

BLACK KID GLOVES

Losing 2–1 in the 1884–85 rubber, Australia was represented by the first West Indian Test cricketer: Sam Morris, a Tasmanian of Caribbean ancestry. Alfred Shaw recalled the response of the visitors to the first coloured cricketer they had seen.

One of our opponents was a 'gentleman of colour' named 'Sammy' Morris, a real good fellow and an excellent cricketer, professional at the time for the Richmond Club. He wore a white shirt, with sleeves reaching down to just above the wrist.

He was fielding 'out in the country' when Johnny Briggs came in to bat, and on the little Lancastrian seeing him, he exclaimed in astonishment: 'Well I'm blest, if there isn't a fellow fielding out there in black kid gloves.'

Alfred Shaw: Cricketer (Pullin) pp86–7

SPECTACLES

Although Australia's batting was in a parlous state at the time, it did uncover successors to Spofforth and Boyle in Charles 'Terror' Turner and J. J. Ferris. When England toured Australia in 1886–87, Turner inflicted on its captain Arthur Shrewsbury the indignity of two ducks in the same match.

A local wag sought an introduction to him and gravely stated he had a memento which he begged him to accept. It consisted of a very diminutive pair of specs, and the presenter intimated that they were presented to keep Arthur in mind of his two ducks in the match with New South Wales the previous week, and of his inability to play Turner's bowling. Shrewsbury took the specs, so as not to spoil the fun. He had been 'b Turner 0' in each innings in the match in question.

Alfred Shaw: Cricketer (Pullin) p99

TOBACCO SPONSORSHIP

When a planned Third Test on that trip did not eventuate, a famous contest between Anglo-Australian combinations of Non-Smokers and Smokers was arranged at the East Melbourne ground in March 1887.

Boyle led the Smokers onto the field 'each blowing a cloud from a cigar of colonial manufacture; but immediately the business of the day commenced butts were thrown away.'

Age, 18 March 1887

Non-Smokers registered a world record score of 803 (Shrewsbury 236), and Smoking Englishman Bill Scotton was given out 'handled the ball'. Alfred Shaw explains this remarkable dismissal.

The last ball of the match was bowled to Scotton and he, playing it gently toward point, ran after it and secured it as a memento of what was in every respect an extraordinary match. The fielding side, the Non-Smokers, who were equally desirous of securing the ball, were quite sold by Scotton's action. They appealed to the umpire as to what should be done. As 'over' had not been called, and as the ball was in play when Scotton seized it, there was no alternative but to rule Scotton out for handling the ball.

Scotton did not mind that in the least. He had secured the memento and he let everyone know he intended to stick to it.

Alfred Shaw: Cricketer (Pullin) pp97–8

BURN OUT

Blackham partly contributed to his own burden when he led Australia to England in 1890 by perpetrating one of our most eccentric selections when, in order to defuse colonial feeling about the rival claims of NSW's Sid Deane and Victoria's John Harry to the reserve keeper's berth, he ignored both in favour of Tasmanian Kenny Burn. It was not until the SS Liguria moored in Adelaide before setting off to England in April 1890 that Blackham learned something was amiss.

Monday morning saw most of the team about town together, and then it was discovered that Kenny Burn had, to use his own words, 'never kept wickets in his life'. This caused considerable amusement at the expense of the crack wicketkeeper [Blackham], who had solved the Deane–Harry puzzle by suggesting the inclusion of the crack Tasmanian. The mistake was the result of a curious misconception. Blackham had seen in print that 'Burn' had stumped men in Tasmania, but that Burn was Kenny's brother and quite an inferior player.

However, the team was consoled by the reflection that the Tasmanian has the reputation of being a fine batsman, a fair bowler and a good field. Extraordinarily heavy work will fall on Blackham's shoulders, or should I say his hands, but like the keen cricketer he is, he looks forward cheerfully to the task.

'Round the Ground' by Felix, the *Australasian*, 26 April 1890

DOCTOR'S WAITING ROOM

The 1890 Australians were beaten 2–1 by W. G. Grace's Englishmen, despite the manful bowling of Turner and Ferris. As the former noted, England's captain was a hard man to remove from the crease even when he was out.

Playing for Gloucestershire against the Australians at Bristol, in 1890, he [Grace] went in first and, after the usual preliminaries took strike to J. J. Ferris, who opened the bowling. To the first delivery he played forward and just touched the ball, giving Trumble at slip a chance which he accepted.

Dr Grace, knowing he was out, immediately commenced to pat the pitch where the ball lodged, evidently to convey the idea that he was waiting for the ball to be returned to the bowler and for the over to be continued; but as this was not done he stood and enquired what was the matter, whereupon he was told he was out. With an apparent air of surprise he exclaimed: 'What! How's that, Umpire?'

'You're out,' the umpire replied.

Dr Grace laughingly retorted: 'I did not carry the bluff far enough.'

Besides enjoying the reputation of being the finest cricketer that ever played the game, Dr Grace was one of the keenest and knew every move on the board.

The Quest for Bowlers (Turner) pp46–7

LITTLE ALICK

Alick Bannerman was an indispensable member of early Australian XIs, noted for his gravity and inexhaustibly patient batting.

He was always very keen and hardworking; in fact his keenness often developed into outright seriousness. I remember once we had an erratic, lightsome player on our side who, to beguile the tedium of waiting between overs, sang snatches of music hall ditties. Alick stood it for a while, then went up to our merry friend and — with the seriousness of a judge sentencing a murderer to death — made this speech: 'Do you know, my friend, you are playing cricket? If you want to play cricket, play it; and if you want to sing, go and sing, but for heaven's sake don't sing comic songs in the slips!'

With Bat and Ball (Giffen) pp146–7

It is said that in order to get into the good graces of an umpire, Alick Bannerman gave him a tip for the races prior to the commencements of a match. 'May Queen is a good thing in the handicap,' he said. 'Give 'em out when they're out, you know, son.'

The Game's the Thing (Noble) p241

Perhaps Alick had learned a few lessons in hard ball from his brother Charles. Certainly when they batted together — as in one Australia–The Rest match — it was every man for himself.

After some confusion between wickets, the two brothers found themselves at one end of the pitch while the ball was already on its way to the other end. One of them had to be run out and Charles was in no doubt who it would be. He said to Alick: 'You're better out than me.' And, stepping inside the crease, gave his brother a shove out.

True to the Blue (Derriman) p22

Playing The Angora

Bannerman was also a fine mid-off fielder. An instance of his skill was recalled by Tom Horan from a game against Yorkshire at Harrogate.

Peate kept dodging a yard or so out of his crease and back again, 'playing the Angora' as George Bonnor in his refined way termed it. Alick noticed this, but did not pretend to throw at the wickets, until presently Peate advanced about an extra foot. Then, with surprising dash and rapidity of action, Alick picked up and, letting fly at the stumps, knocked the middle peg out before the astonished Peate could get back.

Never before have I seen a batsman more utterly crestfallen than Peate seemed as he walked to the pavilion amidst the assembled thousands. The only persons who did not laugh were Peate himself and little Alick, whose dander was up to such an extent that his moustache bristled as he said: 'Play the Angora with me, will you?'

'About Fielding' by Felix, the Australasian, 16 October 1897

21

ANGUISH

Bannerman's highest test score was 91 against England at Sydney in 1891–92: an effort taking seven and a half hours, during which he scored from only five of the 204 balls bowled to him by William Attewell, but which underwrote an Australian victory.

I shall never forget the sight of the field round him as he stonewalled. There was WG at point, almost on the point of his bat; Lohmann a couple of yards away at slip; Peel at silly point; Stoddart only a dozen yards away at mid-off; and Briggs at silly mid-on. One gentleman remarked that it reminded him of the famous painting 'Anguish' in which a bevy of crows are swarming round a dead lamb over which the mother is watching. A barracker called out: 'Look out Alick, or WG will have his hand in your pocket!'

But Alick stonewalled on, imperturbably blocking the straight ones, sardonically smiling at the off-theory and judiciously tapping a rare loose one to leg. Suddenly he swished at an off ball, and cut it past WG's ear to the boundary, and then what a yell rent the air!

He was eventually caught by WG off Briggs, who had simply tossed balls down slowly with as much twizzle on them as possible, in the hope that he might lead Alick into an indiscretion. But the Englishmen had to wait seven and a half hours for that indiscretion! Truly patience is a virtue.

With Bat and Ball (Giffen) p126

THOUGHTS FOR YOUR PENNY

Australia won that 1891–92 series, thanks in no small measure to Blackham winning a critical toss at Melbourne ... though not without heavy scrutiny from his English rival Dr Grace.

The Australian used a fearfully battered, favourite penny, which he had carried for many years. It was apparently so hard to distinguish one side from the other that Grace tossed it up two or three times to see whether it was loaded to come down on a particular side. After careful investigation he seemed satisfied enough to lead his men into the field.

W. G. Down Under (Smith & Williams) p113

Hot To Trott

Melbourne postman Harry Trott was confident of getting to the UK in 1893.

HT is asked what chance he has of getting into the team for England and he replies: 'Well, that 196 against East Melbourne got me as far as Albany; the 63 in the first innings against NSW got me to Colombo; the 70 not out in the second innings carried me as far as Suez; and being put on to bowl first against SA placed me in the Mediterranean; once there, nothing can keep me back, you know, so I am safe in England.'

'Round the Ground' by Felix, the Australasian, 14 January 1893

Got A Match?

Arctic conditions when the 1893 Australians played XVIII of Blackpool inspired the mercurial Queensland bowler Arthur Coningham to an ingenious solution, related by his contemporary Charlie Turner.

Arthur Coningham was fielding in the country. It was a cold, raw day and the Australians were fielding in their sweaters. The batting not being too brilliant or lively, the outfields had little to do and the idea evidently struck Coningham that he would like to get warm. So he gathered some bits of sticks and grass, piled them up, and then asked one of the spectators for a match. Having obtained this, he set fire to the little pile of grass and commenced to warm his hands. It amused a section of the spectators who applauded him, and one wag suggested that he go inside and get a couple of hot potatoes to put in his pockets.

The Quest for Bowlers (Turner) p46

Quiet Achievement

The Australians left England on the SS Germanic at the end of their tour and headed for a tour of North America, where cricket was played with vigour and interest. While going from Detroit to Vancouver, Trumble and Blackham stopped in Winnipeg and gave an interview.

They stopped at Winnipeg for two or three days, and in their hotel had quite a long interview with a deaf-and-dumb cricketer. The latter was an enthusiast and when he found that Blackham was Blackham and Trumble Trumble his joy was great.

With pencil and paper questions and answers were kept up for a long time, much to the entertainment of several gentlemen present and finally Messrs Blackham and Trumble said Good-bye after the strangest and most silent cricket interview ever experienced by them.

'Round the Ground' by Felix, the *Australasian*, 13 January 1894

THE VILLARRICA ASHES

Another Australian tour occurred in 1893: almost 500 Australians led by William Lane left for Paraguay with the aim of creating a socialist utopia based on equality and temperance. One of the few distractions from their enterprise was a cricket match the pilgrims played against British residents at Villarrica.

It was the first cricket match ever played in Paraguay, and the results were telegraphed to Asuncion after every innings. Frank Birks and John Black rode from Loma Rugua to Villarrica but missed the first innings in which the English XI had made 63 to the Australians' 56.

Birks and Black joined the other Australians from Las Ovejas at the best hotel in Villarrica, where they all sat down to an eleven-course dinner with the Englishmen. 'After dinner,' wrote Birks, 'we had songs and boxes of cigars which are very cheap, and as we New Australians couldn't get drunk on wine we tried ginger ale and iced lemonade leaving the wine to the Englishmen, who were not slow in putting it away.'

Perhaps benefiting by this abstinence, the Australians scored 71 to the English team's 63 in the second innings, thus winning the match by one run.

On their way back to New Australia the cricketers found the Tebicuary swollen so much by rain that they hired a boatman to tow their horses across. They lost their way in the dark, ended up at Ajos, and then had to hire a guide to take them along a bridle path through the monte to Las Ovejas.

The forest at night seemed like fairyland to Frank Birks. 'If you can fancy riding through miles of foliage just like that in the summer houses at the Botanical Gardens you will have a faint idea of it,' he wrote. 'But it was far better than any summer house ... ' Next morning the cricketers were back amongst the cares and complaints of Loma Rugua.

A Peculiar People (Souter) pp105–6

PEELED

The First Test of the 1894–95 series at the SCG is one of cricket's most celebrated contests. Australia, led by John Blackham, set a new Test record with 586, Syd Gregory making 201 on the SCG pitch tended by his father Ned. Having enforced the follow-on, Australia was set 177 to win and finished the fifth day 2–113. But as Sydney slept, the elements took a hand.

The Australian cricketers went down to breakfast at the Baden Baden Hotel, Coogee with great anticipation. 'It's all right boys. The weather is beautiful!' roared Ernie Jones, who was first out of bed that morning.

Giffen was confident too as he looked through the window at the bright blue sky — until he bumped into his skipper. Blackham, who had worried about the weather throughout the previous day, had a face 'long as a coffee-pot', and forecast bad things as they took off for the SCG, the carriage leaving deep furrows in the soft ground. It had rained heavily during the night. The uncovered pitch was saturated, transformed into a batsman's nightmare.

Some of Stoddart's men, feeling the match was lost, had got drunk on the Wednesday night, and it now fell to the captain to get the booziest of them all, Bobby Peel, sobered up for action. He was put under a cold shower and told of the duty which lay before him now that a blazing sun on the wet pitch had given England an unexpected opportunity to fight back for a victory which had seemed utterly impossible for the previous few days. Peel, as oblivious as any to the night's rainfall at first thought someone had watered the pitch. As it gradually dawned on his befuddled brain that England were back in with a chance, he is supposed to have said to his skipper: 'Give me the ball, Mr Stoddart, and I'll get t'boogers out before loonch!"

Stoddy's Mission (Frith) pp95–7

Which he did. Peel took 6–67 and Johnny Briggs 3–25 as Australia's last eight wickets fell for 36 runs. 'Observer' of the Australasian *describes the closing scenes as England won by 10 runs, one of only two occasions in Test cricket history where a team has won after following on.*

The crowd were all on their feet, yet the silence, except for the roar when a wicket fell, was the tragic stillness of death, and for an hour people suffered, in silence, that unpleasant sinking about the waistband which is a manifestation of anxiety, and almost painful while it lasts. Blackham walked up and down the balcony like a caged lion, muttering 'Cruel luck

— cruel luck', and George Giffen, half-dressed, stood with a singlet in one hand and a shirt in the other, blankly watching the procession … In short, the team were thoroughly cut up seeing the victory thus snatched away … 'The rain beat us,' said some of them. 'No! the sun beat us,' said Blackham. Those who bet were heavy losers, a well-known Sydney jockey dropping £100, while another was fool enough to lay £40 to £5 on the Australians on Thursday morning. He was an admirable judge of horses but a poor judge of cricket.

Australasian, 21 December 1894

Bring Him On Both Ends

The loss was rough justice for George Giffen, whose all-round contribution to the match was unprecedented: 161 and 41, 8–239 from 118 overs and two catches. Not surprisingly, when he was given the captaincy at the MCG, he retained a faith in his own faculties.

The first time he had the say in a Test, he bowled 78.2 overs in England's 333 at Melbourne — 23 more overs than anyone else. Other players at last persuaded … Hugh Trumble to ask George to take himself off. Giffen: 'Yes, I think I'll go on the other end.'

Telling the story against himself years later, Trumble grinned: 'He did — and finished with six wickets.'

On Top Down Under (Robinson) p46

Nothing Doing, Cricket Mad, Stoddart Out

A dramatic five-match series decided only in the final game, the 1894–95 series was followed with unprecedented fanaticism on both sides of the globe.

At peak times during the Test series business stood still — even at the Ballarat Stock Exchange where victory and defeat sent a London-born sharebroker soaring off into Rule Britannia in a 'tenor voice of high register', soon to be challenged by some Australian brokers who raised the Southern Cross to flap alongside the British flag and lustily sang The Men of Australia.

Then a Cornishman leapt onto a chair and hollered: 'Look here you! It's all very well you talking about Hingland and Horstralia, but where would you be without Cornwall, eh?' And they all burst into God Save The Queen.

Communications between the Melbourne Exchange and Ballarat were limited one afternoon to a wire which read: 'Nothing doing; cricket mad; Stoddart out.'

To be there was everything for there was no TV substitute, or even action close-ups in the newspapers. A Captain Lee, in command of *Arawatta*, even delayed her sailing from the Port of Melbourne during the Second Test match so that he could witness more of the cricket in person. Hunger for news of the Tests even spread to the maritime species. When the mail steamer *Arcadia* berthed at Adelaide, passengers raced to the Oval to watch the stirring Third Test, with many of the crew making do with updates as various launches came to and fro. When *Arcadia* sailed on the Saturday evening with Australia well-placed, she passed sister ship *Himalaya* out of Melbourne and flying the signal: 'How's The Cricket?' The score was flown in reply.

Stoddy's Mission (Frith) p58

WRONG TICKET!

Stewards for the Members' Enclosure at the Melbourne Cricket Ground had also acquired new levels of efficiency, as Tom Horan discovered.

The fact is I pulled out the wrong ticket, but the same colour as MCC, just to see if the old man is awake. Awake! Rather! He scarcely saw half an inch of colour when he yelled out: 'Wrong ticket!' and I must confess that I was sold. The old man beat me hollow; he is fairly lynx-eyed.

'Round the Ground' with Felix, the *Australasian*, 11 January 1896

A LUCKY BLACK CAT

Harry Trott's 1896 Australians lost the First Test at Lord's, though not before a stirring fightback. Bowled out for 53, they trailed by 239 on first innings and at once were 2–3 in their second dig. But Trott joined Syd Gregory at 3–62, and they set a Test partnership record at the time for any wicket of 231 that had the blessing of a pavilion feline.

The wicket was still a joy to batsmen, and if the Australians believed in mascots they surely were heartened by the black cat which ran about in front of the picturesque ivy-clad tennis court that used to be where the Mound Stand now rears itself in huge proportions — a gaunt tribute to the growing popularity of cricket …

Time after time little Gregory sent the ball betwen the covers to where that cat had been taking a sun-bath inside the boundary. I hope that he, as a foe to superstitious fetish, had no designs on that black cat. Gregory's drives to the off almost printed a pattern on the grass, so beautiful and frequent were they …

Gregory and Trott did great deeds, but I shall always believe that Trott was caught in the slips by Hayward when 61. At that time the Press Box at Lord's was beneath the old grandstand scoring board, and the view was broadside, so that one could see the slip fielders at each end. It appeared as if Tom Hayward had made a clean catch — although the ball was near the ground.

He tossed the ball into the air, but Trott stood still, and on appeal one of the umpires gave him not out as he was entitled to do … During luncheon I ventured to ask Hayward if the catch was above suspicion and for my pains I got this reply: 'Do you think I should have tossed the ball up if I had any doubt about it?'

William Gunn, who happened to be fielding close to the wicket, was equally sure that Trott must be out, and another cricketer, whose name I shall suppress went so far as to say that 'no one but a ------ Australian would have stood still.'

Wickets and Goals (Catton) pp80–1

LOCAL RAIN

England was only 80 ahead of Trott's Australians with only five second innings wickets in hand as the penultimate day of the 1896 Oval Test ended, and even WG had virtually capitulated. But dark deeds were afoot, as Joe Darling recalled.

As soon as stumps were drawn the late Dr Grace came into our dressing room and said: 'Well Trott, you are going to beat us, as now the weather is settled there will be a good wicket tomorrow.'

During the night it remained lovely and fine and we went down to the Oval very sanguine of winning … One can well imagine our surprise when we found that there had been a 'local rain' of about 22 yards long and 6 feet wide, just where the wicket was.

At first we did not realise what had happened, until we started to bowl on the wicket ... England set us 113 runs to win and we made only 44. The wicket was absolutely at its worst in our second innings, and this in spite of the fact that it had not seen any rain since 3pm on the Monday.

Test Tussles On and Off the Field (Darling) p32

A RUM RUN OUT

Darling began the 1897–98 series against Andrew Stoddart's tourists at the SCG with the first Test century by a left-hander, although equal discussion centred on the run out while batting with him of Charlie McLeod. 'Lightning' McLeod was deaf as a stump and, bowled by a no-ball from Tom Richardson, had strayed from his ground and been run out by English keeper Bill Storer. Prince Ranjitsinhji recalled the perplexity of the tourists when sharp criticism followed.

The incident began by Richardson bowling him off a no-ball; the full-pitch, after hitting the wicket, travelled to short slip; the batsman, meanwhile, not hearing the call of the umpire, left his wicket and was walking away to the pavilion. The ball, being smartly fielded by slip, was thrown to the wicketkeeper, who, seeing the batsman out of his ground, pulled up the stumps and appealed for a run-out, the umpire answering the appeal against the batsman.

This incident gave rise to a lot of excitement, argument, and talk all round the ground, but, as usual, the majority of critics harped in a point that had no bearing on the question. The great point was: was the ball dead or not at the time the man was out of his ground, and the stump pulled up? If dead, the man was not out; if otherwise, the decision of the umpire was the right one.

In this case, the ball was in play the whole time, therefore the decision given was the only possible one.

The England team came in for much abuse, owing to what the public considered its unfair play and unsportsmanlike conduct in taking advantage of a batsman's mistake. It is needless to say that such criticisms came from persons who might do well to study the game more closely. Our opponents, the players, upheld our action.

With Stoddart's Team in Australia (Ranjitsinhji) pp116–7

Joe Darling made two more centuries that series, including 178 at the Adelaide Oval which finally convinced a stubborn Scottish father John that cricket was a worthwhile career for his son.

Joe was a great cricketer at school — he made 252 for his college on Adelaide Oval — but his father, a prominent South Australian politician and in business a keen wheat-buyer, apprenticed him to a farmer in the dry northern areas of South Australia.

Joe, however, after about two years of farming, rebelled, returned to Adelaide and started a cricket depot, much to parental disgust. Joe's cricket prowess put him into the SA XI against Stoddart's last team and he thumped their bowling mercilessly, making a century in one innings.

Gradually, the old man relented and he much astonished the family by happening down to cricket matches when the lad was batting. By and by there came a reconciliation. On top of a big score the Hon John D walked into his son's dressing-room: 'Joe ma boy, I think you're best at cricket. Here's your gold watch and a cheque on ye representing one poun' per run of your score today.'

Joe was speechless. That year the old man followed his offspring to Melbourne, and when he got there said: 'I don't keer about beezness so much noo', and went from there to Sydney. And now the Hon John — who five years ago had never seen a cricket match — is always there provided that Joe is there too, and the score of 178 against England on Friday week brought a cheque for £78.

The old man only makes it £1 a run over the hundred now — 'One has to be canny wi' Joe, who bats better when the siller is up.'

Bulletin, 29 January 1898

'Cut Out All This Rubbish'

Four years Darling's junior at Prince Alfred College, twenty-year-old Clem Hill also made a remarkable impact on that series with an innings of 188 in five hours out of 323 in the Fourth Test at the MCG. As he explained, Hill owed a considerable debt to Hugh Trumble who joined him at 6–58 and added 165.

It looked as if we would be all out before lunch for less than 100 when in walked, or rather stalked, Hughie Trumble.

I strolled across to meet him to give a tip or two about the wicket, when he started on me with: 'Now cut out all this rubbish. You leave that ball outside the stump alone. Do you hear me?'

The records tell you that I made 188 and Hughie got 46. They never tell you the real story. Hughie Trumble made every run I got that day.

The Golden Age of Cricket (Trumble) p62

Heat And Dust

The Tests in Melbourne were played in a devouring heat, so great that birds literally tumbled from the sky, allowing Prince Ranjitsinhji to prove himself a true humanitarian.

While Ranji is sitting in the private balcony watching the intercolonial, an unfledged minah tumbles from the roof into the balcony, and Ranji picks up the callow nestling, puts a finger into its mouth and wishes to have it placed again on the roof.

He asks an enthusiastic boy cricketer named Dougall of Boundary Road to climb up the post and put the bird back, but the post is so hot in the terrible heat that young Dougall cannot undertake the climb. The prince, however, was not satisfied until the little squeaker was restored to its nest above.

'Round the Ground' by Felix, the *Australasian*, 11 January 1898

The Adelaide Test was also played in enervating weather culminating in a dust storm so thick that it blotted the town from view. Penrith apiarist/off-spinner Bill Howell, who bowled 94 overs in his first Test, showed a novel approach to slaking a cricketing thirst.

Most first-class cricketers, when they are thirsty, have a drink brought out to them, but when Howell felt the need for refreshment, he simply bent down to an Oval hosepipe and quenched his thirst. The effect was immediate, and his next over was a maiden.

Adelaide Oval Test Cricket 1884–1984 (Whimpress & Hart) p23

Jonah

The fastest bowler in Darling's armoury was the moustachioed Broken Hill miner Ernie Jones, tirelessly aggressive but a playful character behind his menacing mien.

It was Jones who in the England v Australia match at Lord's in 1896 bowled the first ball — a very fast and short one — through W. G. Grace's beard for four byes, the champion walking up the wicket and saying: 'What the h--- are you doing Jonah?'

To which Jones replied: 'Sorry Doctor, she slipped!'

My Cricketing Life (Warner) p106

On an occasion when Australia was playing against Gloucestershire and Charlie Townsend came in to bat, I commented that he was the thinnest man I had ever seen, being well over six feet tall and fine as a match. When Townsend was taking strike to Jones the latter came up to me and said: 'Joe I do not like bowling at this man.' And when asked why not, Jones replied: 'I am frightened that if I hit him, the ball will go right through him.'

Test Tussles On and Off the Field (Darling) p38

It was Ernie's practice to carry a stick and, when overtaking his teammates, the nearest to Ernie would get a smart smack on the rear that was not too gentle. In due course Joe got one and laughed with the rest of them, but next day in Sydney he visited one of the tobacconists' shops and from a wide assortment of sticks selected a light malacca cane.

After dinner that night, like the others, Joe sat out under the Norfolk pines in front of the hotel until he saw Ernie, with a couple of his mates, get up and stick in hand saunter off for the evening stroll.

This was the signal for Joe and his companions to make a move. Joe of course was MC and when he caught up with Ernie that gentleman was the recipient of such a beauty in the right place that it proved an antidote to Ernie's affectionate but peculiar way of passing the time of day with his cricketing friends.

Not Test Cricket (Monfries) pp69–70

Jones survived and prospered. Even thirty years after his last Test match, he was a popular figure at the wharves, one side only of his head having turned grey, welcoming English sides to Australia with stentorian cries of: 'You haven't got a chance!' This was the man who, when asked by King Edward VII if he had attended St Peter's College Adelaide, replied: 'Yes I drive the dust cart there every week.'

The Fast Men (Frith) p60

The Coming Of Trumper

The twenty-one-year-old Victor Trumper made 135 not out as Australia seized the 1899 Lord's Test, then became the first Australian triple-centurion in England at Hove in a manner so easeful that even his captain was overwhelmed.

When he made 300 (not out) against Sussex in 1899, I asked Joe Darling who was 70 (not out) when the innings was closed: 'What do you think of the boy?'

'What do I think of him?' he replied. 'I thought I could bat.'

The Game's the Thing (Noble) p177

Dear Rubbish ...

Away from home for almost eight months, much of the Australians' time was consumed letter writing. Frank Iredale, though, took too long one day in a Cambridge hotel and his teammates started teasing him.

Many furtive calls were made for him to hurry up, when Alf Johns, our second keeper, yelled at him, 'Come on, Nossy, never mind writing to rubbish!'

Iredale heatedly replied: 'It has nothing to do with you, Alf Johns, if I do call my wife a pet name.'

The Game's the Thing (Noble) p241

Rising Sons

Test debutants Reg Duff (104) and Warwick Armstrong (45 not out), held back to make best use of a rain-affected MCG wicket in the Second Test of 1901–02, added 120 for the last wicket with the heartfelt moral support of their fathers.

The veteran South Melbourne player George Major is seated under the elm and tells me that Warwick Armstrong's father was in the MCC reserve. Sitting next to him was a stoutish man, who said: 'I do hope my boy makes a hundred'.

Mr Armstrong said: 'Who's your boy?'

And his friend replied: 'Duff.'

Strange that two fathers, utterly unknown to one another, should sit side by side in the pavilion and talk in this strain while their sons were batting.

'Round the Ground' with Felix, the *Australasian*, 12 January 1902

PLEASE EXPLAIN

Clem Hill made 99 himself at the MCG but looked like atoning for that oversight as he confidently approached a Third Test century before his Adelaide home crowd.

Nobody thought he would commit a further indiscretion but, with his score on 98 he tried to bring up his century with a big hit off Braund. He lifted the ball long and high, but saw it fall straight into the hands of Tyldesley who was standing on the asphalt bicycle track which then ran round the Oval.

On many grounds, the stroke would have brought Hill a certain five runs and achieved his century. The crowd yelled 'Not out!' but the local rules did not favour the batsman, and the protests only faded when MacLaren explained the situation to the crowd.

Adelaide Oval Test Cricket 1884–1984 (Whimpress & Hart) p29

It also required explanation to the Fourth Test crowd at the SCG when debutant Albert Hopkins was caught at the wicket for 43 off Len Braund by Arthur Lilley. England's keeper recalled that he had his opposite number to thank.

I caught the ball and also knocked the bails off, and when they saw Mr Hopkins leaving the wickets they immediately commenced to hurl uncomplimentary epithets at my offending head. They are very keen, and it was obvious that he was not stumped; but they failed to observe that he was given out by Argill, and were under the impression that the decision had been given by Crockett for stumping. J. J. Kelly the Australian wicketkeeper thereupon went to the crowd and explained to them that Mr Hopkins had been caught at the wicket, and that the decision was a perfectly correct one. They at once altered their demeanour and commenced shouting: 'Good old Lilley!'

Twenty-Four Years of Cricket (Lilley) pp177–8

Tasmanian Charles Eady, who represented Australia in the last Test of the 1901–02 series, set an Australian record unlikely to be surpassed at the end of that season: his club cricket score of 566 for Break O'Day has been surpassed only once anywhere in non-first-class cricket since. Time had lapsed after three consecutive weekends in Break O'Day's game against Wellington, in which the team had reached 6–652 and Eady 419 not out, and Rick Finlay records how the record hunt was renewed.

Who actually reopened the issue of the Break O'Day v Wellington match is not clear, but those who wanted it continued had on their side the original condition that each side was to complete an innings — and Break O'Day had not finished theirs yet.

There can be no doubt that those people were actually motivated by the desire to see Eady extend his score to even more massive proportions and perhaps to have a tilt at the world senior record: A. E. Stoddart's 485 made at Hampstead in 1886. One thing was certain and it is testimony to the eloquence of their opponents that they were persuaded to continue.

So on April 5 the teams arrived once more at the Domain Ground for Day 4 of this 'contest'. Wellington did well under the circumstances to round up eight of the original team, not forgetting that [Kenneth] Burn was still too ill to take part. Ward, a country lad, and Donoghue were also absent but, contrary to what has been insinuated in the past, their places in the field were taken by adequate substitutes: the energetic Morrison, 15-year-old Keith Eltham (a future Tasmanian player) and Duthoit, an amateur photographer of indeterminate age who by an incredible quirk had been at the match in England in which Stoddart had made his 485 — the record that Eady was about to eclipse. It must be said, therefore, that Eady at no time was opposed by fewer than 11 opponents …

A large crowd by Hobart standards gathered to view history being made, and Eady did not let them down. He was much more belligerent on this day, taking the number of fives hit from seven to 13 and being finally dismissed for 566 stumped in attemping his 14th. In all his innings occupied 477 minutes and contained in addition to his 13 hits over the boundary, 68 fours, 16 threes and 38 twos. He was ninth out at 908 and the innings, mercifully for Wellington, closed three runs later.

Wisden Cricket Monthly, January 1987 p32

Old Sol

Australia's 1902 tour was bedevilled from its beginning by weather that saw virtually every member of the team laid low at some stage. Team members thought longingly of the sun at home.

Reggie Duff found a picture of 'Old Sol' and pasted it inside his hat. Someone saw him staring into it and asked: 'What are you looking at Reg?'

'I'm having a look at the sun,' he said. 'I have not seen it for a month.'

Sydney Sun, 28 May 1930

The Evil Weed

At the peak of the team's flu epidemic, when Bill Howell, Joe Darling and Monty Noble were lying sick in Manchester, they became victims of incorrigible prankster Hugh Trumble. Noble tells the story.

Majors Wardill and Morcombe (team managers), after listening to the subtle suggestion of the arch leg-puller Trumble, decided to visit us, as we thought sympathetically, but, as we learned afterwards, for the purpose of smoking us out.

With pipes at full blast, the Victorian contingent first visited Darling and puffed great clouds of smoke all round him. Knowing that he was a non-smoker, the enjoyment of the South Australian's discomfiture was all the more keen.

After revelling in their self-imposed entertainment at his expense they sailed gaily into my room, ordered whisky and soda for four and repeated the smoke nuisance but, being a smoker I rather enjoyed their visit.

During their occupation of my room I noticed that Trumble temporarily left on some pretence, but returned a few minutes later and helped in the fumigation process. When the atmosphere was so thick you could almost cut it, Hughie suddenly said: 'It's no use, Ben' — this to Major Wardill — 'we can't smoke him out. Let's give Bill Howell a doing.' So they left me with the smoke and what remained of the whisky.

Now Howell detested tobacco smoke; but it so happened he had great faith in the efficacy of sulphur fumes as a cure for influenza, and, prior to retiring for the night, usually sat over a burning mass of it, inhaling the fumes as though they were the sweet scent of the burning grass-tree.

During his absence from my room Hughie had not been idle. He went to Bill, informed him of the intended visit and its object and suggested he immediately get the sulphur going. At the same time he took the precaution to place the key of the door of Howell's room on the outside. When he had given Bill sufficient time to fill the room, he suggested that the party should then visit Howell, and so, in high glee, they proceeded on their journey.

Opening the door in response to a call of 'come in', they confidently walked into the trap, Hughie bringing up the rear. Bill, lamb-like, welcomed them, and, before they could speak, Trumble locked the door from outside. For five minutes the air was filled with short-sharp cries, much coughing and spluttering and almost vicious hammering at the door. When it was eventually opened they came out with a rush, gasping for breath, with eyes watering rivers of tears, vowing vengeance on their late colleague, who by this time had retired from the field of action and was not seen again until the following morning.

The Game's the Thing (Noble) pp233–5

Is Vic Aboard?

Notwithstanding the cold and wet wickets, Victor Trumper scored 2570 runs and eleven hundreds — both records — and became the one team member his captain considered indispensable.

In those days there were no motor coaches in England, and the team would be conveyed from its hotel to the cricket ground by a four-horse-drawn brake, and the story goes that before the brake moved off, Joe Darling would call out: 'Is Vic aboard?' It was only then that the coachman would be given the order to drive off.

Test Tussles On and Off the Field (Darling) p27

Keep Victor Quiet

Trumper, with partner Reg Duff, opened the Australian innings in the Fourth Test at Old Trafford with a stand of 135 in an hour and a quarter and proceeded to the first Test century before lunch on the first day, despite the Machiavellian planning of England's captain Archie MacLaren.

MacLaren often reconstructed Victor's innings for me in our many talks together, a match-winning achievement if ever there was one. When MacLaren won the toss (in a three-day match remember) the wicket was soft after rain — no 'covering' in those olden times. My plan, narrated MacLaren, was to keep Victor quiet for two hours.

Lockwood was unable to bowl more than a few overs before lunch, because the ground was so damp that he could scarcely find a foothold. So, MacLaren commanded his other bowlers, F. S. Jackson, Tate, Braund and Rhodes, to keep Victor quiet until lunch, whatever else you do. Thus one of cricket's subtlest skippers with his tactics put into force by experienced and skilful masters of spin and length, sought to reduce Trumper to inactivity.

The field was set to stop the fours, on a turf which robbed strokes of much power. 'In the second over,' said MacLaren, 'Victor drove Jackson over the sightboard into the practice ground — and I couldn't ruddy well set one of my long fields in the practice ground, could I?'

Neville Cardus in Cricket: The Great Ones p39

WE'VE GOT YOU THIS TIME

When he could get a foothold after lunch, Lockwood did run amok and took 6–48 in Australia's eventual 299. And England — 0–36 at lunch on the final day with MacLaren and Palairet batting smoothly — needed only 87 to win. When England's captain expressed his confidence in the match's fate during the break, Darling had a ready reply.

We were sitting at lunch when Archie came into the room. 'Ah Joe,' he said to Darling, our skipper, 'I think we've got you this time.'

'Oh have you?' said Joe; 'why we've only got to get two or three of you out and the rest will shiver with fright.'

The Game's the Thing (Noble) p225

A BALLY FLUKE

England got as far as 3–92 before, to Trumble and left-armer Jack Saunders, they began to stumble. Six wickets fell for 24, including a catch from Trumble by Clem Hill of England's wicketkeeper Arthur Lilley that bordered on the miraculous.

I raced after the ball with not the slightest idea of bringing off a catch, but with the full determination of saving a fourer. Almost on the boundary, after having run the best part of 25 yards, I threw everything to chance and made a dive at the leather. No one was more surprised than myself to find the ball stuck in my hand. As a matter of fact for the fraction of a second I could hardly believe I had brought off the catch ... but the next instant I was the proudest man on the ground ... Poor Dick Lilley passing me on the way to the pavilion said: 'Oh Clem, what a bally fluke!'

For appearance sake I had to reply: 'Never on your life!' But the England wicketkeeper knew the truth and spoke it.

Maurice Tate (Brodribb) p8

FRED FAILS

Fred Tate, as last man at 9–116, french-cut Saunders for four. But two deliveries later, the Australians won the match, retained the Ashes and put Fred Tate into history forever.

Now Saunders ran in with his left arm extended parallel to his body, signifying to his comrades 'a fast one coming'. It pitched straight and came on through as poor Fred Tate played forward, too late. The ball, keeping low sent the leg stump somersaulting. The massed crowd sat horrified and silent at the spectacle and even the Australians were momentarily bemused, not fully aware they had won by just three runs. Suddenly they leapt in the air excitedly, shaking hands as they sprinted for their dressing-room.

Victor Trumper and the 1902 Australians (Brown) p131

No Test for more than half a century generated as much tension as the closing stages of Tate's match.

The wife of Major Wardill, who had been doing some crochet work prior to the last stages of the match, involuntarily ran one of the needles through the palm of her hand. My mother [Hugh Trumble's wife], who was sitting with Mrs Wardill, often told me that the strain and suspense were impossible to express adequately in words.

The Golden Age of Cricket (Trumble) p32

Jessop's Wager

MacLaren finally got the better of the Australians at the Oval, where Gilbert Jessop played his momentous hand of 104 in 75 minutes. Coming in at 5–48, the Gloucester man was stimulated by a wager he had placed on his team's chances.

Personally I was most uncomfortable for I had foolishly embarked the night before at dinner at the Great Central Hotel, which one or two of us had made our quarters for the match, on a wager which bordered on the ridiculous.

In pleading guilty to so grave a misdemeanour as betting I throw myself on the mercy of the court, for though betting at cricket is an anathema to me, on this occasion it was not so much the desire quickly to become proprietor of lordly demesne as it was to assist in the laudable object of raising drooping spirits.

We had sat down to dinner that night before an open window from which could be perceived a cloudless sky giving hope of a welcome change in the weather. The first glass of 'Pommery' had scarce time to produce that feeling which for want of a better word may be described as moreish, when pitter-patter, pitter-patter, the change came. It rained harder.

… When the flow had subsided save for an intermittent trickle, I rashly offered to take 10 to one that I for one would make 50, and 20 to one as regards double that figure. As this seemed such a clear case of money for nothing the offer was snatched up immediately. Let me say at once that the sum at stake would have sufficed to have paid for no more than the paint on the lodge gate of the aforementioned demesne.

A Cricketer's Log (Jessop) pp196–7

Paddy Goes Mad

Darling was again an outstanding leader who produced his share of runs, including a barnstorming 116 against Hampshire that Noble attributed to a terpsichorean motivation.

When we began that partnership a band of pipers, ten strong, arrived on the ground and played with might and main. Probably this stimulated our captain who, by the way, is a Scot. Anyhow Reggie Duff said afterwards: 'As soon as the pipers came on the ground, Paddy went mad.'

Those 'Ashes' (Noble) pp28–9

Debagged

No matter how revered the leader, though, even he needed his leg pulled at times. Clem Hill narrated this story of a sartorial strike at the skipper.

We were on our way home from the 1902 tour and Joe had a pair of tweed trousers which he had had for about six years and we thought it time he got rid of them. Of course you would not suggest such a thing to him. He was a dominant personality and had his own opinions.

Somebody proposed that the trousers should be dumped overboard. But who was to do it? If Joe found out there would be ructions. So a document was prepared marked 'Secret', which every member of the team signed agreeing to do the deed if they should have the misfortune to draw from the hat the piece of paper which named the perpetrator.

When Joe came to pack his clothes prior to leaving the boat at Cape Town, he missed the trousers.

'That's strange,' he remarked to Howell. 'I suppose one of those natives at Trinidad took a fancy to them.'

Howell, who was one of the conspirators, said he supposed that was right, he recalled that he had seen a dark chap about the deck!

Adelaide News, 3 March 1933

Mary Ann

For the Test tour by Warner's MCC side the following season, Australian players in Darling's absence elected as their captain Montague Alfred Noble. One of Australia's finest all-rounders and eventually shrewdest leaders, Noble was known universally as 'Mary Ann'. It peeved his mother no end.

My old mother went to see an interstate game in Sydney. As I led NSW onto the field, two male occupants of the grandstand sat immediately behind her. One said: 'There's Mary Ann.'

'Where?' said the other.

'Why there, in front of the team. Don't you know him by his big feet?'

The old lady turned and said: 'Excuse me, sir, do you know you are referring to my son?'

This brought an immediate apology. Later, she said to me: 'My boy, had I known they would call you that name I'd have given you different initials.'

The Game's the Thing (Noble) p243

CROCK CROCK CROCK

The First Test at the SCG in 1903–04 was an unforgettable affair. Noble made 133 in Australia's 285, but his team's score was more than doubled. Victor Trumper then commenced an immortal Test innings that drove the Hill into frenzied adulation.

Braund came on to bowl from the Randwick End. Trumper late cut his first ball to the fence for four. It was a stroke of sheer elegance and the crowd roared appreciation. The next ball was also cut to the fence, finer, but again for four. The crowd roared louder. This was the superb touch, the highly skilled placement, the whippy wrist work of the master. Braund tried to trick Trumper by a faster ball, but it was wide and went through for four byes. Then the whole Hill and the Members' Stand rose and cheered as Trumper with perfect timing scorched the grass wide of cover for yet another four. A stroke, that, to live in the memory. And now from the crowd came gales of laughter at an anticlimax, for Trumper played the next ball quietly back along the pitch.

'You've got him tied down, Braund,' called a wag from the Hill.

The last ball of the over Trumper drove wide of mid-off. It went toward the grandstand with Hirst in pursuit. The batsmen ran one; they ran two — the crowd yelling as if it were a game of football — they ran three; and they turned for a four as Hirst threw. It would be a close thing and Hill and Trumper sprinted. The crowd was roaring continuously.

But the throw slipped out of Hirst's hand and veered off towards the sightboard. Hill had clapped on such speed that he overran his end by about 10 yards and had a long way to go when Trumper called him for the overthrow, the fifth run.

The four runs had made the crowd delirious. The overthrow, as an overthrow always will, brought yells of 'Go again!' and 'There's more in it!' The excitement bubbled, with the crowd urging Hill on and on. Relf had the ball now and returned well towards the pavilion end, towards which Hill was running.

The ball passed behind Hill, and Lilley, taking it, whipped the bails off. Hill had run some 15 yards past the wicket and on returning was told that he had been given out.

Hill stood in amazement. Apparently he couldn't conceive that he was out, as the ball had passed behind him. Nor could the crowd at right angles to the wicket believe that Hill had not beaten the ball home.

A crowd in ecstasy now turned into one in an ugly mood. Hill's reception of the decision spurred them on, and from the Outer — and also from the Members' Stand — came bursts of booing. Crockett was the umpire who had given Hill out and the crowd began to croak, 'Crock-Crock-Crock'. The noise went on undiminished for minutes from all the ground and when Noble came to bat he found that Warner was very agitated. The English captain had walked toward the Members' Stand to ask for silence, but to no avail. The ground re-echoed to 'Crock-Crock-Crock-Crock'. It was like a marsh full of bull frogs on a rainy night.

Masters of Cricket (Fingleton) pp91–2

ALL OUT 15

Trumper stood alone as Australia lost the Second Test at the MCG on a rain-affected wicket, top-scoring with 74 from 122 and 35 from 111. But the rout was nowhere near as complete as that the MCC inflicted on Victoria in the tour match. Here is a contemporary account of Australia's lowest first-class total, by 'Looker-On' of the Sheffield Daily Telegraph.

On the first innings the Victorians led by 51 runs — just enough, one would have thought, to make the game interesting if the wicket continued bad.

The wicket was bad, but not nearly so bad as the Victorian batting for in 45 minutes cricket Rhodes and Arnold disposed of the whole side for 15, and of these Trott, with two lives given him, made 9.

McAlister was out to the third ball bowled by Rhodes, Armstrong the fourth, and the bowler was only deprived of the hat-trick through Bosanquet missing Trott ...

At the other end, Arnold got McLeod with his first ball and Ransford with his second, so that four wickets were down in eight balls with no runs scored.

When Rhodes yorked Laver, his record was 3–1 from 20 balls. Arnold then nearly succeeded in catching Trott at point and when Baker jumped out to one of Arnold's and was stumped six wickets had fallen for 12.

Trott was caught by Arnold at point, Scott went out to Arnold and was stumped and Fry was held at the extra slip off the second ball bowled to him. With Saunders too unwell to take the field, the innings closed for 15 (one extra).

Bringing Back the Ashes: The Story of the MCC Tour of Australia (Looker-On) p50

In 1903–04 Australia discovered a successor to Jones in the indefatigable Albert 'Tibby' Cotter, a bowler from Glebe with a slinging action and a massive heart, fast enough to break bushels of stumps. Warren Bardsley described him thus.

Strong, big, never got tired. He broke more stumps than any other fast bowler I knew. We were always running out of stumps down at Wentworth Park. Tibby loved to break stumps and he loved to 'pink' a batsman. Every fast bowler does. Gregory, McDonald, Larwood — the whole ruddy lot of 'em. Just as soon hit a batsman as hit the stumps. And no harm in that I suppose.

We were playing North Sydney one day and Tibby was in great form. Knocking stumps over in all directions. In came Stud White and the first ball Tibby smashed Stud's fingers against the handle of the bat. A sickening crunch. They took Stud off to hospital. Never forget Tibby's remark. 'Well that's one of the -------- out of the way.'

About an hour later Stud came back to bat again with his fingers heavily bandaged. Very brave man, Stud. Tibby took one look at him and snorted, 'Give me the ball. I'll break the -------'s neck this time.' Tibby reckoned that when he pinked a batsman, he should remain pinked.

Masters of Cricket (Fingleton) p55

Johnny Moyes left behind this image of Cotter bowling for NSW versus SA.

I recall seeing him one day bowling at the South Australians with a gale behind him. The ball flew fast and high, too fast indeed for one batsman who could only turn his back and take the full force of the ball, which burrowed into his flesh and left a hole into which the ball could have been placed sometime later …

Cotter was not always accurate, but he had the stamina of a marathon runner. He could bowl from noon until the adjournment at half on, wringing the perspiration out of his cap and then going on with the job. He was the type of fast bowler who like to bowl. To suggest that he needed a 'spell' was to suggest that he lacked the will to endure and that would be just too silly. Perhaps his greatest asset was the ability to make the ball lift quickly under the arm pits, a wicked business, and he could do it from a good length without recourse to bumping. And if you hit him for four his 'Good shot!' would come floating down the pitch, an expression of appreciation, and not the signal to expect one at your head next ball.

Australian Bowlers (Moyes) pp61–2

'DON'T WORRY ABOUT THAT, BILL'

Darling emerged again to lead Australia to England in 1905, a side including Trumper, Duff, Noble and Armstrong. Among the newcomers was baggage master Bill Ferguson, who would be factotum for countless cricket tours over the next half-century. One of his hardest tasks on that initial tour was taking care of Victor Trumper.

Probably the neatest and most elegant bat in the world at that time, Vic was anything but neat when he was in the dressing room or at an hotel. He was the despair of his charming wife, and the not-so-charming baggage master, because he simply refused to worry about the condition of his clothes and equipment. Any old bat would do for him, whether there was rubber on the handle or not, and I can still see him now after slaughtering the best bowling in England taking his flannels off in the dressing room, rolling them into a ball and cramming them into an already overloaded cricket bag — there to remain until they were worn next day.

Mrs Trumper used to say to me: 'Just look at Victor's clothes. Whatever does he do with them?' On such occasions I would often fold his clothes neatly and repack his bag but within 24 hours chaos again reigned supreme. The Trumpers were real aces for my money. If Victor caught me packing his bag he would say: 'Don't worry about that Bill. You have enough work to do without me causing you extra trouble.'

Mr Cricket (Ferguson) p21

'HE'S THERE AGAIN JOE!'

Warwick Armstrong emerged on the tour as both a fine all-rounder and a forceful character, with a self-belief so strong it occasionally needed some restraint.

Warwick Armstrong had such a run of missed catches in the slips that Joe Darling told him he wouldn't have him there anymore. Warwick knew enough about Joe to keep away from the slips but, after two or three games, when a right and a left-handed batsman were in and things a bit mixed, he attempted a try on (Warwick loved fielding in slips as it meant very little chasing to prevent four).

Tibby Cotter was the bowler and, choosing the right moment, Warwick sneaked into the slips. For a great wonder this move was unnoticed by Darling and Cotter, running to the wicket, was just about to deliver the next ball when Hill at mid-off throwing both arms in the air yelled: 'Hey!'

Wondering what on earth was the matter, Cotter stopped abruptly to find Hill pointing at Armstrong but looking straight at Darling and saying: 'He's there again Joe!'

'Come out of that,' said Joe, and before a big crowd of spectators away went poor Warwick very sheepishly to another position. Knowing Armstrong as I did, I can imagine he later got even with Clem.

Not Test Cricket (Monfries) pp70–1

FARMER JOE

The Ashes were left behind with unlucky defeats at Trent Bridge and Old Trafford, though Englishman C. B. Fry recalled that Australia could have avoided defeat in the former match had it not been for Darling's sportsmanship.

Towards the end of the Australians' second innings, when they were well in the soup, the light became very poor.

Charles McLeod, when his partner got out, ran to the pavilion and signalled. The big brown moustache of Joe Darling emerged. There was a consultation at the gate. Joe Darling surveyed the quarters of the sky as a farmer would, then shook his head, slowly indeed, but not without emphasis, turned his broad back and went in.

McLeod had wanted to know whether he should appeal against the light. The light was bad. If Joe Darling had allowed the appeal I think it certain the umpires would have stopped play, and Australia would have drawn the match. Joe Darling was a sportsman of the best. We had by that time morally won the game, and Joe Darling was not the man to slide out on a side issue. And mark you, McLeod need not have discussed the question: he could have appealed himself, but he, too, felt disinclined to escape when his side was beaten on the play.

Life Worth Living (Fry) p238

LIGHTNING

Charlie McLeod, known as Lightning, was himself a relishable character whose deafness often resulted in humorous proceedings, as Monty Noble recalled from an Australian game against Essex.

A. P. Lucas … had been playing well and making strokes many younger players might envy. He was deaf in one ear.

Fielding mid-on for us was Charlie McLeod, who also was deaf on one side. Between overs Charlie made several attempts to open up conversation with Lucas, but the batsman took no notice. This annoyed Charlie very much and he mentioned the fact to Hughie Trumble — of all people.

Hugh looked very serious and replied: 'Yes Charlie, he has a reputation of being very particular about those to whom he speaks.'

Soon afterwards Lucas asked Trumble what sort of fellow McLeod was. 'I've been trying to talk to him for half an hour,' he said, 'but he won't take any notice.'

'No,' said Hughie, 'Charlie is a bit stuck-up, you know.' And so the practical joker had the two glaring at each other during the remainder of the innings.

The Game's the Thing (Noble) p231

The 1905 Oval Test, indeed, almost occurred without him.

Clem tells the story of how, during a Test match in England, Charlie came down to breakfast at the hotel at a quarter past eleven and seeing the room empty of guests said to the waiter: 'Am I first down?'

'Yes,' replied the waiter. 'First down to lunch!'

In that case Charlie, minus a breakfast, landed at the ground just in time but on another occasion he told me that he entered a bus to go to the Surrey Oval, and after reaching the terminus and seeing no signs to denote there was a cricket match in the vicinity he said to the driver: 'Where is the Surrey Cricket Ground, driver?'

'Oh that's miles away,' was the reply. 'You've taken the wrong bus.'

Then poor 'Lightning' listened to a set of directions that made him wonder if he would ever see his companions again, but this he did manage to do in time to be abused roundly and later fined a fiver — his third fine for late arrivals. Poor Charlie was always in trouble, and in his opinion it was always due to his abominable luck!

Not Test Cricket (Monfries) pp90–1

POSSUM SOUP

The 1905 Australians must also have been the terror of waiters across England, if this despatch from all-rounder Frank Laver is to be believed.

Nearly all the waiters in England are foreigners. Many are in the country for the purpose of learning the language. Well connected people of

Germany and elsewhere take positions in leading hotels without salary solely for the object of acquiring the accent and pronunciation of the better class people. I never, however, met any who refused a tip. So little do some understand the language that we have often played tricks upon them. We would look at the menu card and order possum soup, roast bustard on kangaroo tails, emu wings with lizard sauce or some other ridiculous dish — whatever happened to enter our heads. The waiter would say: 'Yes sir!' and hurry away. Later he would return and say: 'I am sorry, sir, there is no more, it is just off.'

An Australian Cricketer on Tour (Laver) p221

THE TIE THAT WASN'T

A. O. Jones's English tourists lost the First Test of their 1907–08 Ashes series but won the second by a wicket in an extraordinary finish at the MCG when Syd Barnes and Arthur Fielder added 39 for the last wicket. As the former recalled, had Australia's Gerry Hazlitt had the dead eye of the West Indies' Joe Solomon, Test cricket might have had its first Test tie half a century early.

It was like this. When we wanted two runs to win, Fielder was facing Armstrong and played one to Saunders at rather deep mid-off. Although it was quite a sharp run we made it easily through.

The next ball I drew away to leg and played Armstrong with a gentle push on the off-side. He was bowling leg stuff with only two men on the off, Hazlitt at deep mid-off and cover nearly square with the wicket and I judged it to be a safe move.

On playing the stroke I dashed off for the run, which was really a run and a half, but imagine my consternation to find when half-way down the pitch that Fielder was still leaning on his bat, dreaming no doubt of the run he had just made.

I shouted: 'For God's sake, get off, Pip', and off he went like a hare, but in the meantime Hazlitt had dashed in and grabbed the ball and, had he kept his head and just lobbed it to the wicketkeeper, Fielder would have been out by yards.

Instead, however, he had a wild shy at the sticks, missed and the match was over. I have often thought that if he had been run out, the verdict would have been I had lost my head (and the match) at the critical moment, but it was certainly an exciting finish.

Pip kept on running flat out and my last view was of him disappearing into the crowd around the pavilion. Had not the pavilion been in the

way I think he would have finished up in England and been the first to
bear the good news.

Cricketer International, February 1978 p16

Hartigan's RDO

Australia was barely a hundred ahead of England when its seventh second-
innings wicket fell at Adelaide Oval in the Fourth Test of January 1908. But,
in the heat of 42.5°C, Queenslander Roger Hartigan (playing in his first Test)
and Clem Hill (playing with a bad fever) added 243 for the eighth wicket.
Hartigan's 116, as well as helping Hill win the match for Australia, earned
him a few extra days off.

He worked for a Brisbane auctioneer, who had given him only a few
days leave in order to play in the Test. At the end of the fourth day,
when Hartigan was 105 not out, his leave had come to an end, but
fortunately his employer sent him a telegram saying: 'Stay as long as you
are making runs.'

Adelaide Oval Test Cricket 1884–1984 (Whimpress & Hart) p39

'The Governor-General'

Also unearthed during that series was a brilliant twenty-one-year-old all-rounder
Charlie Macartney, who at once acquired a nickname he never lost.

It was during the English tour of Australia in 1907–8 that I was first
dubbed the 'Governor-General'. K. L. Hutchings was responsible for this,
and it has stuck to me through all my career.

In this connection, my wife relates with glee a conversation overheard
by her at a match. One small boy said to another: 'Why do they call
Mac the GG?' 'Because he's so cocky, of course, was the reply.'

My Cricketing Days (Macartney) p39

'Ranji'

A NSW contemporary who attracted an equally adhesive nickname was H.
V. Hordern, known as 'Ranji' because of his swarthy complexion. Though
he played only seven Tests (for 46 wickets at 23) he deserves better

remembrance: he was the first Australian bowler, one afternoon in the nets at the SCG, to master the fiendish wrong'un pioneered by B. J. T. Bosanquet.

Practising one afternoon at the SCG, I asked my old friend Alec MacKenzie would he mind if I tried something on him. He was one of the state's best players at the time and only out of our friendship did I have the courage to ask him. He kindly said: 'Bowl anything you like.'

I started my usual leg-breaks and then timidly tried my newly discovered 'wrong un'. It was a full toss and was promptly hit from one end of the ground to the other. Another period of leg-breaks and then my googly full toss again with the same result. But, just before his practice was over, I made my third effort; luckily, this time, it hit the ground first and he played the wrong way for it

I rushed up and said: 'Why didn't you hit that one, Alec?'

And he said: 'I don't now, I just missed it.'

But I knew that if such a fine player had played the wrong way for the break, well, I had it.

Googlies (Hordern) pp48–9

How Many Do You Want Curly?

When Monty Noble's 1909 Australians arrived in England, one member shone from the first. Left-handed opener Warren Bardsley opened the tour with 63, 76 and 63 not out, then at Chelmsford participated with Vernon Ransford in a 200-minute stand of 355 against Essex before a lesson in the team ethic from Victor Trumper.

While I was resting on the grass I thought that, being near 200 with almost three hours to go, I might have the luck to go past Warwick Armstrong's 303 and set a new record for an Australian in England. On 219 I pushed a ball into the covers, called Trumper and ran. By the time I noticed Vic was not running I was too far to get back.

When Vic came in I asked him why he'd left me stranded when it was my call. Vic said: 'How many more did you want Curly? Remember, there are others in the side who'd like an innings.'

On Top Down Under (Robinson) p114

ONE MAN'S TRIPE

1909 was Trumper's last English tour, by which time he was well-established as national favourite. On his own wickets, Trumper remained a supreme stylist. Batting for Paddington, related the brilliant leg-spinner 'Ranji' Hordern, he was the young bowler's supreme challenge.

I met Trumper in opposition in a grade match at Chatswood Oval. If I had ordered the wicket, it could not have been more to my liking. It was what we get so rarely in this country, a fiery one; in other words, fastish, inclined to kick, and the ball easily turnable on it. No slow bowler could ask for better, and I was in absolute top-hole form.

Trumper collected 12 runs off my first over. My second was delivered to F. A. Iredale (at that period still a fine batsman) and tied him up very badly. My third was to Trumper. He started to operate on me again, and one ball in particular stands out in my memory because, for a fraction of a second, I thought it had bowled him. It was the perfect leg-break, pitched some three or four inches outside the leg-stump, and broke sharply into the wicket. Trumper played so late that I almost saw it hit his wicket, but within a few inches of the stumps his bat flashed and he cut the ball to the boundary past point.

Now what could one do? That individual ball could not have been better if a machine had delivered it, and yet it was brilliantly hit for four! As I sorrowfully watched it speed on its way to the boundary, Frank Iredale said to me: 'You never bowl me any of that tripe when I'm down that end.' I turned to him and said: 'My dear Frank, it's the same tripe that's got you tied up, which Victor is hitting for four.'

Googlies (Hordern) pp140–2

I'VE NEVER BOWLED BETTER BUT ...

When South Africa toured Australia for the first time in 1910–11 under Percy Sherwell, Trumper attained the highest score of his Test career at the Adelaide Oval: 214 not out in three and a half hours that reduced bowlers to impotence.

Percy Sherwell, compelled to watch his dreams of a South African victory fading with every mighty clout, was still big enough to describe Trumper's knock as 'the perfect innings'. Talking to the tourists during the tea interval, I remember Buck Llewellyn chiding bowler Sid Pegler with: 'What are you playing at? Isn't it time you got Vic Trumper out?'

Pegler's reply was, in itself, perfect testimony to the batsman. 'I've never bowled better, but Vic seems to make me bowl exactly as he wants all the time.'

That was what happened at Adelaide. A good ball from Pegler was made to look a bad one, while the occasional bad delivery was murdered quite ruthlessly. At close of play, Victor Trumper went straight back to the hotel, had a hot bath, and retired early to bed — as if he had achieved nothing out of the ordinary; he had simply done a normal day's work.

Mr Cricket (Ferguson) p110

THE BLUNDERBAT

A novice batmaker approached Trumper before the Fourth Test at the MCG and asked Trumper if he would trial one of his new ones.

He would have had in his bag several bats that suited him in weight and balance but, nevertheless, he didn't hesitate about accepting the young applicant's gruesome-looking bat. It weighed almost 3 lb 6 oz and it staggered his teammates.

'Surely,' one of them said, 'you won't use that blunderbuss, Vic?'

'He's only a young chap and he's starting out in business,' replied Trumper. 'If I can get a few runs with this it might help him.'

He made 87 (probably wearying of lifting it!), inscribed it on the back with a hearty recommendation, and gave it back to the delighted young man.

Masters of Cricket (Fingleton) p25

TIGER, THEY THINK I'M FINISHED

While in the grip of poor health, Trumper played what proved his last Tests during the Ashes rubber of 1911–12. But his method and manner left an indelible impression on the young English wicketkeeper 'Tiger' Smith.

I got to know him well on the 1911–12 tour of Australia and I don't think a kinder man ever lived ... When I kept to him in Australia he only had three years to live; he was tubercular then and coughing a little when he batted, but he never complained.

The off-field incidents in the Australian dressing room saddened Victor. Stronger men like Warwick Armstrong pressurised him into supporting the players' demands to have Frank Laver as their manager on the forthcoming tour of England. So Victor didn't come to England in 1912 and I think he was bewildered by it all. He also heard that some of the Test selectors didn't rate him all that highly, yet he got a beautiful hundred in the First Test and fifty in the last. In that last Test, Victor turned to me at one stage and said: 'Tiger, they think I'm finished.' All I could think of was: 'I wish I could play like you Victor.'

One example of his sportsmanship on that tour. He was captaining an Australian XI against us and Jack Hearne skied a ball to J. N. Crawford off Roy Minnett. Jack was walking to the pavilion when Victor called him back because someone in the crowd had shouted 'no ball' when Jack was about to play his shot. Can you see a skipper doing something like that today?

A very superstitious man, Victor. If he got runs wearing a particular pair of trousers or using a special bat, nothing would persuade him to change either. As a result Victor's bat was normally black with age.

Like Jack Hobbs, I don't think he had a weakness in his batting apart from his ill-health. A most un-Australian person, he was a champion and one of the most endearing men I've ever met.

'Tiger' Smith (Smith) pp14–15

Johnny Won't Hit Today

Australia was defeated 4–1 by an outstanding England team that summer led, when Pelham Warner fell ill, by John William Henry Tyler Douglas, a pace-bowling all-rounder, league footballer and Olympic boxer. He rose to the task of leading England, and even won a famous nickname from Australians.

His response to the address of welcome at the Town Hall in Melbourne had been one of the shortest but most famous speeches ever made by a captain of MCC: 'I hate speeches. As Bob Fitzsimmons once said: 'I ain't no bloomin' orator, but I'll fight any man in this blinkin' country'.'

It was in Melbourne, too, in the match against Victoria that an anonymous wag in the crowd had dubbed him 'Johnny Won't Hit Today' when he was in the middle of one of his most dour efforts with the bat, having moved into one of those states where he became totally becalmed. The nickname stuck, and little that Douglas did with the bat over the next 17 years was calculated to rid him of this title. In truth, he was rather proud of it.

Johnny Won't Hit Today (Lemmon) p50

BARNES STORMING

Douglas's men included a superb pair of opening bowlers, Sydney Barnes and Frank Foster. Barnes's devastating opening spell in the Second Test at the MCG, and the crowd's ill-tempered response, are here recalled by H. V. Hordern.

Australia won the toss, went in on a perfect wicket and promptly lost six of the best batsmen for 36 runs. Barnes at one period had four wickets for four, and that after bowling for nearly an hour; his bowling on this occasion is generally conceded to be the finest ever done on a plumb wicket in Australia. The crowd gave him wonderful recognition, round after round of applause coming from all parts of the ground.

I happened to be the advanced guard of the tailend, and was batting with our wicketkeeper 'Sep' Carter — a very fine bat he was, too. Australia was in a desperate plight and we were doing our little best to pull the match round. Carter had a fine repertoire of strokes, and in particular cut beautifully, whereas my shots were decidedly limited.

The late J.W.H.T. Douglas captaining the English side very naturally had a man deep on the boundary for Carter's cut, and brought him close up for me. There is not much in that surely to start a riot, but it did. Sending the man out and bringing him back took up a certain amount of time, and during one of these periods a few hoodlums called out: 'Get on with the game!'

Barnes, evidently strung up to concert pitch, suddenly lost his temper, foolishly threw the ball on the ground, facing the crowd and, folding his arms, stood glaring at them. Then he got what he was looking for: they howled at him just as heartily as they had previously cheered, and I am sorry to say hooting came from every part of the ground.

As Barnes ran to bowl, pandemonium broke loose. I stepped away from the wicket and sat on my bat, plainly asking the crowd to 'shut up' and behave itself. This happened three times and I sat so long the last time that the hooting abated and the game proceeded, and only sectional booing took place from time to time. These are absolute facts; and wasn't it all so very wrong and so very silly?

Googlies (Hordern) pp163–5

A CANNY CONDUCTOR

Barnes took 32 wickets in the series, Foster 31, the latter baffling the locals with a slower ball so subtle that he signalled it to his Warwickshire wicketkeeping teammate Tiger Smith by a change of step. It seems that the only Australian not hoodwinked was a lone tram conductor whom Foster met.

I love trams and riding in them far better than motor cars. One day in Australia I got into conversation with the conductor of a tram I was riding in. He astounded me with his knowledge of the game, and I sat and sat, looked and looked, until the man must have thought I was potty!

My mouth was opened, my nostrils were distended, and I answered 'Yes' and 'No' just like a fool! Anyhow, he knew more than I did so I kept 'como'.

'You get off here,' he finally said, 'and I shall be watching you myself in an hour. So take my advice and bowl that slow one a bit more often, and when you bowl it — don't change your step!'

Dear reader as true as I sit here, I fondly imagined that there was only one person who knew of my sign to Tiger Smith and you may guess who THAT person was. I left that Australian tram a sadder but wiser member of the XI playing for England v Australia that day.

Cricketing Memories (Foster) p66

SIX OF THE BEST

Much of the action in that series, however, came off the field. A lingering dispute between the cricketers and the nascent Australian Cricket Board about whether the former should be entitled to appoint their own tour managers led to ill-feeling between Australian captain Clem Hill and the Victorian player/selector Peter McAlister. On 3 February 1912, Clem Hill arrived at the NSWCA to select the team to play England in the final Test at the SCG with McAlister and fellow selector Frank Iredale. Secretary Syd Smith recorded the exchanges — verbal and physical — whose repercussions were felt for decades afterwards.

The conversation was started in regard to the match being played in Melbourne on that day, Mr Hill remarking that it was strange that one of the best bowlers in Australia — Mr Laver — should have been omitted from the State team, and one who should be playing in the Test matches.

Mr McAlister then remarked that in his opinion Mr Hill had not sufficiently used Messrs Kelleway and Minnett in the bowling department, so as to rest Messrs Cotter and Hordern. Hill stated that he considered that neither of the bowlers in question were any good on the Melbourne and Adelaide wickets. Mr Davis in answer to a question from Mr Hill, also participated in the conversation and remarked that whatever Frank Laver may have been on English wickets he did not consider he was a good bowler on Australian wickets and quoted that gentleman's average for the last 19 years, and at the same time informed the selectors that he would be only too pleased to go down to the office and bring his assistance to them in their work.

He also remarked that he considered Minnett a splendid bowler in so much as he had seen of him on NSW wickets.

In view of his remarks, Hill informed Mr Davis that he did not consider that he was any judge of cricket.

The discussion again got round to the captaincy question, when McAlister reiterated his statement with regard to the using of Kelleway and Minnett. Hill remarked that Minnett had better take over the captaincy, and that he was quite prepared to hand his resignation to the honorary secretary at once. McAlister stated that he was not giving his view as a captain, but as a judge of cricket.

At this stage Mr Davis, at my request, left the room. I had some telegrams ready to show the selectors with regard to Mr McLaren being available for the Fourth Test match, and was only awaiting an opportunity to give them this information before leaving the meeting myself.

Hill then asked McAlister where he got his experience as a captain, and he (McAlister) replied that he had captained teams in Australia, and he captained several matches as vice-captain of the Australian XI in England, and he considered that he had done all that was necessary.

Hill remarked, was it not a fact that Warwick Armstrong had refused to play under him as captain in the old country. This McAlister denied, and Hill asked him to name any match in which Armstrong took part, and in which he (McAlister) acted as captain. McAlister replied that he played under him as captain at Lord's on one occasion when Mr Noble had to leave the field, but that he did not play under his captaincy in other matches because he always stood down when Mr Noble was not playing.

Hill then asked McAlister what matches he had ever won as captain and asked him to write them down on a sheet of paper. McAlister numerated several, and Hill remarked that they were very second-rate matches.

McAlister said: 'At all events I did quite as well as Victor Trumper had done in captaining the Australian XI against Gloucestershire, when he almost made a hash of things.'

Hill then stated: 'Fancy you comparing yourself to men like Trumper and Armstrong.'

McAlister replied: 'At all events I consider I am as good a skipper, if not better, than the two players you've mentioned.'

Hill then informed McAlister that he had no idea of captaincy and McAlister replied: 'At all events I reckon I am a better skipper than either Trumper, Armstrong or yourself.'

Hill got up from his chair and informed McAlister that he had better take the position of captain and pick the team himself. Hill then sat down and informed McAlister that he knew absolutely nothing about skippering a side which brought forth a retort from McAlister that he (Hill) was the worst skipper he had ever seen.

When this remark was passed, McAlister was leaning with his two hands in front of him, and Hill immediately jumped up and said: 'You've been asking for a punch in the jaw all night and I'll give you one', immediately leaning across the table and dealing McAlister a violent blow on the side of the face.

McAlister was somewhat dazed but jumped up and rushed round the table to where Hill was standing and a fight ensued, both selectors grappling and trying to punch each other in the small space between the table and the wall. McAlister sat down between the telephone box and the table and Hill leant over him but did not strike him whilst on the floor. I eventually managed to separate the two combatants and I might state here that when the scuffle took place the table slewed round and Mr Iredale was jammed into the corner and thus powerless to act.

I urged Hill to get out of the room, but he went to the other end of the table near the door. As soon as McAlister got to his feet I tried to stop him from rushing Hill but they again got to holts. The furniture was knocked all over the room, the pictures were broken, and Hill grappled with McAlister and forced him onto the table and the window-sill — another couple of feet and both selectors would have been out the window into the street, three floors below, but this was prevented by Mr Iredale leaning across and catching McAlister by the arm, whilst I pulled Hill off by the coat-tails. As soon as I got Hill away, I at once shoved him out of the door and told him he 'had better stay outside'. While Mr Iredale and myself were holding McAlister he shouted to Hill: 'You coward! You coward!' Blood flowed from McAlister's face copiously and it presented a sorry spectacle. My clothes, collar, hat etc were covered in blood.

After getting McAlister to sit down I went outside and interviewed Hill and told him he had better go home. He said: 'Syd, I will not be a member of the selection committee any longer, as I refuse to sit with McAlister as a co-selector.' I replied that I could not take that as official, but if he would put the matter in writing, I would place it before the board. He said he would write it out at the hotel and I would call for it.

NSWCA Archives (quoted in *Bat & Pad* pp131–4)

MADE A MESS OF IT

When the Australian Board continued to insist on naming its own manager for the tour of England that year, the so-called Big Six (Hill, Trumper, Armstrong, Cotter, Carter and Victorian left-hander Vernon Ransford) withdrew from the team. Suddenly, young Charlie Macartney was the mainspring of the batting. At Lord's he had a dashing 99, a victim only of his own impetuosity.

Macartney played the best innings of the tour with 99 at Lord's and the manner of his dismissal typified the man and his outlook to cricket. Most batsmen of the period were wont to creep toward a century like a cat-burglar on his objective. Not so Macartney. He tried to hit F. R. Foster into St John's Wood Road.

'I thought I could have hit it for six,' he declared later. 'Should have, too. Full toss. Made a mess of it.'

Masters of Cricket (Fingleton) pp178–9

TURNING THREE INTO NONE

Australia was led by forty-year-old Syd Gregory, who showed only a shadow of his former batting form although he remained an exemplar at cover-point.

He [Macartney] told me that C. B. Fry and Plum Warner were batting in a Test match at Lord's. Charlie Kelleway bowled to Warner who hit the ball out to the covers and, thinking it was going between the fields-men, Warner called Fry and as the batsmen passed each other on the pitch Warner said: 'Two Charles, perhaps three.'

Off they went. The Australian captain S. E. Gregory was fielding at cover point, a position where he excelled; he was alert and anticipated the shot, moved across to intercept, which he did and, gathering the ball cleanly, he returned it to the bowler's end on the full. The ball hit the wicket with Warner a yard out of his crease. It was not a case of 'two Charles, perhaps three', but run out on the first. What a reward for anticipation!

The Rattle of the Stumps (Oldfield) pp153–4

EXIT PURSUED BY BEAR

Australia made its first tour of North America the following year, taking civilisation to the natives of Winnipeg by bowling their local team out for six (including four byes) and watching as the pavilion collapsed. The best, however, was to come when the players left in the evening for Minneapolis.

On our way back, the train stopped near a small town named Theodore and from the windows we saw a bear chained to a post nearby. Sid Emery thought he would like to get a picture of this bear, so taking his camera he left the train and set off.

To secure a good picture he advanced within the circle made by the captive in his wanderings about the post at the full length of his chain. While trying to focus his camera, Sid took his eyes off the animal which at that moment was standing at full height against the post.

Looking up a minute later Emery discovered the bear almost upon him, and in a wild effort to get out its reach, tripped and fell. The bear made a savage lunge at him with its paw, but fortunately Emery was able to roll out of its reach and escaped in the nick of time. He returned to the train fully determined never more to photograph a bear!

My Cricketing Days (Macartney) p94

'I'VE BOWLED MY LAST BALL'

With the outbreak of the Great War, many first-class and Test cricketers enlisted in the AIF. Australia's most grievous loss was the valiant fast bowler 'Tibby' Cotter, who perished at Beersheba, and whose last days are remembered here by a colleague named simply as 'Bluey'.

I was Tibby Cotter's cobber in the 12th Light Horse and on the night of October 30, 1917, we were at Khallassa in Southern Palestine, the most remote portion of the southern position. We watered our horses there and prepared to move off in the attack on Beersheba.

'Tibby' was one of the best foragers in the AIF. He would come to light with a bottle of champagne in the middle of the desert and the lads in the section all looked to him to turn up with something unusual.

About 1.30 on the morning of the attack, 'Tibby', who had received instructions to report to Echolon on a guard, turned up at the unit. He said to me: 'Bluey, I've skittled a Turk in one hit; and what do you think he had on him — a yard of ling.'

He wasn't going to Echolon, he insisted; but said he would treat the boys to a Stammell fish supper in Beersheba; and be damned to the consequences.

We moved off at 4.30am from Khallassa and attacked Beersheba that afternoon. 'Tibby' was next to me on one side in the charge, and Trooper Jack Beasley on the other. Rex Cowley was there also. The other three were skittled by a machine gun and, after we had cleared the Turks out, the troops went back half an hour later to bury the dead.

'Tibby' was still alive when I got to him and he recognised me. 'Blue,' he said. 'You can have the fish supper on your own.' He died shortly afterwards.

He should never have been in the charge. Had he obeyed orders he would probably have been alive today.

Just before we left Khallassa, 'Tibby' — who in a bowling competition at Tel-el-Fara bowled over 18 single stumps at full pace out of 24 — took up a ball of mud and, throwing it into the air, said: 'That's my last ball, Blue; something is going to happen.'

NSWCA Archives (quoted in Bat & Pad)

STARSEARCH

The first notable cricket played by Australians after the Great War was by the Australian Imperial Forces XI in England in 1919, whose recruitment unearthed many future Test stars. It was when NSW opener Herbie Collins oversaw a selection day at the Oval that he clapped eyes on one particular talent.

Collins was one of the selectors and the team was to include 14 players. They had agreed upon 13 and were stuck for the last man. Then someone pointed out a gangling youth who was heaving arms and legs in all directions as he bowled. The selectors called him up. Had he played cricket in Australia? Yes, he had, a little — with the North Sydney third-grade and Veterans' teams.

'Well,' said Collins, 'we have to get somebody to fill the last place so it might as well be him.'

Nobody had thought to ask the Cornstalk his name, so they sent for him again. His name was Gregory. That was a good start anyway, the selectors told themselves. It didn't occur to them that he might have been one of THE Gregory family, the most famous cricket family in history; nor, of course, did they foresee that they had in their grasp one of the greatest all-rounders the game of cricket was to know — J. M. (Jack) Gregory. He got the final place in the team simply because he was unusual in appearance and the selectors had to fill in with somebody. 'Give the job to the long bloke,' they said.

Masters of Cricket (Fingleton) p101

Gregory proved to be a fast bowler of such speed that, not only did he take bushels of wickets, he incapacitated the team's keeper Ted Long. Collins went to look for a replacement.

The search for one was conducted through various units, and at head-quarters in Horseferry Road somebody told the questing and worried Collins that in the neighbourhood was a young chap who had done a bit of wicketkeeping somewhere. The informant didn't know his name but offered to take Collins to where this man lived.

Very soon, then, Collins was led to a dingy apartment near Horseferry Road, beneath street-level, and there he found a smallish, quietly-spoken chap, in khaki, writing letters home.

'I believe you keep wickets?' said Collins.

'Well, yes, I have a little, back in Australia.'

'How would you like to keep wickets for the AIF team?' asked Collins.

'Oh no,' said the other, 'I'm not in that class.'

'Well we have to go to Oxford tonight on the 9.30 train. Be at Paddington at nine. Got any flannels?'

'Not even a shirt.'

Then began a feverish hunt for some cricket togs. Collins remembers the new chap sat in a corner of the railway compartment, a few cricketing odds and ends tied in a bundle, and scarcely uttered a word during the whole of the run to Oxford.

In the first over of the match, the new wicketkeeper caused whistles of excitement among the team-fellows. What is more, by the end of the morning's play, a new star had come into cricket's firmament. He was W. A. Oldfield, and he was the best wicketkeeper Collins ever saw.

Masters of Cricket (Fingleton) p103

HOBBS NAILED

Batsmen-fielders Johnny Taylor and 'Nip' Pellew were the other discoveries, and Oldfield himself sensed at once the sagacity as skipper of Collins.

I remember sharing a taxi-cab with him and Jack Gregory to Kennington Oval, where the AIF side was playing Surrey. He discussed how we might dismiss Jack Hobbs and I can see him now, leaning forward and patting his forehead, as he exclaimed: 'Look here Long 'un (referring to Jack Gregory) I think we might have a bit of success if we put an extra man at deep square leg on the fence and, by pitching short outside leg stump, Jack Hobbs might fall for the plot.'

61

And how well his prophecy turned out. The famous Surrey man was out for 51 caught by Johnny Taylor off Jack Gregory in just the very position he described.

The Rattle of the Stumps (Oldfield) p20

Not all the AIF team's matches were against first-class opposition: they did play by invitation at the stately home of a peer of the realm.

The main requirement was that His Lordship should have some success with the bat, but this was partly in the hands of fate and the acquiescence of the umpires, who in this case happened to be His Lordship's butler and the under-gardener.

The latter, unused to the heavy beverage, was officiating when His Lordship glanced Docker to leg and a joking appeal brought the response: 'I'm sorry, but His Lordship is out.'

All the fury of countless generations was in the regal retort: 'What for?' The gardener replied sternly: 'For the rest of the afternoon, Your Lordship.'

The AIF Cricket Team (Cardwell) p51

PELTING PENTRIDGE

Gordon Robinson (1888–1969) was a strapping twelve-and-a-half-stone six-footer who scored prolifically for Brighton in the Melbourne sub-district competition, but whose cricketing career was stunted by his engineering work for the Gas & Fuel Corporation. He often worked at weekends and was late for matches and, on the second day of one contest with Coburg near Pentridge Gaol, it seemed he would be incapable of resuming his innings.

At this moment he came in through the gate so they ran to him and took him onto the ground, took his jacket, handed him a bat and got him to resume his innings. He had no sprigs so it was a bit difficult for him.

Anyway, at the end of each over they would run out and change his shoes, took his tie, until in the end there he was with a cricket shirt on, but still grey pants and grey socks. In the course of his innings he hit seven sixes; one of the sixes climbed over the wall of Pentridge Gaol. The ball never came back. It was one of the jokes of the players at the time that that shows you what sort of people are in Pentridge these days.

Ray Robinson interview, National Library of Australia

Australia's Biggest Hit?

Gordon told nephew Ray, who would become one of Australia's finest cricket writers, that the biggest hit he'd made was one at Glenferrie Oval in 1919 against Hawthorn-East Melbourne.

'Batting with my back to the railway,' he said, 'I ran down the pitch to drive googly bowler E. A. (Dick) Goss. Dick fooled me in the flight by bowling a top-spinner which dipped in.' Instead of going on with the drive Gordon swung across with a sweep which connected with the meat of the bat. Bob Grieve VC, who was next in, filled in part of the story: 'I was sitting on the old pavilion padded up when the ball sailed overhead. I stood up, waved my bat, and called to them that it was still going up.' Calculations and measurements showed me that if the pitch was in the middle of the field, the ball had travelled 87 yards by the time it passed over the boundary fence. Edgar Brown of the MMTB scaled it on a board map and made it a hundred and eighty-six yards to the old railway. It was believed that the hit was probably longer than that recorded in *Wisden* by the Rev. W. Fellowes practising at Christchurch ground, Oxford, in 1866.

Ray Robinson interview, National Library of Australia

'Don't Expect Gifts From Anyone'

The 1920–21 Test series introduced to Test cricket Jack Gregory. As a dashing left-hand batsman, he had 460 runs, as a constantly express bowler, he took 23 wickets. Future commentator Alan McGilvray provided this vivid memoir of facing Gregory in a grade match at Trumper Park.

In his first over he caught one of our fellows in the face and broke his jaw, then bowled the next batsman so comprehensively he snapped a stump in two. Enter McGilvray shaking! I can still see the sight of Gregory coming at me, every muscle and blood vessel in his neck straining and glowering at me. Through the first over I faced I could not lay a bat on him.

Eight balls. Eight shots. Eight air swings.

I had been getting runs at the time and eventually I snicked enough of Gregory's deliveries and picked up sufficient runs from the other end to get to 99. Gregory then offered some gentle encouragement.

'Don't worry lad, you'll get this over,' he said. There was a comforting smile on his face and I thought to myself that the great man was going to give me a run and my first century.

There followed the fastest over of the day. It was brutal stuff and, though I survived, I was out a few balls later for 99. After the game Gregory came into the dressing room looking for me.

'You thought I'd give you that one didn't you?' he said. I nodded. 'Well,' he said, 'when you get your first hundred son, you'll earn it. Don't expect gifts from anybody.' A hard lesson but a good one.

The Game is Not the Same (McGilvray) p186

'A DEVIL OF A SCRAMBLE'

By taking 15 catches in his first Test series, Gregory also proved himself one of the most gymnastic slip catchers Australia has possessed. Leg-spinner Arthur Mailey furnished this instance of Gregory's astonishing intuition.

On one of those occasions when Hobbs threatened to spend the weekend with us, I entered into a pact with Jack Gregory during the lunch interval. The idea was that my first ball to Jack [Hobbs] in the second over was to be an obvious wrong 'un pitched, if possible, on middle and leg stumps. The moment this ball was bowled, Gregory was to spring round the back of Oldfield and wait at leg-slip for Hobbs to snick an easy catch.

Gregory remembered the plan but I forgot it, and instead of the planned ball being a wrong 'un it was a perfect leg-break on off-stump. When I saw Gregory dashing behind the wicket I realised the blunder I had made. But Gregory, keeping his eye on the ball in flight, saw it spinning the opposite way to what he expected, hurtled back to the slips and was just in time to grab the ball almost off Jack's bat.

Gregory wasn't particularly pleased about the incident. He said I was trying to make a fool of him.

That night I asked Jack Hobbs if he knew what had happened. 'Not quite,' he said. 'But I heard a devil of a scramble going on behind the stumps.'

10 for 66 and All That (Mailey) p77

MAINLY MAILEY

Mailey himself took a record 36 wickets in his first five Tests, and demonstrated a charm and quick wit that often deflected trouble.

Mailey hit the pads in a Test match at Adelaide Oval.

'How's that!' he demanded.

'Not out,' replied umpire George Hele.

'Bloody cheat,' muttered Mailey.

Hele almost leapt at him. 'Who's a cheat?' he barked.

'I am,' said Arthur, and all was well.

The Vic Richardson Story (Richardson) p99

Although it was against the law, I must break down and confess that I always carried powdered resin in my piocket and, when the umpire wasn't looking, lifted the seam for Jack Gregory and Ted McDonald. And I am still as unashamed as a Yorkshireman who appeals for lbw off a ball that pitches two feet outside the leg-stump.

Anyhow I was in pretty good company. One day in Sydney, Johnny Douglas the England captain asked me to show him my hand. He held it for a while and then said: 'Arthur, you've been using resin. I'll report you to the umpire.'

I asked him to show me his right hand and, looking at the thumb-nail, I noticed it was worn to the flesh on the outside.

'You've been lifting the seam, Johnny,' I said.

My co-rebel grinned and the matter was dropped.

10 for 66 and All That (Mailey) p133

DOCTOR PARK'S HOUSE CALL

Doctor Roy Park was a formidable all-round sportsman who played football for Footscray and Melbourne and cricket for Victoria from 1912 to 1925. Yet Australian cricket's post-war strength confined him to a single melancholy Test appearance at the MCG in December 1920, where he was bowled first ball by England's Harry Howell.

He didn't tell anyone at the time — he didn't let on until years later when he told his son-in-law Ian Johnson — but Roy Park had not been to bed the night before his Test debut. He had been called to a maternity case at Footscray. It was a difficult birth and Dr Park stayed with the patient all night.

'That was typical of the man,' said Mr Johnson, secretary of the MCC and one of the bursary's four trustees. 'Not only did he place the welfare of his patient first, but he never told anybody. He didn't make excuses.'

The story goes that Dr Park's wife, who was knitting in the stand, dropped a ball of wool as the bowler ran in. She bent to retrieve it — and missed her husband's only Test innings!

Herald, 9 June 1979

'I May As Well Stop As Long As I Can'

Australia trailed England by 93 on the first innings in the Third Test at Adelaide Oval, and were 3–45 in the second dig, when the monumentally-patient Charles Kelleway was dropped first ball. Keeper Herbert Strudwick recalls how the tourists came to rue the error.

At the close he was 19 not out. Only two wickets fell next day, and Kelleway was still in with 115 to his credit! Armstrong made 121 — he and Kelleway put on 194 runs.

On Wednesday, Kelleway and Pellew were the batsmen, and I spoke to Kelleway when he came in to bat. 'Good morning Charlie! I said good morning and good night to you yesterday, but I hope I'm not doing the same today! I'm sick of seeing you in here.'

He replied, 'Oh I may as well stop as long as I can!' He finished up with 147 made in seven hours. It seemed a lifetime to me behind the stumps, but he had done his share in winning the match for Australia.

Twenty-Five Years Behind the Stumps (Strudwick) p196

'Me Losee My Friends'

Warwick Armstrong's 1921 Australians were among the strongest battalions Australia has sent abroad, and undertook one of the most elongated excursions: nine months in which they lost only two first-class matches. The tour commenced with an overland journey through Europe where, Bert Oldfield recalled, the team almost lost one of its number.

We had decided to get out at Invalides station but, to our surprise, Ryder was taking his time and was left in the train. The door had slammed quickly, as it does on all overseas undergrounds. I was detailed to follow him on the next train and restore him to the team.

When I arrived at the next station, Ryder was surrounded by a host of railway officials and I found him gesticulating and saying: 'Me losee my friends' in quaint pidgin English and continuing to try and explain his dilemma. One of the officials said to him: 'If you would please speak zee good English I would probably understand you, yes!'

Behind the Wicket (Oldfield) p131

The Big Ship

Armstrong was a towering presence, both psychologically and physically, as his frame had filled out to twenty-one stone.

June was at its sunniest when the Australians played Hampshire in 1921 and a Southampton newspaper reported that Armstrong, strolling round the ground while Bardsley and Macartney made centuries, became aware of a little boy dogging his heels.

He thought it manifestation of hero worship, but the boy's persistency at last made him say: 'Here, give me your autograph book and I'll sign it.'

The boy: 'I ain't got one.'

Armstrong: 'Then what do you want?'

The boy: 'Please sir, you are the only decent bit of shade in the place.'

On Top Down Under (Robinson) p99

Often on a warm June afternoon on the mellow county grounds of England, Warwick would doze at point and allow the game to drift like a ship left in the hands of its crew. There were very few batsmen in England who could back-cut and Warwick, after having a couple of glasses of ale at lunch, knew that there was a sanctuary in one part of the field where his siesta had little chance of being interrupted.

Early in that tour he did make the mistake of fielding in the slips at Leicester, and a ball, after hitting him on the slope of his stomach, ricocheted past his nose and after fifty or sixty feet in the air was caught by Carter the wicketkeeper who had hardly moved from his original position. Warwick opened his eyes lazily, affected a Falstaffian smile, and after muttering something about 'wasps being bad today', moved over to point.

10 for 66 and All That (Mailey) p61

Charms And Amulets

With their prior record, the Australians needed little supernatural support. But they took precautions.

During the early part of the tour, a rubber kangaroo which could be inflated was presented to Warwick Armstrong by Walter Brearley, England's fast bowler of some years before, as a mascot for the team. At the beginning of a match it was blown up and placed in a prominent position in the dressing room and at the conclusion of the match was deflated and packed away in readiness for the next occasion. Later on we acquired a horseshoe, which was gaily attired in green and gold ribbons and also hung in a prominent place next to the kangaroo.

Jack Gregory's cricket bag was generally the receptacle for these mascots after the games. I have read and heard that these two mascots were missing from the dressing room while the two matches we lost were being played.

My Cricketing Days (Macartney) p126

Too Far To Run

Macartney himself was in full gubernatorial bloom, making 2335 runs at 58.

Macartney … held that every ball had 'a look on its face' as it came up the pitch towards him.

'It was labelled,' he said, 'either 1, 2, 3, 4, or 6. I leave out the 5. Too far to run.'

Masters of Cricket (Fingleton) p180

Some of my happiest days in the sun were spent watching Macartney from the other end and marvelling as he flicked the ball from the off-stump to the long-leg fence while the bowler waved his arms and then wiped his brow in perplexity. And Charlie would say, 'Don't take any notice of me. I'm just mad.'

The Changing Face of Cricket (Moyes) p45

Six Of The Best

Jack Gregory established his reputation in England during a single over in the First Test.

The match was only four or five overs old, the score was up to 18 only, when Gregory whipped one away off the seam, Knight moved his bat but not his feet and Carter took the thick snick in triumph. Not a happy moment for Ernest Tyldesley, also in his first Test, rushed into the breach before a proper breath could be drawn. This was unkind luck enough, but his first ball was worse, it was one of Gregory's fastest and it spat savagely back from the line of the off-stump. Tyldesley's defence was as good as any Number Three's in England, but though he came down hard on it, he was too late for anything but a thick inside edge, and it had his leg-stump in the spasmodic smother.

The next ball beat Hendren to the wide, and the last of the over, testified to by all responsible spectators as the best and fastest of the whole cumulative sequence shot his off-stump yards out of the ground, a completely unplayable back-break delivered at the peak of speed. *The Cricketer* solemnly declared that this ball would have bowled the best batsman in the world at any time of an innings; no doubt Hendren would have gladly endorsed this sentiment with his initials and the date if in the heat and horror of the moment he could have recalled either to his memory. England 18 for three; with that single over Gregory destroyed the morale of English cricket for the best part of a season.

Warwick Armstrong's Australians (Mason) pp46–7

'NOT TOO CLEVER'

Warren Bardsley top-scored during Australia's eight-wicket win in the Second Test at Lord's with a diligent 88, on a pitch whose vagaries he tried to explain to his monarch.

When the Test teams were presented to King George V at Lord's in 1921 the King asked Australia's top-scorer, Bardsley: 'How is the wicket?'

Bardsley replied with an Australianism: 'Not too clever, sir.'

The King turned to an aide and said: 'What does that mean?'

From the Boundary (Robinson) pp237–8

CAUGHT ON THE REBOUND

A plucky batsman, Johnny Taylor forged a reputation as one of the finest outfielders the game has seen. One of his victims on that tour was the Notts man George Gunn.

One one occasion Gunn hit Arthur Mailey over mid-on to a deserted place in the outfield. Collins, fielding at silly point, heard the batsman call down to his partner, 'Two — maybe three.' But Johnny Taylor took off from deep mid-off, ran some 40 yards in even time — as Taylor could — dived, and took an unforgettable catch. 'Well,' exclaimed the staggered Gunn, 'I'll be well and truly ------!'

Masters of Cricket (Fingleton) p110

SAMMY SAVES THE DAY

The Australians were in strife only once against England, during the Fourth Test at Manchester where the elements took a hand. It was their gnomic wicketkeeper Hanson Carter who saved them, recalled Hunter Hendry, though not before Warwick Armstrong had entered the record books uniquely.

Rain ruined the first day's play and consequently altered the rules of play to a two-day match. England batted on a wet wicket — not sticky but one which favoured batsmen because the ball became wet and soggy and difficult to control. Russell was batting very well and we were in a precarious situation. Lots of runs were on the board and the possibility of a sticky wicket faced us when it was our turn to occupy the crease.

'Sammy' Carter, our keeper and an encyclopaedia of cricket laws, said to Warwick Armstrong: 'If they don't close before 10 to 5 they can't close today' and put the law book open on his locker at the correct page before we took the field after the tea adjournment. Play went on and we were anxiously watching the clock and heaved great sighs of relief when 5pm came.

The Hon. Lionel Tennyson came on to their dressing room balcony and in a very jubilant mood called out that he had closed their innings. Warwick made several attempts to show him we were not going off but as Lionel had disappeared into the dressing room there was nothing for us to do but go off.

Warwick then produced the rule book after everyone including selectors and administrators disputed the decision. It was an unusual occasion to point out they did not know their own rules!

The Sydney Hill was noted in those days for barracking but I never heard worse than when we trooped back onto the field. Even when passing through the members' enclosure we were abused and bustled. Bedlam broke out across the ground. So Warwick, who was 20-stone, sat down on the wicket like a bull elephant and waited until Tennyson came onto the ground and walked round the whole arena with an umpire explaining it wasn't the Australians' fault.

Play was resumed and Warwick who had bowled the last over before we left the field picked up the ball and bowled another over!

Cricketer, December 1980 p35

Hit Wicket B McDonald

Having vanquished the Englishmen, Gregory and McDonald had a similarly shattering effect on the South Africans when on the way home Australia won the last of three Tests there by 10 wickets.

It was here that Jack Zulch, opening for South Africa, innocently asked Herbie Collins, who'd taken over the Australian captaincy from Armstrong, if Ted McDonald was really fast.

'Fairly quick,' said the droll Collins. 'But he needs to warm up.'

McDonald did warm up — behind the pavilion before the innings began.

His second ball shattered Zulch's bat, sending a fragment into the stumps. The scorecard simply reads: 'Hit wkt bowled McDonald'. But there was more to it than that.

The Fast Men (Frith) p94

Left, Right?

Victoria won the Sheffield Shield in 1921–22 for only the fourth time in the twentieth century, although captain Edgar Mayne occasionally did not trouble to discover his teammates' abilities.

Captain Edgar Mayne was not always well briefed on newcomers to the Victorian XI. As Edgar walked onto the field another time with right-handed batsman Bryan Cosgrave, he said: 'You bat left-handed, don't you son?'

Cosgrave: 'No, but I'll try.'

On Top Down Under (Robinson) p123

Schadenfreude

A well-travelled leg-spinner called Clarrie Grimmett had similar problems with Mayne, and did not make an impact until he transferred to South Australia.

This afforded the chance of revenge on his old skipper, whom he caught and bowled at their first meeting as opponents.

On the Sunday players from both teams visited a nearby Adelaide winery in the foothills, where a sheep was turned over the hot coals. The players and the officials tucked into their meal with relish, but Clarrie reserved the skeletal head of the poor beast for the Victorian captain.

Edgar Mayne was a prized scalp for Clarrie. The Fox never forgot the enemy, and he regarded Mayne thus, for Mayne's non-recognition of his bowling skill in Victoria … As Victorian captain he had shown scant regard for Clarrie's ability.

Clarrie slammed the sheep's head in Mayne's empty soup dish and laughed: 'There you are Mr Mayne. Your head on a platter, caught and bowled!' There was the odd snigger from the Victorians, but nothing to the roar of delight from the South Australian corner. If Clarrie hadn't won his teammates with his marvellous bowling, this timely act against Mayne was something they'd never forget.

Clarrie Grimmett (Mallett) p54

THE TIGER MEETS THE DON

Clarrie Grimmett's future partner Bill O'Reilly was at the time a primary school teacher playing occasionally for his home town of Wingello in country New South Wales. In 1924–25 he had an auspicious encounter with another rising star, Don Bradman of Bowral, and later wrote this evocative if perhaps somewhat embroidered account.

Play began.

In my first over I hit the stumps of one of Bowral's openers. That warmed me up for the entrance of a diminutive figure, approaching with what appeared the diffident gait of a stopgap performer sent in to hold the fort for long enough for the real number three in the batting order to get his pads on.

What struck me most about him was the difficulty he seemed to have in taking normal steps as he approached. His pads seemed to reach right up to his navel. His bat was small and had reached the sere and yellow stage, where the yellow was turning to dark tobacco.

Still, he shaped up as though he knew what the game was all about, and the expression on his face publicised the fact that he felt quite at home and was ready to cope with anything I had in store for him.

The battle was joined. As the game proceeded I was quick to realise that I had come into contact with my first 'problem child'. My training as a primary teacher was supposed to have prepared me for dealing with the occasional hard case who would turn up from time to time, but nothing could have prepared me for the confrontation with this particular youth.

As the precocious lad began to handle my quickish leg-breaks, bouncing high off the coir mat which always favoured spin, I was made aware that here at last I had a real job of work on my hands, and I wondered what I should say to Len Kelsey next time I saw him.

I had a bit of bad luck early in that memorable afternoon. Twice before he had reached 30 the youngster was dropped in the slips off my bowling. To elucidate it is necessary that I give an honest pen-picture of the captain who led Wingello in that great struggle.

Selby Jeffrey was a railway fettler. He had worn the Australian uniform which proudly displayed the big brass 'A' denoting the fact that he was present on the Sunday morning of 25 April 1915, when the Australian and New Zealand forces went into action at Gallipoli in their attempt to open up the Dardanelles. Selby was an ANZAC, and as such held the unbounded respect of every man on the field. He sported a fairly robust black moustache. His face was rosy with blatant good health and his persistent good humour was heralded by the most pleasant smile one could wish to see.

His snow-white shirt and duck trousers were immaculate, as were his rubber boots. He wore a black waistcoat over his shirt, unbuttoned. The idea of the waistcoat was quite original: it held his pipe, tobacco and his matches. It was not unusual in those far-off days for a country cricketer to light up and take a few draws on a pipe or cigarette. Nobody took umbrage at it …

Selby used to slip his big-boled bent-stemmed Captain Peterson pipe into the top pocket of his unbuttoned waistcoat. His tobacco pouch fitted snugly into the other top pocket, with the tin box holding his Wax Vestas matches in the bottom pocket along with a pen-knife for cutting the plug of dark 'Conqueror' tobacco.

It would have been senseless for him to field in any position where it had been necessary for him to raise the occasional canter. Had he run there would have been a scattering of smoking paraphernalia in all directions. Wisely therefore he placed himself at slip where he was splendidly covered by a magnificent keeper named Tommy Lynam and always supported by an active and mobile second slip.

Very early in the day I got one to lift and bite. Young Bradman edged it and the ball travelled speedily and straight in the direction of Selby's midriff. It would have been an extraordinary effort had the catch been taken. It struck him in the solar plexus just at the moment when he was, with both hands well and truly occupied, lighting his pipe.

Bradman soon gave our skipper a chance to redeem himself by snicking my quicker ball straight to him again. This second time Selby made a manful attempt with both hands to make the catch, but he had blown such a dense cloud of bluish smoke from his startled lungs that he must have lost sight of the ball well before it reached him.

'Sorry Bill,' he called, as if nothing untoward had happened. Selby's inconsistencies at slip were part and parcel of the Wingello team's programme. I was probably the only one among us who felt that he might have been wise to deny himself just a little longer.

Who in the name of all that is holy could ever possibly hope to get away unscathed when Don Bradman had been given two early lives? If I said earlier that I experienced some early worries as the boyish Bradman started his innings by methodical employment of the middle of his bat, I could certainly go much further in describing my own mental reactions as this young man tore the Wingello attack apart. Even though his size suggested that he would have been better fitted physically to have been riding winners at Randwick racecourse, he summoned up the energy required to land the ball over the fence on half a dozen occasions. One wondered where the battery was that generated the power.

To draw a convenient veil over the desolate scene, Selby Jeffrey's team finished the day a crestfallen crowd who listened more to the rattles of the old Model T Ford than to any animated flow of conversation on the thirty mile return trip to Wingello. Their chief bowling hope had nothing whatsoever so say. The boy Bradman was 234 not out.

Back at home I questioned my mother's wisdom in aiding and abetting my downfall by so carefully collecting my gear, but she seemed to think I had come to little harm, really, and that I should have considered myself lucky to have spent such a lovely day out in the fresh air playing cricket.

As the game was to be continued on our Wingello wicket the following Saturday afternoon, I could not help feeling that I was due to face up to another hammering from this pint-sized powerhouse a week later. I saw no hope ahead for me. All was gloom … My pride had been badly injured.

The next Saturday afternoon arrived. I lined myself up manfully for another serve of what the game I had loved so much might have to offer. The first ball was again mine to bowl, and the not out Bradman was there to deal with it. I let go my accustomed leg-break, aimed at the leg stump. It spun sharply past the Bradman bat and crashed into the top of off stump. Suddenly, I thought, the grass round our Wingello ground began to look greener than ever it had done before. The birds began to sing. The sun shone becomingly. One ball changed my whole sporting outlook. Gone were the dismaying plans to give the game away forever, I was prepared to go on and take whatever it had in store for me, and I made a personal pledge that as I was taking it on the chin in future I would be unsparing in my efforts to deal out as much as I could of what I was getting.

There were lots of encounters for the two of us in the years that were to follow. There were times when I felt the full weight of Don Bradman's bat — many of them indeed — but there were many occasions too when I had ample reason to rejoice in the lesson I learned on those afternoons at Bowral and Wingello in 1925.

Tiger (O'Reilly) pp49–53

PONNY'S POISE

Bill Ponsford made his debut in the First Test of the 1924–25 series against Arthur Gilligan's Englishmen and, for perhaps the one occasion of his life, looked impermanent against the brilliant medium-pacer Maurice Tate. England's Herbert Strudwick saw it all.

Ponsford came in and Tate almost bowled him half a dozen times in the first two overs. Ponsford turned to me and said: 'I've never played against such bowling before!'

I replied: 'No it doesn't look as if you had!'

He went on and made his 100. It was a great performance and I admired him for his pluck …

Each time that Tate just missed bowling Ponsford, he put his hand to his head and looked up into the sky. While he was doing this one wag in the crowd shouted: 'It's no good Tate, He won't help you.'

Twenty-Five Years Behind the Stumps (Strudwick) pp220–21

KING OF COLLINGWOOD

Australia was 6–119 in the Fourth Test at the Adelaide Oval against Gilligan's men when Victorian all-rounder Jack Ryder took the game by the scruff of the neck. He was 72 at stumps and, as he equalled the Australian record score against England by proceeding to an unbeaten 201, ratified his nickname 'The King of Collingwood'.

The following morning the postal authorities did a brisk trade delivering telegrams to Ryder and the more runs he scored the more work there was for the Adelaide post office. Former Collingwood footballer Ted Rowell and the celebrated Collingwood coach Jock McHale jointly sent a telegram which read: 'Congratulations fine stand. Hope you get a century today.' From Caulfield racetrack the controversial business figure John Wren wired to say: 'Congratulations on upholding Collingwood's reputation.'

A Life-Long Innings (Fiddian) p88

BERT'S GREAT GRAB

Bert Oldfield, who took 78 catches and made 52 stumpings in his 54 Tests, nominated as his favourite dismissal a leg-side grab that dismissed Jack Hobbs in the first innings of the Sydney Test a month later.

Pitched just outside the leg-stump and with the assistance of the wind, it swung well away to the leg-side, aided by the firm glance from Hobbs' bat, but having had those first two deliveries as a guide and seeing that the fourth ball was pitched on the leg-side, I anticipated its course by covering a greater distance, and as soon as I heard the snick I stretched my arms full length while in my stride, probably four or five yards wide of the wicket, and brought off a catch which certainly thrilled me and brought the spectators to a man to their feet.

The roar of the crowd brought home to me the sensation of the catch. There was no describing my delight at the achievement in dismissing such a redoubtable opponent. I can still see Gregory continuing his run down the wicket to greet me with a smile, while Hobbs quietly left the scene no doubt amazed by the suddenness of it all.

Behind the Wicket (Oldfield) p14

VICE-REGAL APPROVAL

Grimmett made his Test debut in the same match, and his 11–82 devastated the tourists.

Clarrie loved to talk of his Test debut; his pride shone, yet he did not boast. He simply told it as it happened. 'It must have been my lucky day, because as we left the field some friends called me over to the grandstand dividing fence to congratulate me,' Clarrie recalled. 'As we chatted there was a heavy thud. I looked down and saw a heavy battery box at my feet. It had been accidentally dropped by the broadcasting technician from the balcony above' ...

As he left the SCG, well satisfied with his bag of five English scalps, a large black limousine pulled up. A man sitting inside waved his hand at Clarrie and called: 'Congratulations Grimmett.' The car was some distance away before Clarrie realised that the occupant was Lord Forster, the Australian Governor-General. A night out with his old Sydney baseball mates, which included dinner in Circular Quay and the theatre, rounded off a great day in the life of Clarrie Grimmett.

Clarrie Grimmett (Mallett) p63

CROCK AND THE CLOCK

That Sydney Test was also the last in which Bob Crockett presided. The 'Chief Justice' had stood in 32 Tests, and his 38-year first-class umpiring career was rewarded the following season by a testimonial, but he remained to the end the complete professional.

To mark Bob Crockett's retirement from umpiring in March 1926, during the tea interval of the district final Sir Leo Cussen presented him with a cheque for £1043 which had been raised by public subscription. Crockett was deeply moved and began a speech of thanks. Then, in a widely-publicised gesture characteristic of the man, he looked at his watch and told the astonished assembly: 'Well, it's time to get out again.'

Seasons in the Sun (Coleman) p338

QUESTION OF DEGREE

Collins' vice-captain on the 1926 tour of England, forty-year-old Warren Bardsley batted through the Australian innings in the Lord's Test for 193. But, at his age, he seems to have been feeling the lack of a formal education.

He was congratulated on that feat by Dr H. V. Evatt, then a rising young barrister. Bardsley's acknowledgement was typical. 'I'd swap it for one of your degrees,' he told Evatt.

'Well,' said Evatt, 'give me the 93. You keep the 100 and the not out and you can have any of the degrees I've got.'

Masters of Cricket (Fingleton) p56

Bardsley was out at once when England's Arthur Carr sent Australia in at Headingley, but it set the scene for an innings of premeditated violence from Charlie Macartney.

It was not often that the pugnacious Macartney feared a bowler. But he did Macaulay. 'This chap,' he said on the eve of the Test, 'could go through us. There's no better bowler in England. I want permission to murder him immediately.'

Collins the captain was ill, and Bardsley was to take over the leadership for this match.

'You don't often talk like that, Charlie,' said Bardsley.

'No but I know what Macaulay can do to us if we don't nobble him first.'

So Bardsley agreed that Macartney could do as he wished.

It is well to know this background because it gave rise to one of the most brilliant innings in the history of cricket.

There were storms during the night and the groundsman switched to a new pitch next day because the original one had been flooded through the covers. The Australians all of them, gathered in an anxious band around the pitch while the Englishmen were having great trouble in choosing their final team in the pavilion — also no doubt wondering what Carr should do if he won the toss.

The three Australian selectors — Bardsley, Macartney and Ryder — locked themselves in a bathroom while they finalised their team. They too had to discuss what to do in the event of winning the toss. But fortunately for them Carr called correctly — and he put Australia in …

Bardsley was out off the first ball of the match — something that had happened only once previously, when MacLaren fell to Coningham in Melbourne. Sutcliffe caught Bardsley low at first slip off Tate.

In strode Macartney. He glided Tate's third ball though slips for two, but then, off the fifth ball, he snicked Tate to Carr, of all people, in the slips — and Carr dropped the catch. That was the most publicised catch in all history by the end of the day, because Australia, instead of being 2–2, didn't lose the next wicket until 235! …

Macaulay, playing his first Test for England, opened the bowling from the pavilion end. His first delivery was a no-ball, which Woodfull hit for a single. Up came Macartney. He took guard, studied the field, twirled his bat, cocked his left foot at the bowler, as was his wont, and hit Macaulay for two to the off. The next ball he smashed almost for six. The 'murdering' of Macaulay had begun.

The whole Leeds crowd (which had uttered a painful 'Oh!' as Carr dropped Macartney) now began to exclaim 'Ah!' as Macartney unfolded his artistry. He smacked Macaulay for two more fours in his next over and in 40 minutes Australia had 50 on the board — 40 of them to Macartney. In 79 minutes up came the 100, Macartney's share being 83. In 103 minutes Macartney had scored 100, the first batsman since Trumper to hit a century before lunch.

Masters of Cricket (Fingleton) pp181–3

LONG ENOUGH

Over the next few years, Bill Ponsford became renowned for his astronomical scoring: he is still the only man to have passed 400 twice in first-class cricket. When no bowler seemed capable of taming him, it took former Victorian all-rounder Allie Lampard to re-establish the status quo.

Lampard had been a St Kilda teammate of Ponsford through the Saints' glory reign. In a charity match he was a relieving umpire. 'Maybe another Ponsford 100 would have suited the crowd,' he said, 'but it would have made the game one sided. I told the bowler Charles Winning: 'If you hit his legs I'll give him out'.

'The bat was always there, though, so in an undertone I prompted the bowler to appeal for a ball that Ponny had let pass well off the wicket when he was 40.'

Ponsford: 'What am I out for?'

Lampard: 'You've been there long enough.'

Ken Piesse, *Cricketer*, November 1979 p19

EYES FRONT

Although Ponsford's faculties always seemed superhuman, Ray Robinson subsequently discovered that his eyesight was sub-par.

After all that had been said about Ponsford's wonderful sight, the doctor that examined him when he volunteered for the airforce was astonished to find that he was colour blind; he could not distinguish between red and green. A dialogue like this followed:

Dr: What colour did the new ball look to you?

Ponsford: Red.

Dr: What colour did it look after it became worn?

Ponsford: I never noticed its colour then, only its size.

Between Wickets (Robinson) p149

LONG-PLAYING RECORD

In the annual match at the MCG, NSW were dismissed for 221 on Christmas Eve. After rest days for Christmas and Boxing Day, the home side replied with a first-class record.

The story is told that when he made 352 of Victoria's record score of 1107 against NSW, Ponsford looked as if he would bat on into eternity; but at 352, enough runs for any team's total, Ponsford played a ball from outside his stumps onto the wicket. As he turned to see that his ears had not played him false he made this remark in a most doleful voice: 'By cripes, I am unlucky.'

Cricket Crisis (Fingleton) p121

LONG LIVE VICTORIA

Woodfull made 133, Hunter Hendry 100, Jack Ryder a fearsome 295 and Victoria was steered past 1000 by wicketkeeper Jack Ellis.

Jack Ellis was — he still is — a vital, cheerful fellow. As he made the eventful stroke to the outfield he whooped: 'Come on, there's three in it. Three in it and the thousand up! Long live Victoria!'

Masters of Cricket (Fingleton) p120

MAILEY ON THE MAULING

The carnage did not end until Tommy Andrews ran out Ellis for 63, and figures of 4–362 from 64 overs in the final total of 1107 provoked from Arthur Mailey some of his most famous lines.

After he [Ryder] had cruelly hit me into the members' reserve, Andrews said: 'Put a man there, that's his weak spot.' It was rather a pity that Ellis was run out at the finish, because I was just striking a length.

Very few chances were given, although I think a chap in a tweed coat dropped Jack Ryder just near the shilling stand, or was it the members' stand. Here I would like to thank the spectators who fielded so well. They never let up during their long stay on the other side of the fence.

The next time I come to Melbourne (I'm afraid nobody but a statistician would ask me again) I think it would be a graceful act if the spectators came inside the fence and gave a little support in the field.

To the scoring board officials I humbly apologise. I do hope they were on piece work.

Sun-News Pictorial quoted in *Seasons in the Sun* (Coleman) pp342–3

Jack Ryder himself provided this interesting vignette of Mailey and his young leg-spin protege James Campbell.

I guess that 1107 back in December 1926 will always stand out in my mind ... And I will always remember Arthur Mailey telling the NSW captain Alan Kippax not to expose a young spinner Campbell to all this punishment. Arthur volunteered to keep bowling, though he finished with 4–362.

Jack Ryder, *Australian Cricket*, February 1975

When Ryder received an MBE in the Queen's Birthday honours list of 1958, the leggie sent the Victorian the following note.

'May I extend my sincere appreciation of the honour Her Majesty has bestowed on you. You have richly deserved it despite the fact that you belted the cover off me in 1927 or was it 1928? I'm trying to forget it all.'

A Life-Long Innings (Fiddian) pp 161–2

AUSTRALIA EXPECTS

All Australia looked forward to England's visit in 1928–29, as Charlie Macartney discovered when touring Europe with his wife ...

One day while we were traversing the miles of art in the Vatican Museum intently gazing at the wonderful sculpture, tapestries, paintings and other works of art, I was touched on the shoulder by a man who introduced himself as from North Queensland and promptly asked me what I thought about the coming Test matches in Australia.

I was speechless for a moment, as I cannot think of a place in the world where the mind is so devoid of any thoughts of cricket as the Vatican

Museum. However, satisfying him that I had no idea which side would win, I heard him question the guide with the next breath as to why so many cats were kept in the Trajan Forum.

My Cricketing Days (Macartney) p224

... and as England's captain Percy Chapman discovered when his team disembarked from the SS Otranto *at Fremantle.*

As we were walking down the gangway when we landed in Australia, a wharf labourer yelled: 'Good luck to you Chapman! Have you brought the Ashes with you?'

'We're going to take them back — I'll show them to you when we go,' Percy shouted, grinning.

'I'll have a quid with you on that,' challenged the wharfie.

'Done!' called Chapman. 'Have the money ready for me when we leave.'

He had, too, but Percy just grinned all over and told him to drink our healths with it.

Cricket My Destiny (Hammond) p40

AN ENGLISHMAN ABROAD

English supporters were few and far between, though England's fast bowler Harold Larwood remembered one.

I can recall that at Sydney in a NSW–England match in 1928, one lone figure sat there constantly calling out: 'I'm a Pommie and I'm proud of it.'

The crowd around him shouted back: 'Shut your bloody mouth and watch the cricket.'

The Larwood Story (Larwood) p107

AL AND HAL

NSW was 9–113 in reply to Victoria's 376 on Christmas Day 1928 when Alan Kippax was joined by last man Halford Hooker. Kippax was 20, but so short of recent runs that his Test place was in jeopardy. Hooker had reached 20 once in first-class cricket.

As Hooker took centre, talkative wicketkeeper Jack Ellis said: 'Have a go Hal, the bowling's easy.' Ellis talked so incessantly, as if to break his concentration that Hooker turned and said: 'My word you talk to yourself a lot, Jack.' But when Hooker was still there after several overs, Ellis encouraged him by saying: 'Stick there, Hal.'

'When I had the strike for the last over,' recalled Hooker, 'captain Jack Ryder put on an opening batsman Fred Baring — the slowest off-spinner I ever saw — to tempt me into a stupid shot. 'Kip' signalled to me to be careful, reinforcing my resolve not to risk a change of style.'

The tailender survived all that a'Beckett, Ebeling, Ironmonger and Hendry could fire before lunch but nobody thought NSW had a chance. Hal said: 'The partisan crowd had booed 'Kip' at the toss because he had held his place in two Tests. But by six o'clock they were supporting us.'

During the day Victorian cricketlovers tuned in their crystal sets and, as news of the defiant NSW partnership came through the earphones, many left their Christmas dinners to flock to the ground. Some were even said to have used sixpences and threepences from Christmas puddings to pay their way in.

As the NSW score improved, the pressure and the fielding became more intent. 'As the scores came closer, Ryder had fieldsman packed close round me,' Hooker said. ' 'Kip' came along to say that, as two of them had boots on the wicket, I would be entitled to ask the umpire to have them moved back. I said to him: 'What surprises me is that the bowlers are so straight that they can get the ball through without touching the infielders!'

'For my club Mosman I usually went in No 10 or No 11, but I had absorbed enough from watching such great batsmen as Hobbs ... to avoid giving a chance until we'd topped Victoria's 376.

'Our aim was to give 'Kip' most of the strike but once he found that I was set, he no longer forfeited singles if they left me to play most of an over. From lunch to tea on a hot day I went from 18 to 22. The scorer told me that through the innings I averaged five balls out of eight.

'I have never been so close for so long to such a magnificent batsman in top flight. His back-cut, a lost art today, often passed between first and second slip.

'At tea Alan looked at the board and said: 'We're going pretty well. We'll get these. We only need 193.'

'I said: 'Do that sum again. We only need 93.'

'Alan finished the day on 222 and we were nine short overnight. The trouble was to put the bowling out of my mind and get to sleep. Next morning I asked him: 'How did you sleep?'

'Completely relaxed, Kip said: 'I always sleep well'.

'Next morning Kip faced Bert Ironmonger, who'd impressed Walter Hammond with the way he could swing the ball from off to leg then turn it across.

'When he cut two and four I walked up to Kip and said: 'Don't take such risks please'.

'Kip replied: 'Listen, son, it's like a football'.

'When a classic cut off Ironmonger put NSW in front a loud laugh came from the pavilion where St Kilda captain Bert Cohen collected a bet.

'Bert had said early in the match he thought Kippax, Jackson and Bradman made NSW's batting too strong for Victoria. Friends laughed him down. One scoffed: 'You can have 500 to one.' Cohen said: 'I'll have a bob of that.' He collected 25 pounds ...

'We were 44 ahead when Ryder caught me at slip off Ted a'Beckett for 62,' Hooker said. 'Though I was in good nick, using different muscles I had never batted so long, five hours and four minutes, and I was sore for a couple of days.'

Ray Robinson, Cricketer, March 1982

'THIS KID'LL GET 100'

In an unsuccessful series against England, Australians sought solace in the performances of its young batsmen. Archie Jackson's 164 on debut at Adelaide suggested a strokeplayer cut from the Trumper cloth.

The Scotland-born Jackson leaned forward to the first ball he faced from Maurice Tate, one directed in line with his leg-stump. Believing the ball had struck Jackson's pads, Tate threw up his arms and appealed for lbw. The ball had flashed to the boundary at fine-leg. When Tate realised the youngster had glanced it, he turned to Hele and said: 'This kid'll get 100.'

Bodyline Umpire (Whitington & Hele) p60

Australia lost three early wickets, but Jackson had stormed to 70 out of 3–131 at the end of the second day. Another promising newcomer, Don Bradman, joined the youngster early next day, and had accompanied Jackson into the nineties when lunch was taken.

I was Jackson's partner when we resumed after an interval. If my memory is correct, Archie's score was 96 or 97, and being so much older than he (just about a year to be precise) I had the temerity to offer him some advice. Jackson was about to take strike against Larwood, who had a new ball, so I suggested to him that there was no hurry. 'Take your time,' I said, 'and the century will come.'

Those who saw his next stroke will agree with me that no more glorious square drive could be played. He didn't care about Larwood or the new ball which travelled like a bullet to the pickets in front of the members' stand.

The youthful genius went on to make 164 and became the youngest player in history to make a Test century. The score did not matter so much. It was the manner in which he scored his runs. The English players joined in the applause, for cricketers like to see artistry even when they are on the receiving end.

To think that four years later I should be called upon to act as one of the pall-bearers when this glorious young player's remains were carried to rest, a victim of that dread scourge, tuberculosis.

Farewell to Cricket (Bradman) p23

Clickety-Click

Clarrie Grimmett took an amazing 82 wickets in 11 matches in the 1929–30 summer, his top-spinner especially murderous. And, although talented Sydney teen Stan McCabe noticed at one stage that Grimmett betrayed his toppie by clicking his fingers, he then erred by telling the bowler.

'I can read you Scarlet,' Stan declared triumphantly. 'You give that ball away with a click of the fingers. Whenever I hear that I know what's coming.'

Next time Grimmett bowled to McCabe he let go a big leg-break. The fingers clicked loudly, McCabe played for the top-spinner, only to be caught at slip as the ball turned off the pitch. Nonplussed, McCabe asked how he did it.

'I've got a left hand too, you know,' Grimmett laughed.

The Game is Not the Same (McGilvray) p122

Napper

McCabe's 844 runs in 1929–30, however, guaranteed his selection in Bill Woodfull's touring team to England in 1930. And it was while the team was staying in Paris at the historic Elysee Palace Hotel en route, that McCabe was delivered of his famous moniker 'Napper' by Victor Richardson and Alan Kippax.

The dawn would sometimes race them to sleep; and one morning Kippax exclaimed: 'All we need now Vic, is for Napoleon to walk through the door.'

As he spoke, the great double doors opened and in came Stan McCabe. At 19, his features resembled remarkably those of the first French Emperor, and he still had his hair.

'Well, Kip, there's your Napoleon,' Vic said; and the name stayed.

Fours Galore (Whitington) pp54–5

THE DON'S FIRST DAY OUT

The twenty-one-year-old Donald Bradman needed precious little time adapting to foreign wickets on his first tour of England. At the first opportunity, he scored 236 at Worcester.

The new ball was taken at 430 and Bradman immediately hit a four, then a single, and was 200. He was given a great ovation as the Cathedral bells were appropriately chiming 'The Last Rose of Summer'. His score occupied 250 minutes, and it was an Australian's highest individual score against Worcester.

Sydney Sun, 2 May 1930

THIS BOOGER

An unbeaten 185 followed against Leicestershire, before a stern encounter with Yorkshire at Bramall Lane where a story was played out that was handed down in the local dressing-room for years to come.

Don Bradman had been batting only a short time and, as usual, looked to be in ominous form. Macaulay, who had been known to quail batsmen with a glare and a mutter, asked for the ball and in a loud voice declared: 'Let me 'ave a go at this booger.'

His first over was a maiden to Bradman, but in the next he was hit for five boundaries and a further 16 runs in his third over. As silently he took his sweater, a voice with the strength of a loudhailer came from the crowd: 'Tha should have kept tha bloody mouth shut George.'

Fifty Years in Cricket (Hutton) p80

Similarly insatiable where runs were at issue was Bill Ponsford. It was almost, recalled wicketkeeper Bert Oldfield, as though the Victorian couldn't help himself.

In a previous county match Ponsford had scored a double century and had vowed afterwards: 'Never again! Too much like hard work!' At Cambridge before the game against the University he repeated that, and added: 'Today if I get 50, I'll throw my wicket away.'

Surely enough he made a chanceless 50, whereon one of our players called to Archie Jackson who was next in the batting list: 'Get your bat Archie! Ponny will be out any minute now.'

But to our surprise, instead of throwing his wicket away, Ponsford took block for his next 50 and by his renowned solid type of batting, went on to score another double century.

The Rattle of the Stumps (Oldfield) p32

ILL MET BY MOONLIGHT

The other sensation of the tour was Grimmett, whose wrong 'un caused consternation even to the delivery's pioneer.

During the 1930 tour he [Grimmett] met Bosanquet who asked: 'Am I responsible for you?' Not surprisingly, the spin brethren talked for hours, their scientific discussion at the end of the pier at Hove ending at two in the morning. Grimmett took 28 Test wickets on that tour, a return which, in truth, had as much to do with Australia's success as Bradman's 974 runs.

The Slow Men (Frith) p106

ALL THUMBS

Though Australia lost the First Test at Trent Bridge by 93 runs, there came a century from Bradman, 10 wickets from Grimmett and some spirited fast bowling by Tim Wall who thrice hit Yorkshireman Herbert Sutcliffe on the thumb and finally forced him to retire hurt.

When Sutcliffe withdrew his batting glove after the third blow, the top of his thumb was seen to have burst open like a rose in bloom. For some time after this, Wall received abusive letters from English fans accusing him of bowling deliberately at Sutcliffe's thumb. Tim's reaction was to exclaim: 'I wish I was as accurate as they think.'

The Vic Richardson Story (Richardson) p21

Australia's First Tie

In some ways the most remarkable game of the tour was Australia's meeting with Gloucestershire, the first tie involving an Australian team. England's Walter Hammond describes its closing scene.

Hornibrook and Walker were batting together, the last two Australians and the score — was level. Goddard was handling the ball, looking closely at it, ready to begin an over. I believe you could have heard a pin drop.

The ball went down. Hornibrook played it carefully — I'll bet he was sweating, too! No score. Another ball. Another. A shout to split the welkin: 'Howzat?'

The ball had hit Hornibrook on the pad. The world stood still while the umpire stared deliberately up the pitch. The appeal was dismissed.

More balls. No score. Over. Parker coming up to the wicket. Parker knows where there is a spot, the ball pitches on it, and the batsman Walker is hopelessly beaten. But — the ball goes past the sticks, apparently touching them. The bails remain in place. Walker does not let it happen twice; he plays with grim care. Each ball Hornibrook sneaks up the pitch past half-way, ready to risk everything on a stolen single that will win the game. As the ball reaches Walker, Hornibrook bolts home again.

Over. Still no run. Tom Goddard takes the ball once more. Tom, who used to be a fast bowler, must feel his blood boil within him to send down an 'express', just because this is a situation where violence seems the only adequate expression of the terrific tension. But he fights the devil down. His arm comes over again, with the slow precision of a machine. The ball goes down. It goes down again. Again.

'How wuz her, then?'

Tom's familiar yell follows the clip of the ball on Hornibrook's pad as if part of the same sound. The earth stands still and the sun stands still. Then — the umpire's finger goes up.

Pandemonium breaks loose! A tie! The only tie the Australians have ever played in this country. The crowd surges onto the grass as if the walls of a dam had burst. Above the great surge of dark clothes froths a white foam of hands and programmes. We are inundated. Players are slung up onto shoulders with as little care as sacks of wheat. Tom Goddard's arms and legs jerk like semaphores as he tries to keep his balance. What do they care about balance! A continuous deafening shouting stupefies the senses and a thousand hands beat our backs and wring our arms almost from their sockets. Somehow we have to get to the station to catch the train for Swansea. I do not know how it was done. All I remember is the vast confusion and my aching back and arms. The approach to the station, the booking office, the platforms seethed and thundered with hilarious mobs shouting, singing yelling: 'Speech!' And then again: 'Speech!'

Next day in the dressing room at Swansea we compared backs. We were black and blue. It looked as though we had been cruelly beaten.

Cricket My Destiny (Hammond) p72

A Quarter Of A Thousand

Bradman then really hit his straps, essaying probably his finest technical innings at Lord's: a chanceless 254.

One of the spectators that day, the late Mr H. F. Mathews of New Malden, recalled the impact: 'I well remember when he reached 250 the people round me expressing their amazement and dismay very volubly, when what must have been a cockney retorted: "Blimey, what are you worrying about? It's only a quarter of a thousand."'

Sir Donald Bradman (Rosenwater) p109

No Love Lost

Not everyone was satisfied by the innings. The cricket-loving playwright Ben Travers recalled that Bradman was not, among his teammates, a universally popular figure.

On the Sunday of that match I played golf with Tom Webster against Victor Richardson and Alan Kippax. The latter had joined Bradman at the wicket in the late evening with only about half an hour's play still to go. Bradman had by that time made a goodly proportion of his 254 and, being Bradman, had only thoughts for the morrow. Kippax confided to me his utter, bottled-up resentment of Bradman, who had taken care that he, Kippax, the newcomer, had the strike wherever possible. Bradman's Test record on that tour undoubtedly raised jealousy within the Australian camp, Woodfull apart.

94 Declared (Travers) p55

READY FOR TOMORROW

Bradman was irrepressible, however, and scored an unequalled 309 not out on a single day in the Leeds Test in which he scarcely raised a sweat.

McCabe joined Bradman about 45 minutes before stumps, when Don had been batting almost throughout the day. After they had been together for less than a half hour, Stan, two years younger than Don, walked down the pitch between overs and exclaimed: 'You'll have to stop running these short singles, Braddles, or you'll have me completely blown out.'

When they returned to the dressing-room at stumps, Don received congratulations from us all on his superb batting. He turned to Bill Woodfull and confided: 'That wasn't a bad bit of practice. I'll be able to have a go at them tomorrow.'

The Vic Richardson Story (Richardson) pp26–7

SOFT SOAP

Bradman reached 334 next day and, while fielding later on the leg boundary, was conveyed a telegram by Woodfull.

It said: 'Kindly convey my congratulations to Bradman. Tell him I wish him to accept £1000 as a token of my admiration of his wonderful performance. (Signed) Arthur Whitelaw, Australia House.'

Bradman thought it was another practical joke, but Woodfull and Kelly assured him it was genuine. A. E. Whitelaw, an Australian, had settled in England and become a wealthy soap manufacturer. He said later: 'I thought Bradman's performance merited such recognition ... we must encourage our cricketers in every way possible, since cricket is the greatest of all games. This is not so much a gift as a mark of appreciation on behalf of all Australians.'

Bradman (Page) p65

POSTMAN'S KNOCK

When Australia played Northamptonshire a month later, Bradman got an inkling of his new renown.

It was at Northampton that Bradman received a letter without delay addressed simply to: 'Mr Don Bradman, Champion Cricketer, England.'

Sir Donald Bradman (Rosenwater) p120

LARWOOD'S HOPE

Bradman made 232 at the Oval and took as his companion for much of the innings Archie Jackson, who scored a brave 73 against the fiercest fast bowling that Harold Larwood could manage.

There is nothing more heartening for the fast bowler than to get a little lift from the wicket. It is like icy champagne to the palate. The ball popped sharply as I hurled myself into every delivery. I pinked Archie several times. He took it like a man and stood up to me, playing the game of his life.

Don didn't like the balls rising on his body. He was hit once or twice, but the real significance in his play was the fact that he kept drawing away. It wasn't all that obvious to me at first, because I was mainly concerned with getting the ball up off a length, but I began to notice that he flinched. Others saw it too and we talked about it after the match. I thought Bradman was a bit frightened of the ball that got up sharply. I may have been wrong but that was my impression. I wasn't dropping them short — the ball was popping from a good length.

The Larwood Story (Larwood) p71

STINGS IN THE TAIL

The Australians also played an agreeable game against Glamorgan, where Swansea's tannoy impressed Vic Richardson (so much so, in fact, that he later pressed SACA secretary Bill Jeanes to install one at the Adelaide Oval).

I was leading the Australian side and the announcer came across to me at the fall of each wicket to discover the identity of the next batsman. When our eighth wicket fell I said: 'Wall is next, but you may as well announce Wall and Walker together. They won't take long out there.'

As Wall walked onto the field, the fellow announced: 'The next batsman is Mr Wall of South Australia, but Mr Richardson has asked me to announce Mr Wall and Mr Walker together as they won't take long.'

91

Like true South Australians, Tim and Charlie did not let me down. Three balls were enough to dispose of the pair of them.

The Vic Richardson Story (Richardson) p33

The scoreboard for Victoria's match at the MCG against NSW at Christmas 1931 ends allusively: H. H. Alexander absent 0. And therein hangs a tale. The fast bowler, nicknamed 'Bull', had popped off for a little recreation with his side two wickets down overnight.

Returning from it 90 minutes later, he boarded a tram at the corner of Flinders and Spencer Streets ...

'What's the score, connie?' Alexander enquired of the conductor.

'We're all out,' he replied.

'I mean the match at the MCG.'

'We're all out, sir.'

'We can't be all out,' said Bull. 'I'm the last batsman!'

The conductor did his utmost to hurry that tram along Flinders Street and Wellington Parade. Bull was there for the first over of the NSW innings. Watchers remarked, however, upon the mysterious decline in his speed and hostility. He'd lost at the races.

Bodyline Umpire (Whitington & Hele) pp73–4

BRADMAN'S BACK

Bradman averaged a staggering 201.5 against a visiting South African team in 1931–32, a performance that not surprisingly filled the tireless Springbok paceman Sandy Bell with awe.

One morning some of the South Africans were sitting in my office discussing cricket. Bradman came in for a few minutes and then left. As he walked along the corridor, 'Sandy' Bell looked after him and said in a voice resonant with wonder and admiration: 'That's the first time on this tour I've seen his back.'

Bradman (Moyes) p30

TIGER LEARNS TO ROAR

Making a belated Test debut in that match was the leg-spinner Bill O'Reilly, who already had a reputation for ear-splitting appeals. A reputation, moreover, he was proud of.

That his maiden Test wicket against South Africa was delayed, O'Reilly ascribed to bad pre-match advice from his friend and Australian selector Chappie Dwyer.

As O'Reilly prepared to take the field for the first time, Dwyer confided: 'Keep your wits about you. They're already starting to say that you appeal too much for lbw.'

In his first over, O'Reilly struck the pads of opener James Christy. Wicketkeeper Bert Oldfield did not appeal and neither, in an act of monumental self-control, did O'Reilly. Another two overs had elapsed when umpire George Hele muttered in passing: 'Don't you appeal for lbws?'

'Did you think he was out George?' O'Reilly asked.

Replied Hele: 'It would have been wise, I think, for you to have asked me.'

O'Reilly bowled Christy not long after, and his assault from that day forward was unblinking.

NLA interview published in *Wisden Cricket Monthly*, January 1995 p33

'WILD MAN OF THE WICKET'

An Australian team managed by Arthur Mailey toured North America during winter which resulted, on Wednesday 20 July 1932 as the visitors were in New York watching the Yankees play the White Sox, in a meeting between Don Bradman and Babe Ruth.

Perhaps fortuitously for the Australians, Babe Ruth was injured and the great player entertained them in his private box at Yankee Stadium. So the two greatest hitters of a moving ball in the history of sport met. According to the New York press, the Babe sat resplendent in a brown sports coat, white striped trousers, buckskin shoes and white cap — the true nabob.

The two looked each other over and began to chat. The Babe was surprised by Bradman's lack of size and weight … a scientist rather than a powerhouse …

'I thought you were a husky guy, but us little fellows can hit em harder than the big ones,' roared the Babe, and at once the proper spirit of camaraderie was established. Babe asked Don what impressed him about baseball: 'In two hours or so the match is finished. Each batter comes up four or five times. Each afternoon's play stands on its own. Yes cricket could learn a lot from baseball … There is more snap and dash to baseball.'

The *New York Times* enjoyed the editorial opportunities the Australian visit afforded and called Don Bradman 'The wild man of the wicket' and 'the ring tailed wallaby of the cricket crease'.

The Don Meets the Babe (Sissons) p28

THE IRON DUKE

When Douglas Jardine brought the England team of 1932–33, he at once became noted for his unparliamentary manner. When local journalist Claude Corbett criticised Jardine's team for taking the field late in their opening match at Adelaide, he was sent for by the English captain and his manager Plum Warner.

Jardine said, 'Mr Corbett, I have received a number of letters from Australians, abusive letters. These I disregard. I have also received a letter from an English friend of mine living in Australia. Of course, I shall reply to him. In view of what I have told you, is there anything you would like me to add to the letter as a comment from yourself?'

Corbett said: 'Yes Mr Jardine. There is something you can add. You can tell him from me that my comment is "Go and get f-----!"'

Corbett's phrasing was decidedly Anglo-Saxon. Mr Warner intoned plaintively: 'Gentlemen, let's keep the conversation on a higher plane.'

The Larwood Story (Larwood) p93

'YOU MUST PLAY, DON'

Bradman himself was locked in a struggle with the Australian Board of Control. He had agreed to write for R. C. Packer's Associated Newspapers, but the Board had then refused to grant him its permission. It seemed for a time that the Don might not be available to play against Jardine's men.

There was one very tempting offer from overseas. An English newspaper group cabled him an offer of £3000, a huge sum for those days, if he would abandon any hopes of playing in the Tests and cover the series for them.

By that time Associated Newspapers were under fire for 'holding Bradman to his contract', and some members of the board had begun to flinch under the steady bombardment of abuse and criticism. They asked A. G. Moyes, then the sport editor of the *Sun*, to introduce them to R. C. Packer, of the editorial board of the newspaper group, so that they might ask him to release Bradman from his contract.

Packer agreed to do so, but Bradman steadily insisted that he was under a moral obligation to fulfil the contract. His only offer of concession was to accept the English bid, drop out of the Tests and write for the overseas newspapers and pay the huge fee over to Associated Newspapers.

Packer rejected this and said: 'You must play, Don.'

He answered: 'You can't force me to write, but there's nothing in the contract which allows you to force me to play.'

Packer replied that Associated Newspapers only wanted him to forget about writing and play for Australia. He spoke so persuasively that Bradman at last agreed to break his own inflexible rule.

Bradman (Page) pp113–4

'SIGNED, TWO'

Bradman fell ill before the First Test, however, and his unexpected omission provided Ray Robinson with an extraordinary scoop. He waited almost fifty years to reveal the source.

One of my Test friends Bill Ponsford had arranged to keep me posted on anything exceptional that happened, using a figure instead of a name for whatever player was involved; in the code that was only possibly going to be used — probably nothing was going to happen — he was the opening batsman with Woodfull so he was number two, Bradman was usually the third batsman and he was number three.

So a telegram arrived addressed to me at the Melbourne *Herald* saying: 'Three declared unfit'. And it was signed 'Two'.

The editor for whom I was working hadn't been there long and, although a very good editor, had his doubts about how authentic this could be, so the only thing that happened as a result of the message was that a guarded paragraph was put in the stop press.

Ray Robinson NLA Interview

CHANGES OF PACE

Three players for England scored centuries in the First Test at the SCG: Herbert Sutcliffe (194), Wally Hammond (112) and the Nawab of Pataudi (102).

The last occupied a laborious five and a quarter hours, which tested a few of the locals' patience.

After watching him potter round for an hour and a half for about 25 runs and then, for a similar period, without any improvement, Vic Richardson crossed the wicket between overs and said to him: 'Pat, what's wrong? Aren't you seeing them too well?'

'Oh,' said the Nawab. 'I'm waiting for the pace of the wicket to change a bit.'

'Good God!' said Richardson. 'It's changed three times while you've been in.'

The Larwood Story (Larwood) p120

'STOP MUM JUMPING THE FENCE'

England's touring party was stacked with fast bowlers including Harold Larwood, Bill Voce, Bill Bowes, Gubby Allen and Maurice Tate. As young Stan McCabe watched with his parents the intensity of the English fast bowling at the SCG, he prepared his parents for the worst.

Stan McCabe was sitting in the front seats of the members' enclosure with his mother and father as the early batsmen began to be hit about the upper bodies by balls from Larwood. Wickets began to fall, and as the 22-year-old McCabe left his parents to don his pads, he called to his father: 'If I get hit Dad, stop Mum from jumping the fence.'

The Vic Richardson Story (Richardson) p69

AS FAST AS HE LOOKED

McCabe's unbeaten 187 is one of the bravest and most stirring innings ever played, for the strength and hostility of the opposition, as Bill O'Reilly attested on the basis of his experience on coming in at the fall of the eighth wicket.

Bill O'Reilly was next and was greeted by Stan with the following advice, which should be enshrined in our cricket folklore for all time: 'Don't worry about him [Larwood], he's not as fast as he looks — I'll handle him.'

Bill took guard and the first delivery received from Larwood cannoned onto the shoulder of his bat before he had time to lift it. O'Reilly, stupefied, called down the pitch to McCabe. 'Not so bloody fast, eh? I'll say you can handle him.'

Stan McCabe (McHarg) p35

You Wouldn't Read About It

The Sunday papers reporting the innings trumpeted variations on 'McCabe the Magnificent', but the player himself was unmoved. He had lunch with 'Chappie' Dwyer at a restaurant on the Pittwater shore.

At that lunch, 'Chappie' ... remarked jokingly, 'I suppose you have a swollen head after reading all that praise in the press.'

'But I haven't read the papers,' replied Stan. 'I thought there might be a lot of exaggerated praise in them it would be better for me not to read.'

Fours Galore (Whitington) p54

Yabba

Stephen Harold Gascoigne (1878–1942), the Balmain rabbito who became an SCG legend for his wit on the Hill as 'Yabba', was at his peak during what became known as the 'Bodyline' series. Here are some authentic yabbaisms.

'Don't worry son, it wouldha bowled me' (to a tailend North Sydney batsman bowled first ball as the crowd laughed unfeelingly)

'Give him one on the big toe Tibby' (to Glebe Test player, Tibby Cotter, a favourite of Yabba)

'Go Back to Africa Pat O'Dea' (to Indian Prince Pataudi of the English tourists 1932–33)

'Hurry up Herbie [Collins] declare the innings before he gets set and scores a century' (advice to NSW captain when the side was over 500 and a rookie batsman crawled to five in 30 minutes)

'It's no use George, you'll have to wait until playtime' (in a schoolboy falsetto to umpire George Borwick as he held his arm aloft for some time waiting for a sightscreen to be moved)

'Look out, it's a black snake' (as a Marrickville fieldsman positioned himself under a skier, which he subsequently dropped)

'Mind your stays old man' (to Jardine in a mock public school accent)

'My God Badcock, what's wrong with you, syphilis or gonorrhea?' (as 15-year-old Badcock let the ball through his legs to the boundary in his first match at the SCG)

'Put a penny in his meter George ... he's stopped registering' (to umpire Borwick, a gas meter inspector, in response to a slow Pataudi innings)

'Put Arthur on and don't waste time — poor Johnny is wanted on the telephone' (encouraging the use of Arthur Mailey to Johnny Douglas)

'Stand up on yer legs. Here's the Governor-General!' (when Charlie Macartney came into bat)

'Thank goodness he's not a flaming centipede' (when Maurice Tate, who took size 13 boots, took a long time to adjust them)

'What about a clap for Captain Bligh' (to Jardine in 1932–33)

'Wide ... WIDE ... DOUBLE WIDE' (after three successive poorly-directed balls)

'You can take the body away Hanson' (to Hanson Carter, keeper and undertaker, after he had caught Hobbs)

Cricketer, April 1984 p25

BODYLINES

Bill O'Reilly, a teacher at Kogarah, received an insight into the emanations of the series immediately after the SCG Test.

Early defeat in the Sydney Test meant that O'Reilly — being a very, very good and I should say unsophisticated public servant — went back to work for the half-day to take his boys to the St George Sports Ground for their afternoon games. 'They all got their gear out and they went down onto the four grounds,' O'Reilly remembered, 'and each one of the bowlers or each one of the captains set a Bodyline field straight away ...

'And I thought to myself: "Well, I'm not going to interfere. I'll let them have a go and find out how they like it". I don't think I stopped any fights ... but there was a tremendous lot of unusual chiacking that went on, as the kids found out it wasn't the brave thing to do as it looked.'

NLA interview published in *Wisden Cricket Monthly*, January 1995 p34

THE DUCK THAT STOPPED A NATION

When Bradman was fit and included in the Second Test at the MCG, the stage was set for one of cricket's most famous incidents. The bowler when Bradman arrived, and the narrator, was Yorkshire's towering right-arm paceman Bill Bowes.

Every step he took toward the wicket was cheered, and Bradman, a cunning campaigner, came from the darkness of the pavilion, and walked towards the wicket in a huge semi-circle. He was giving the crowd time to quieten and also accustomed his eyes to the glare.

He was cheered as he took up his guard, cheered as he looked round the field to see the disposition of the fieldsmen. The cheering continued at the same volume as I ran up to bowl. It was deafening. I had to stop in the middle of the run-up and wait for the noise to subside. To fill in time I asked my mid-on to move up to silly mid-on.

Once again I began my run. Once again came a terrific roar. Once again I had to stop.

This time I moved my fine-leg fieldsman to the boundary edge. I saw Don eyeing those changed positions with a look of determination.

Then the thought flashed into my mind, 'He expects a bouncer — can I fool him?'

I ran up to bowl with the most threatening expression on my face that I could muster. Don stepped across the wicket intending to hit the ball out of sight. But, as the ball flew towards him, he realised it was not a bouncer at all. In a manner that only a really great batsman could achieve, he changed the elevation of his intended shot and got a very feint edge on the ball, but his defensive move was ineffective. He was bowled out.

The crowd was stupified. Bradman walked off the field amid a silence that would have been a theatrical producer's triumph. The spell was broken by a solitary woman's clapping. The feeble sound rippled above the hushed throng, and then an excited chatter broke out all over the ground.

And it was then I noticed Jardine. Jardine, the sphinx, had momentarily forgotten himself for the one and only time in his cricketing life. In his sheer delight at this unexpected stroke of luck he had clasped both his hands above his head and was jigging around like an Indian doing a war dance.

Express Deliveries (Bowes) pp106–7

HAROLD BOWLS WELL

The Adelaide Test was one of the most furious ever played. When Larwood opened with the wind, with Bradman as non-striker, he at once hit Woodfull a fearful blow over the heart.

The batsman staggered back and the crowd, who were spoiling for a fight, howled with rage. Not just the ordinary punters but grey-haired members were up on their feet, shouting imprecations. Jardine walked across to sympathise with Woodfull and then made his way to Larwood at the other end. Hammond was already there, telling Larwood not to be put off by the crowd's behaviour.

'Well bowled, Harold,' said Jardine, loud and clear, as much for the non-striker's ears as for Larwood's.

Douglas Jardine: Spartan Cricketer (Douglas) p131

'This Game Is Too Good To Be Spoiled'

MCC manager Pelham Warner and his deputy R. C. N. Palairet visited Woodfull in the Australian dressing-room to enquire after his health. Their exchange — leaked to Sun journalist Claude Corbett — has gone down in the annals of cricket.

Warner went up to Woodfull and said: 'We have come to say how sorry we are and to offer our sympathies.'

Woodfull answered curtly in some such words as 'I don't want to see you Mr Warner. There are two teams out there. One is trying to play cricket. The other is not. This game is too good to be spoiled. It is time some people got out of it. Good afternoon.'

Bradman (Page) p129

'Someone Will Get Killed'

Larwood stoked the furnace by felling Oldfield with a bouncer although, as he remembered, the blame for the injury was not all his.

I had stopped bowling Bodyline, and the field was set mostly on the off. I wouldn't have pitched one short at Bertie, only he could bat, and he had settled in. The last thing I would have wanted to do was hit him. I pitched it short on off-stump. Bert swung at it, going for a hook, but it came off the wicket slower than he expected. He had spun almost right round, having just about completed the stroke, when it hit him on the right side of the temple. I think the result would have been worse had the peak of his cap not broken the force of the ball. An X-ray revealed more than a black eye — he had suffered a linear fracture of the right frontal bone.

I was the first one up to Bert. I might have broken even with Gubby Allen, who was fielding at short-leg. I was very upset. It was Bert's fault, and he was gentleman and sportsman enough to admit it at once. I am certain the ball came off the edge of the bat and that he walked into it. I was frightened how serious Bert's injury might be; I was also frightened at the abuse and barracking of the crowd. I thought they were going to come at us. It was so bad that Maurice Tate, who was sitting in the enclosure, got up and went into the dressing room saying 'I'm getting out of here — someone will get killed.'

The Larwood Story (Larwood) p148

NEXT MAN IN

Next man in was Bill O'Reilly, who was required to negotiate the seething crowd on the way to taking on the seething Larwood.

After taking minutes to force his way through the recalcitrant members, O'Reilly's whiff of Larwood's pace was short, sharp and pungent. 'I stayed for about five or six balls before he rolled me over and, when he hit the off-stump … I saw the off-bail just disintegrate as it went. So I bent down and picked up all the pieces and brought them back in my pocket as a souvenir.'

NLA interview published in *Wisden Cricket Monthly*, January 1995 p34

THE FAR SIDE OF THE FENCE

The frenzy of the Adelaide Test spread beyond the boundary and into a crowd who, to a man, abandoned all pretence. The future Prime Minister of Australia, Robert Menzies, later told Jack Fingleton of his experiences that day.

I was chatting to the man next to me, whom I didn't know. He was quietly-spoken, cultured and most interesting. We spoke of many things before the game started.

That was the day Woodfull was struck by Larwood. I looked at the man again and he was a changed person. He was on his feet and his face was choleric. He shouted, he raved, he flung imprecations at Larwood and Jardine because of what his eyes had seen.

Cricket Crisis (Fingleton) p84

Feeling continued to run so high that I was not surprised during the Test when I went into an Adelaide theatre one night and overheard a small child, after coming up and looking at me, saying to her mother: 'Mummy. He doesn't look like a murderer.'

The Larwood Story (Larwood) p155

Lost Appetite

Bradman himself was in uncommonly frail form as the 1934 Ashes tour commenced and weight fell on others in the side. Young Arthur Chipperfield went within a run of a century on debut in the First Test at Trent Bridge, and it saddened umpire Frank Chester to have to rule him out.

He was 99 at the luncheon interval and far too anxious to eat a thing. Three balls after lunch he was out, caught Ames, bowled Farnes. I have rarely seen a player so bitterly disappointed, and I almost wish I could have shouted 'No Ball'.

How's That! (Chester) p25

A Ball Change

Bill O'Reilly, on his first tour of England, bowled one of Test cricket's most fruitful overs at Old Trafford after Herbert Sutcliffe and Cyril Walters had begun with a stand of 68.

O'Reilly was then coming into the attack. He took the ball, looked at it, and said to Grimmett: 'This ball is out of shape, Grum.' Grimmett replied that he thought so too. The bowler handed it to Woodfull, who passed it to the umpire. Another ball was requisitioned.

O'Reilly bowled to Walters. It was a 'bosie', and it popped. Walters hit the pitch and at the same time the ball hit high on the blade near the splice to be deflected gently into the air to square-leg. Wyatt appeared, and was bowled first ball. Hammond hit a four, and then he also was bowled — three wickets in four balls, a sensational piece of bowling which began with a bouncing 'bosie'.

The Changing Face of Cricket (Moyes) p124

Nonchalance

O'Reilly also proved an able fielder, claiming at Lord's a singular catch at gully off Tim Wall to dismiss Ern Killick.

I threw out my hand expecting with a bit of luck to take the ball on the half-volley. The ball struck my hand as though I had timed it perfectly for the half-volley, so I quietly returned the ball to Wall. I was dumbfounded to see Killick tucking his bat under his arm and commence to take off his batting gloves as he turned for the dressing room.

I walked across to the slips fieldsmen and told them that I had caught the ball on the half volley. They laughed at me and, telling me I had taken the ball at least three inches from the ground, advised me to take a few more like it.

The press report of the incident read: 'O'Reilly, fielding in the gully, nonchalantly took a brilliant catch to dismiss Killick.'

Cricket Conquest (O'Reilly) p156

'Up Port Melbourne'

Also on his first tour was left-arm wrist spinner Chuck Fleetwood-Smith, whose wiles were complemented by his peculiar pitchside manner.

First the magpie call … arck … arck … arck … screeched out in a gravelly voice. The bewildered batsman looked all ways wondering if they were about to get pecked on the back of the head from an overprotective maggie.

Then the loud chants: 'Up Port Melbourne Go Port Melbourne' in tribute to his favourite football team. Usually by this time the batsmen had realised they were in the vicinity of a madman. Chuck would wander off to first slip, drawing closer to the batsman, and confusing him even more by raising his head to the sky and imitating the whipbird. If he saw someone he knew in the crowd, his enthusiastic waving would be accompanied by the cry: 'Woop woop woop, Gee up there Bess, Woop woop woop, Lord Hawke Lord Hawke Woop woop woop, Doodle Doodle Doodle. Lord Hawke Lord Hawke Woop woop woop.'

Everyone was turning around. So what, back to the magpie calls and 'I'm in the mood for love'. And we were only in the second over.

Up went a skied catch, straight to Chuck, who was too busy dozing to take any interest in catching the ball. The bowler frantically realised that he had better rescue his wicket. After a 20-metre sprint and a mad dive, the exasperated bowler had the ball in his outstretched fingertips. Chuck awoke, saw the bowler sprawled in front of him, and helped him to his feet with the words: 'Well done. I didn't think you were going to get here in time.' And it was only the third over.

By the fourth over, Chuck was giving a comic performance of his golf swing, strutting around with his bottom sticking out and playing to the crowd, miming his delight at getting a hole-in-one. The rest of the day he would build on his opening by intensifying the volume of magpie calls, the chants and the endless diatribe of gibberish. By this time his teammates and even his opponents were nearly sick with laughter.

A *Wayward Genius* (Growden) pp60–1

ABOVE AVERAGES

Australia was 3–39 on the evening of the second day of the Fourth Test, when Neville Cardus ran across the not out Bradman and invited him to dinner. Bradman declined.

'Thanks,' he said. 'But I've got to make 200 tomorrow — at least.'

Cardus could not resist the reminder that in his last innings at Leeds he had passed 300: 'The law of averages is against your getting anywhere near 200 again.'

Firmly enough, Bradman replied: 'I don't believe in the law of averages.'

Sir Donald Bradman (Rosenwater) p229

LONG LIVE THE KING

Bradman duly made 304, followed by 244 at the Oval, and became again the cynosure of all eyes, his feats eclipsing even news of King George V's lingering illness. Bill O'Reilly had an intimation of Bradman's thrall when he made up a foursome for dinner with Arthur Mailey, the great Fleet Streeter Tom Clarke and author Will Dyson at Canterbury.

Tom Clarke, then working with one of the great London morning dailies, was asked what his paper ... would do with the front page were the King to succumb to his illness that very night. 'Right across the page in banner headlines with a photo and nothing else in sight,' was his immediate response.

To me who knew nothing of newspapers, it seemed that Clarke's opinion was absolutely final, because it was the very first opinion that had so far been accepted without rather prolonged discussion. With that resolved Dyson asked what would be done if Edward, Prince of Wales, were to depart this world. Clarke said that he would almost certainly be given the whole front page also, if there happened to be no other piece of Empire-shattering news to claim part of that important area.

Arthur Mailey then wanted to know how the editors would react if both the Prince of Wales and Don Bradman were to make their exits simultaneously. That query from the puckish Australian furrowed the brows of the pundits ranged round the festive board. Talk went on at great length about the relative importance of the news items from so many different angles that I felt I needed Bartholomew's Atlas to help in deciding the many scattered areas of the British Empire which would be deeply concerned with the two items.

It was eventually decided that both would be displayed on the front page. The Prince of Wales would occupy the top left-hand side of the front page, Bradman the top right. Such was the popularity of Bradman in England in 1934.

Tiger (O'Reilly) pp134–5

Don't You Worry About That

Bradman picked up a serious illness in England that kept him from appearing in the 1934–35 season at home, and when he did reappear the following season it was for South Australia. His run appetite, though, had not been sated.

A Tasmanian team visited Adelaide in the summer of 1935–36. Alf Rushfortz was captain of Tasmania and Bradman skipper of South Australia.

When it came Bradman's turn to bat Rushfortz said: 'Don't go throwing your wicket away today, Don, if you can get your hundred; we need all the gate money we can get to balance our budget.'

'Don't worry, I won't,' replied Don. 'I need 182 for my thousand for the season.' Bradman made 369.

Straight Hit (Miller) p109

'Aren't You Playing, Tiger?'

Vic Richardson's stalwart service to his state and country was recognised when he succeeded Woodfull as skipper when Australia toured South Africa in 1935–36. Richardson showed a sound grasp of motivating his team during the First Test.

Bill is of Irish descent. Sometimes he needs something to get his Irish up. One or two doubtful decisions against him will do the trick. So will a lucky snick or two from batsmen. Neither were forthcoming this day so something had to be done. I took Bill off and refused to bowl him again before lunch that day.

Two or three of my team were in the plot and kept needling the Tiger as he toiled in the deep. 'Aren't you playing, Tiger?' they kept calling. His replies are unpublishable even nowadays. The game now had gone into the final day. O'Reilly was not bowled much in the morning session and by lunchtime was ripe (almost rotten) for reprisal.

I purposefully did not lunch with the team and delayed my return from the officials' lunch-room until we were due to return to the field. Bill had been given no chance to get at me during the interval. When we reached the pitch area, I threw him the ball. Although the wicket was much the same as before, Bill finished the game in a few overs.

The Vic Richardson Story (Richardson) p90

MY KINGDOM FOR A NOURSE

At Johannesburg, Australia and South Africa played a Test replete with splendid batting. First there was a dazzling 231 from local Dudley Nourse, which left the Australians impotent.

Richardson tried to control the game, but it was no use. 'Got any ideas, Chuck, about Dudley?' he said once to Fleetwood-Smith.

'Yes,' said that bowler. 'Shoot him.'

Masters of Cricket (Fingleton) p143

WADE'S WORRY

Stan McCabe recorded the second of his career's three great death-defying innings: 189 not out, with strokes so violent that they endangered the fieldsmen. His partner Jack Fingleton describes its climax.

McCabe ran to a flowing century before lunch, joining Macartney and Bradman in the feat, but in the afternoon if it were possible he pulverised the South African attack even more into dust. The Springboks had a plenitude of bowlers to take advantage of the conditions. Langton and Nupen were splendid medium-paced spin bowlers, and Mitchell and Balaskas found that the wicket greatly exaggerated their spin and also hurried it through.

McCabe never put a foot or his bat in a false position. To me at the other end and fully aware of the difficulties of maintaining even a defence on such a wicket, McCabe's batting bordered on the miraculous. He made

100 in 91 minutes, 150 in 145 and in that total was the amazing total of 24 boundaries.

In the middle afternoon, lightning flashed with startling vividness in the mineral-laden Johannesburg air. Peals of thunder rolled over the Wanderers, but not even the wretched light of the impending storm could dim the Australian's brilliance.

No better compliment could have been paid McCabe than this. With Australia still 125 runs behind and three hours of play, Wade the South African skipper did the most extraordinary thing of appealing against the light from the field.

It was quite apparent that the pending heavy rain would stop the match at any moment. There was thus no fear that South Africa would be beaten, but Wade was nonplussed, mesmerised and indeed stampeded by the profuse profligacy of McCabe's boundaries. Some said there was the flavour of unsportsmanship in Wade's appeal, but Wade was one of cricket's gentlemen. I knew from close quarters that McCabe had woven a spell over him.

Cricket Crisis (Fingleton) p248

POT BLACK

Richardson's team were unbeaten on tour although, when they beat Transvaal by an innings, unexpected late resistance was posed by the tailenders Chud Langton and Ernie Nupen.

Langton and Nupen scored freely in the dark and one mighty hit by Langton off O'Reilly went right over the members' stand into the avenue. When this occurred another ball was requested in order to save time. Langton also hit that out of the ground, and a third ball was called for. That also disappeared out of sight and a fourth produced, to suffer the same fate. By the time the seventh had arrived on the scene, fast bowler Ernie McCormick walked over to Richardson and said: 'Well, that's the end of the reds. Now we can get on with the coloureds.'

Vic's Boys (Bassano & Smith) p89

ERNIE MAC

The sardonic Victorian McCormick was one of the wittiest cricketers to take the field in an Australian cap. Bill O'Reilly recalled the Australians' visit to the De Beers diamond mine in Kimberley, where they were instructed in the security arrangements for black miners.

It transpired that, to discourage those who considered swallowing a diamond, these even involved study of workers' stools. 'Ha! So that's where it comes from!' McCormick said at once. 'The old saying: Flash in the pan.' Said O'Reilly: 'He would have done well on the stage with old Harry Lauder or one of those fellers.'

NLA interview published in Wisden Cricket Monthly, February 1995 p39

Making fun of his left-hand batting he told of an innings where he lasted two balls. He played the first one and called 'wait' resonantly to an impetuous partner. The next bowled him.

As he walked away he heard the wicketkeeper say: 'McCormick? Obviously the tenor!'

In Melbourne against Queensland he and Fleetwood-Smith swung their bats like rusty gates to add 90 for the last wicket. Ernie survived 13 chances (a record) and his partner 11. His comment: 'Death takes a holiday'.

Ray Robinson, Cricketer, April 1981 p28

Though McCormick's first two overs in England at Worcester in 1938 contained 17 no-balls, he coped with his overstepping whimsically.

Commenting on the day's events umpire Baldwin said: 'He lost his run. I had to do my duty.'

McCormick said: 'I wish he was hoarse.'

The matter gave rise to a standing joke in the Australian team. If a member of the public greeted McCormick in the street, he would walk straight on without a turn of the head. A colleague would explain to the bemused cricket lover that the shouts of no-ball had affected his hearing.

Cricket's Dawn That Died (Valentine) p67

He had a letter from his sister after that. The McCormicks all have a rich sense of humour. 'Come home,' she said, 'you are making a fool of yourself — and moreover the tradesman won't call on us now.'

The Ashes Crown the Year (Fingleton) p15

Very fast on his day, McCormick inflicted at least one serious injury on that tour when he knocked Leicestershire's Les Berry senseless. Mrs Berry, he explained, absolved him.

'I was bowling pretty quick and one got up a bit and hit a fellow called Berry in the head,' says Ernie. 'He wasn't too good and had to be carted off to hospital for observation.

'The following day-off, most of the Aussies went to an air pageant held nearby. While we were there I was introduced to Berry's charming wife. I felt terrible about what had happened and apologised profusely but I wasn't ready for the reply: "Oh don't worry," she said, "I've been wanting to do that for years."'

The Wit of Cricket (Brayshaw) p74

McCormick retired after that tour, a decision reached with clinical logic.

It's time to retire he says when you take one boot off, and the other half an hour later. 'And when you get old three things happen. You can't remember other people's names … and I can't remember the other two.'

David Frith, *Wisden Cricket Monthly*, April 1988 p13

McCormick remained in the game, however. One of his legacies is the Frank Worrell Trophy — the symbol of supremacy in Test matches between Australia and the West Indies which he, a jeweller, designed for Sir Donald Bradman. He also remained ready with a quip. When conscripted in the 1950s for a Prime Minister's XI match, McCormick stayed with Jack Fingleton.

On this occasion he [Fingleton] had his house full with Hassett, Morris, Loxton, Johnson and company when McCormick arrived. There wasn't a bed spare. Jack parked Ernie on a mattress on the floor under a grand piano. Next morning, anxious to make amends, Jack took him a breakfast tray.

'Sorry about this. How did you make out?' he asked.

'Fine,' replied McCormick. 'I'll never sleep under an upright model again.'

Keith Miller: The Golden Nugget (Whitington) p23

Ernie would never deliberately say a word he thought would harm a fly, but he's not given to flattery. When Fred Titmus had those four toes amputated in the West Indies early in 1968, Ernie quipped: 'At least they can't no-ball him for dragging now.'

The Quiet Australian (Whitington) p151

GUMMED UP

When Gubby Allen's English tourists of 1936–37 brought a mingling of old stagers and first-timers to Australia, the latter began filling in the former on what they could expect as soon as they arrived in Fremantle.

Through the customs they were ushered with alacrity — just a pause to give anxious officials their autographs — and into a posse of motor cars for the 12-mile journey to Perth. 'You see that tree,' Leslie Ames said to [Ken] Farnes, squinting in the great glare as they bumped along at 35mph. 'Well, it's a gum tree and you won't see any other sort for five months.'

Summers in Winter (Meredith) p143

A SUMMONS FROM THE BOARD

With Australia trailing 1–2, McCabe, O'Reilly, O'Brien and Fleetwood-Smith were summonsed to a meeting of the Board of Control at the VCA offices to answer allegations of indiscipline. The incident led to much rancour between O'Reilly and Bradman thereafter.

O'Reilly asked Bradman what was going on. Don said he knew nothing about it, but declined to accompany the four 'miscreants' saying: 'You know what I think of the board.' This was a reference to past troubles Don had experienced in his dealings with the administrators.

It is worth noting that the four were all Catholics of Irish descent. Fingleton, of similar persuasion but a working journalist, was not summonsed. The board members before whom they were paraded included Roger Hartigan (former Test cricketer), Harry Hodgetts (Bradman's chief in an Adelaide stockbroking firm), Dr Robertson (chairman) and Dr Mailer, a Collins Street medical specialist.

Embarrassment was general on both sides and the preliminaries lacked any noticeable rapport between the two groups. Dr Robertson began reading from a lengthy typewritten screed in which unfitness and insubordination were mentioned, but not applied to any specific people. After a couple of minutes, Bill interrupted and asked if he and the other three were the butt of the allegations. Dr Robertson answered: 'No'. Bill then enquired what they were doing there and, after a few more embarrassing moments, the meeting broke up.

Bill O'Reilly: A Cricketing Life (McHarg) p161

CHUCK'S REVENGE

At the Adelaide Oval, Fleetwood-Smith underwrote Australian victory by avenging himself on a batsman who'd previously savaged him: Walter Hammond.

Chuck had taken the first two English wickets when Bradman remembered a remark by the wicketkeeper Sammy Carter during Arthur Mailey's 1932 tour of America. Carter had said to Bradman: 'I'd love to play one Test with Fleetwood-Smith. He could win a match for Australia some day.'

Bradman walked over to Fleetwood-Smith and, trying to inspire him, said in a cool voice: 'Chuck, if ever we wanted you to bowl that unplayable ball, now is the time.'

Fleetwood-Smith responded to the challenge, bowling probably the best and certainly the mosy significant delivery of his career. In the air the heavily-spun ball swerved tantalisingly away from Hammond's bat, and pitched on a worn spot outside off-stump. Hammond was drawn defensively forward, but was then caught in no-man's land when the ball spun viciously back between bat and pad, accelerating from the pace it made from the pitch to conclusively bowl him. Fleetwood-Smith, who slumped to his knees in jubilation, turned to Bradman and shouted with a hint of sarcasm: 'Was that what you wanted?'

A Wayward Genius (Growden) p122

TWISTING THE TIGER'S TAIL

Bill O'Reilly was a hard man to get the better of but, when a youngster from Petersham called Sid Barnes first played him at St George, he proved capable of twisting the Tiger's tail. Arthur Morris was an eyewitness.

I can still remember Siddy the first time I played him. He played a long innings while O'Reilly went through Petersham, and this whipper-snapper strolls up to Bill in the showers and says: 'Well bowled, Tiger. That was some of the best bowling I've faced.' ... Bill just about swallowed the soap.

One Summer, Every Summer (Haigh) p132

Barnes in due course shared the NSW dressing-room with O'Reilly and, as the Victorian Lindsay Hassett observed, the Tiger still had a hard time keeping the young man in his place.

111

Very early in my career I remember being given out caught off Bill O'Reilly in Melbourne to a ball that came off my pad. I chided O'Reilly afterwards telling him the ball had hit my pad not my bat.

'Go on, you hit it,' barked O'Reilly.

'No Tiger, he didn't hit it,' piped up Sid Barnes, very much the junior member of the NSW side.

'And you can mind your own business,' said O'Reilly, giving him a cuff over the ear.

Australian Cricket, February 1975

Hassett himself wasn't bad at raising O'Reilly's dander, when he demonstrated himself a fine, fleet-footed batsman with centuries in each innings for Victoria against NSW in Sydney.

During the second innings as Lindsay — having just on driven a six, and Bill — at the end of his run through, met in the middle of the pitch, Bill scowled at the world at large and growled: 'And the little so-and-so isn't even good-looking.'

Cricket Caravan (Miller) p163

'COME AND LOOK AT THIS!'

Bradman's 1938 tourists included O'Reilly, Hassett, Barnes, Fingleton, Fleetwood-Smith and another dashing kid batsman Jack Badcock. All however were overshadowed in the First Test at Trent Bridge by Stan McCabe who, seeing his side slump to 6–194 in reply to 8–658, made 232 out of 300 added while he was at the wicket. Ray Robinson describes the innings.

That was the signal for McCabe to take the match in his own hands. For the next couple of hours his batting was enchanting. It held everyone under its spell, bowlers as well as spectators. From the players' balcony, Bradman called to a few of his team who were inside the pavilion: 'Come and look at this! You've never seen anything like it.' In the press box, Woodfull was moved to write: 'It is a pity that the whole cricket world could not see this double-century.'

The 30,000 who were lucky enough watched wonderingly as the vice-captain added 170 while his last four partners scored 38 ... The arrival of Fleetwood-Smith was accepted as an infallible sign that the innings was drawing its last breath. Instead his advent inspired McCabe to unfold the most dazzling half-hour's batting of the match. Hammond spread five fieldsmen round the boundary yet could not prevent fours — McCabe had so many strokes and guided them so surely. The Englishmen fared little better when, near the end of the overs, they drew in to encircle him with a net of infielders trying to block the singles he needed to get the strike at the other end instead of his vulnerable partner.

Fleetwood-Smith rose to the occasion by surviving 18 balls and collecting five runs. Stan scored 72 in the last thrilling 28 minutes — something unheard-of in Test cricket even in the days when Bonnor and Jessop were denting pavilion roofs. McCabe's 232 in 235 minutes (34 fours, one six) is the fastest double century in Test history … Despite the urgency of the chase for runs there was not one slogging hit, in fact no show of force because of the precision of his timing. It was power without violence, dash without slap … When McCabe returned to the pavilion, Bradman greeted him with: 'If I could play an innings like that I would be a proud man, Stan.' Surely the highest tribute ever paid a batsman.

Two former English captains, A. E. R. Gilligan and R. E. S. Wyatt, agreed that it was the best Test innings they had seen and their opinion was shared by a renowned cricketer of an earlier generation S. F. Barnes as this dialogue between Neville Cardus and the mighty bowler showed:

Barnes: 'The finest innings I have seen.'

Cardus: 'Think again, you saw Trumper.'

Barnes: 'I can only repeat it is the greatest I ever saw.'

Cardus: 'I'd've liked to see you out there bowling to McCabe.'

Barnes: (after a moment's thought) 'I don't think I could have kept him quiet.'

Between Wickets (Robinson) pp40–1

THE PRAGMATIST

Fingleton took many catches at short-leg for O'Reilly on the tour and, as he recalled against Warwickshire, helped a few on their way.

In an unthinking moment, I allowed myself to go there [to short-leg] for Waite at Birmingham one day and Santall, a massive man of some 15 stone, gave a short ball all he had. I ducked instinctively as I saw the ball coming for the middle of my forehead and it hit me a glancing blow, shooting up, I believe, tens of feet in the air. As I was lapsing into semi-unconsciousness on the ground I could hear Bradman's piping voice from cover, mixing with bird calls, and calling out: 'Catch it! Catch it!' A practical man, Bradman!

Brown and Company (Fingleton) p108

A Pair At HQ

While Bill Brown made a double-century and Bradman a century in a drawn Second Test at Lord's, young Badcock had the misfortune to make a pair. His sympathetic teammates, Ernie McCormick recalled, decided to say nothing when he returned to the dressing-room.

Badcock's unhappiness was only deepened: 'A bloke makes a pair,' Ernie recalls him saying. 'You wouldn't think his mates would give him the arse, too!'

David Frith, Wisden Cricket Monthly, April 1988 p13

O'Reilly's Report Card

O'Reilly took 10–122 and Fleetwood-Smith 7–107 in a grim, low-scoring Fourth Test at Headingley, which excited those at home.

In 1938, after Bill O'Reilly had skittled England twice to win the Leeds Test, his students at Sydney Grammar School sent a cable to him in England which read simply: 'Satisfactory — a trier.'

Bill O'Reilly: A Cricketing Life (McHarg) p25

Bradman's Jam

Australia was left only 107 to win but, hastened by the possibility of a storm, almost made a hash of it. Bradman, fearful of rain, fell to a wild stroke, and was so full of repentance that he could not bear to see the final rites.

The match became so exciting that, for the first time in my life, I could not bear to watch the play. The scene in our dressing-room could hardly be imagined. O'Reilly with the pads on, hoping and praying he would not be needed, was walking up and down on one side of the centre table. On the other side I was doing the same, but, to prevent my teeth chattering in the excitement, was consuming copious amounts of bread and jam augmented by a liberal quantity of tea. We relied on our colleagues to give us a running commentary of the play.

Our manager was even worse. He could not bear to stay in the dressing-room, and had gone outside the ground for a walk, where thousands of people were lined up in queues unable to gain admittance ...

In that electric atmosphere, it was Hassett who forced the issue. The imperturbable Victorian midget, who in a crisis had always been such a masterful player, lofted his drives and threw caution to the winds in a race to beat the weather.

Farewell to Cricket (Bradman) p108

A Thousand For The Taking

'Bosser' Martin, the Oval groundsman, had set himself the task of preparing the perfect batting strip for the Oval Test. On the morning of 20 August 1938, umpire Frank Chester was inclined to agree.

In my opinion there has never been a better wicket anywhere from the batsman's viewpoint. Luckily for England, Wally Hammond won the toss … and the first over bowled from my end, by Stan McCabe, was enough to prove the docility of the wicket.

As I gave McCabe his sweater he declared, 'Frank, they'll get a thousand.' He was not far wrong.

How's That! (Chester) p29

As young Yorkshire batsman Len Hutton settled in to stay, he too studied the Australians' reactions.

I had opened with Bill Edrich, who could not master 'Tiger' O'Reilly. He should be forgiven as O'Reilly was a supreme bowler if ever there was one. Even if the conditions were loaded against him, he was still formidable, and even more so when adversity fired his Irish blood. After a few overs I heard him growl to umpire Frank Chester: 'Where's the groundsman's hut? If I had a gun with me, I'd shoot him.'

Fifty Years in Cricket (Hutton) p25

Going Down

Hutton made 364, passing Bradman's Ashes record score of 334, and Australia's miseries were increased when Fingleton was injured fielding. When Don Bradman came on to bowl, he slipped in a foothold dug by O'Reilly's boot, and broke his ankle. O'Reilly recalled the ensuing kerfuffle.

'You'd swear I was an opal miner,' O'Reilly related. 'I was going down, down and down, and he stepped into that and did his ankle and was carried off. And the crowd that came out to cart him off, you'd have reckoned it was an aeroplane disaster as compared with the departure of Fingleton.

'Well we didn't see Bradman again on the tour. We waved him goodbye as he left the field, never laid eyes on him again until we got on the ship to come home.'

NLA interview published in Wisden Cricket Monthly, February 1995 p40

With the Don incapacitated, Hammond decided he was safe enough to declare at 7–903. Australia were defeated by an innings and 579 runs in what proved, thanks to the outbreak of the Second World War, the last Ashes Test for more than eight years.

LIFE DURING WARTIME

Wartime cricket in England pitted local Test and first-class cricketers against visiting servicemen. One such match in 1943 between 'England' and 'Dominions' introduced Denis Compton to a figure who would become one of his greatest rivals: Keith Ross Miller. Here, the Englishman describes their first encounter.

Luck smiled upon me that day and I felt set for a big score. Finally the ball was thrown to a tall, dark, brush-back-haired fellow who had been racing round the boundary like a young gazelle and whose gigantic throws with an almost nonchalant whip of the wrist and forearm had drawn whistles of admiration from the crowd. He was fifth bowling change.

Not knowing what to expect I turned to wicketkeeper Stan Sismey and asked: 'What does this chap do Stan?' The answer was comforting. 'Oh he's not really a bowler,' said Stan. 'I expect he wants a bit of exercise, but you might find him a bit quick.'

A bit quick! The bowler took only a short run and when he let the ball go my hair nearly stood up on end. That was the fastest ball bowled to me since I played against Ernie McCormick of the 1938 Australian team in England.

Such was my introduction to Keith Miller.

Keith Miller Companion (Miller & Whitington) p5

A Vigorous Man

When peace approached in Europe, the idea was mooted of a tour by a team of Australian servicemen led by Lindsay Hassett and Miller. The plans were well advanced by the time of the German surrender, and the team was in Blackpool playing a preliminary match when its captain was caught up in the VE Day euphoria.

Our team was entertained by the Lord Mayor, one Mr Roberts, who at 78 years was — to grossly understate the fact — a vigorous man. I parted company with him round 4 a.m. on the understanding that he would come to see my side play the North of England on that very same day. He also put in a proviso that I should have a bottle of whisky at the ground. After the exertions of the previous night I doubted whether he would make it, but surely enough he arrived shortly after the start of the game. We had won the toss and I had the pads on to go in at first wicket down. Our openers put on a fairly lengthy partnership and, when someone tapped me on the shoulders and told me that a wicket had fallen, the tide in the whisky bottle had receded dramatically.

I made my confident way to the wicket and took block. Wicketkeeper for the North was George Duckworth. I consider he summed up the position pretty well — when sniffing the fume-laden air, he muttered: 'Aye, ah think ah'd better stand back otherwise we'll both be bloody shicker.'

Hassett in *Centenary Test Souvenir* p34

'The Better The Ball ... '

The team was hurriedly reassembled for the first of a series of five Victory Tests against England. Miller shone during the series, and produced an innings of 185 in the climactic England–Dominions game that earmarked him for greatness. The Englishman J. W. A. Stephenson attested to Miller's indomitable spirit.

I bowled him a late outswinger. It grazed his off-stump. I showed my chagrin. Miller strode up the pitch, patted the spot where the ball had landed, tossed back his mane and glared at me. I bowled him an almost identical ball. He drove it into the stand and again strode up the pitch. 'A better ball, but the better the ball, the bigger the sixer,' he called. Right then I knew he'd be a great batsman.

The Quiet Australian (Whitington) p87

117

Miller continued his magisterial progress on the subsequent tour of India, playing a blazing innings of 82 in the first innings of the Calcutta 'Test' with a bat 'borrowed' from the partner he joined.

'I asked you not to use my bats,' this player complained as Miller reached the wicket. 'Why don't you find one of your own?'

'I'll take care of it. There won't be a mark on it when I've finished. You'll see.'

Keith had to face the left-handed Vinoo Mankad, a bowler who would take 162 wickets at 32.3 in 44 Tests. Beyond the tarpaulined temporary stand behind Mankad's arm and just outside the ground was a water-lily pond. Four of the five remaining balls of Vinoo's over landed among the lilies.

'I thought you said you'd be careful with my bat?' Keith's partner exclaimed.

'I am being. Every one of those hits went off the middle. Here, take a look at your bloody bat.'

It was unmarked.

The Golden Nugget (Whitington) p97

'WHAT DO YOU HAVE TO DO, JACK?'

The Australian Services XI was prevailed on finally, much against its will, to play a further series of matches against Australian states that continued into March 1946. While Hassett and Miller guaranteed they would play a great deal of Test cricket, an incident at the Adelaide Oval involving Don Bradman on the last day of 1945 seemed to ensure that the all-rounder Cec Pepper would play none. Teammate R. S. Whitington tells the story.

Before Don had proceeded very far he moved in that tripping footed confident way of his a couple of steps out of his crease, mis-sighted the ball and was rapped on his right pad. I was at first slip and could not determined whether Don was leg before wicket or not. Pepper thought he was and appealed excitedly and triumphantly to umpire Jack Scott, a man who had been known in his fast bowling days to appeal excitedly and triumphantly himself against batsmen like Charlie Macartney.

Jack disallowed the appeal. Pepper put his hands to his huge forehead and exclaimed: 'What do you have to do Jack?'

On his way back to bowl the next ball Pepper shook his huge head several times and mumbled some words into what, had he been W. G. Grace, would have been his beard.

From the last ball of the over Bradman took a characteristic single past mid-on and, as he completed the run, called to umpire Scott: 'Do we have to put up with this sort of thing?' I heard him.

Now Jack Scott was permanently employed by the SACA and he was not in a financial position to carry on without that appointment. He told Pepper that in view of Bradman's complaint he had no alternative but to report the incident to the authorities. Soon afterwards the matter came before the Board of Control who demanded that Pepper should apologise. I helped Cecil frame the apology and it was a complete apology. It was handed to the Services team's conscientious and kindly manager Keith Johnson, who was a member of the board at the time ... [but] in some way it became lost in transit ...

In the meantime the Australian team to tour New Zealand was selected and Pepper's name was not among those chosen. The board asked Pepper for another apology. He came to me and asked whether I thought he should send one.

'That all depends upon whether you want to play for Australia again or not Cecil,' I replied, knowing my Board of Control.

'Well in view of my non-selection for the New Zealand tour I have agreed to go to the Lancashire League,' he said. Finally Pepper reasoned that if his word wasn't good enough for the board he would not send another apology, and he didn't.

Gods or Flannelled Fools? (Miller & Whitington) pp31–2

PEPPER SEASONS

Henceforward, the salty Pepper was confined to the northern hemisphere. He made thousands of runs and took hundreds of wickets for Rochdale, Burnley, Radcliffe, Oldham, Royton and North Staffordshire, becoming renowned for his combative mien and ear-splitting appeals. Pepper did not always intimidate umpires, however. The most repeated Pepper story is of an exchange with umpire Harry Wood, when the Australian pulled himself up after an over of vociferous but frustrated 'Howzats'.

At the end of the over Pepper realised that perhaps he had gone a little too far. So as he took his sweater from the umpire he muttered some apologies, saying he had temporarily lost control of himself. The old umpire merely smiled and said: 'You're reet lad, ah likes somebody who speaks their mind.'

This was music to Pepper's ears, so when he rapped the batsman on the pad with the first ball of his next over he really let fly with one of his juiciest appeals. The old umpire, calm as a mill pond and without even flickering an eyelid, replied: 'Not out, you fast Australian bastard.'

Over the Wicket (Brayshaw) p49

Pepper became a first-class umpire himself from 1964 to 1979, though pomp and circumstance always eluded him.

In my debut for the Derbyshire first team I encountered Cec Pepper, who had the disconcerting habit of breaking wind like a bus backfiring as the bowler was about to deliver. When I was non-striker he asked me after yet another resounding blast: 'Just kick that one to the boundary would you John?'

Christmas in Rarotonga (Wright) p71

Political correctness where players of colour were concerned didn't always come easy either. He was umpiring a Warwickshire–Scotland game at Edgbaston, for instance, when Bill Blenkiron replaced the Barbadian Bill Bourne.

Brian Hardie [the batsman] was informed loudly by Cec: 'Batsman, change of bowler, same action, different colour'.

Such light-hearted indiscretions would have brought charges of racialism in today's more structured times but at the time such irreverence was accepted by all as part of the Pepper personality.

Simon Wilde, *Wisden Cricket Monthly*, September 1989 p40

It was the onset of helmets that finally persuaded Pepper to give the game away. As this story suggests, he took a dim view of cricket's protection racket.

Dennis Amiss had strolled to the wicket in a Warwickshire–Kent game with a helmet. Pepper asked him where he'd parked the moped; then Amiss requested he hold it while he was at the non-striker's end.

The umpire's reply was one of rude finality: 'You hold it mate and use it as a bloody pisspot.'

Simon Wilde, *Wisden Cricket Monthly*, October 1989 p37

TIGER'S CUB

The team for which Pepper missed selection was a transitional one. Senior statesmen Bill Brown and Bill O'Reilly led likely lads like Keith Miller, Ian Johnson, Ray Lindwall, Sid Barnes and Colin McCool on a tour to New Zealand. O'Reilly took care to chaperone his young St George teammate Lindwall as he grew used to Test life.

Lindwall only bowled seven overs in Auckland's first innings, dismissing opener Pearson, but in the second innings bowled 26 overs — one of the longest spells he had ever had in first-class cricket ...

In the dressing-room at the end of play, O'Reilly found Lindwall exhausted, too tired to get under the shower and saw immediately that refreshment was needed.

'Have a beer, Ray,' he said.

'Oh no I don't drink,' Lindwall replied.

'You've got to replace that lost fluid,' O'Reilly said. 'If you try to do it with lemonade or Holy Water or something like that you haven't got much chance because you can't drink enough.'

Lindwall took the advice on board. From that time he enjoyed a few beers after a hard day in the field and often contemplated the wisdom of his mentor's words.

Ray Lindwall: Cricket Legend (Ringwood) p40

BOOTS BOOTS BOOTS

O'Reilly took 8–33 in the Test at Wellington's Basin Reserve but, handicapped by an agonising knee injury, acknowledged it would be his last Test.

When I walked off the field my old knee felt so crook that I thought: 'Well this is it mate'. And I walked in and the first boot I took off was my left one, and I whooshed it out the window in amongst a team of kids. And then I chucked the other one, too. So probably somewhere over round Wellington, New Zealand, there's a pair of very good boots still alive, some kid getting a few wickets with them.

NLA interview published in *Wisden Cricket Monthly*, February 1995 p40

SID THE SAMARITAN

The Australians left a good impression on spectators and opposition, and were solicitous when New Zealand's skipper Walter Hadlee shrugged off injury for Otago to make a noble 198 not out from 347.

While the Australians were in Dunedin I got to know Sid Barnes well. He was a kind-hearted person. When I was struggling with the injury to the left hand, he walked up and said: 'Having trouble mate?'

I indicated that was an understatement as Lindwall, fairly enough, was still bouncing me. I could not hold my bat with my left hand. Sid said: 'Try getting onto the back foot and steering them backwards of square. There's nobody there if the ball's in the air.'

It worked long enough for my grip to return to sufficient strength to hold the bat. Not many players would suggest something to help an injured opponent.

The Innings of a Lifetime (Hadlee) p156

'YOU'LL NEVER MOVE BRADMAN WITH THAT STUFF'

England arrived at Fremantle on its first post-war Ashes tour in October 1946 and, at practice near the WACA, captain Wally Hammond discovered that Australians did not need a match in progress to express their competitive spirit.

While we were playing at the nets getting the shipboard stiffness out of our wrists and clearing our eyes for the Australian sunlight, there were plenty of comments for us gratis and not a little free advice. It is deflating to listen to Australian youth sizing you up!

'That Hammond's not half the size they said he was!' growled one disgusted youth watching me bat. 'I'm going home — I've had enough of this!' I was sorry to disappoint him, but I couldn't look any bigger.

'This Edrich don't look much — pretty weak off the back foot I guess,' declared another child of about four feet nothing. 'Get yer nose over the ball there — you won't never do nothing like that.'

And another: 'I don't like the look of this Yardley's wrists — look weak to me. Lindwall'll cut his bat out of his hands, won't he!'

Best of all was the eight-year-old with the huge cap who critically watched Wright bowling, clicked his tongue in despair, and said: 'I'd rap the pickets with that myself Pommy; you'll never move Bradman with that stuff!'

That is the hallmark of Australia — free speech.

Cricket My World (Hammond) p15

THE CATCH THAT WASN'T

Don Bradman made a faltering comeback to Test cricket at Brisbane, batting sketchily for an hour against Alec Bedser and Bill Voce before an incident that had a profound impact on post-war cricket relations. This is Norman Yardley's account.

Bill Voce was bowling. Bradman had got 28, and suddenly attempting one of his favourite strokes, a drive just wide of cover-point, the ball flew from the top edge of his bat and straight towards second slip where Jack Ikin caught it beautifully.

Now I want to be precise about this. As the photograph in this book shows, I was in the best position on the field, even better than the umpire himself, to see exactly what happened. I watched the ball bounce from the turf onto the top edge of the bat and go from there straight into Ikin's hands. According to the Laws of Cricket, it was 'Out!' Ikin held the ball waiting for Bradman to leave the crease. He stared at the ground and did not move. Astounded, Ikin called 'Owzat?' The umpire looked straight at him and said: 'Not out'.

Everyone on our side looked in blank amazement, and Hammond in particular seemed to be wondering what to do next. Bradman still looked down. The point was this. The umpire, according to subsequent statements, supposed that the ball had been chopped down from the bat onto the ground, and had bounced. But you do not have to play cricket for years to know that a ball chopped down at that speed bounces steeply up. It does not travel parallel with the ground at chest height …

I am not intending any slight to Don, nor suggesting anything except that Umpire Borwick made a mistake. All human beings make mistakes sometimes. All the same, it was an unfortunate moment at which to make one. Don Bradman was out, three wickets were down cheaply on a batsman's wicket in the first Test after the long wartime break. It might have made a world of difference if only …

Cricket Campaigns (Yardley) p124

THE ICEMAN COMETH

Bradman eventually rediscovered his touch, dominating in the last stages of his 187 in Australia's 645. Brisbane's notoriously fickle weather turned foul, and a hailstorm offered Sid Barnes the opportunity for a famous practical joke.

Those who went through the Brisbane storm of 1946 will never forget it. It was a terrifying experience and, in no time, the Cricket Ground was a sheet of ice. The dressing-room there is next to the Members' Pavilion, the scene of so many rows in the cricket world and as hard to enter as paradise. This is fenced with barbed wire and once led an English pressman to term it Belsen.

Drinks in the dressing-room are contained in a large tub with a block of ice in its middle. Barnes struggled out with this block of ice in the middle of the storm and tipped it over the fence into the Sacred Pavilion. Down it slithered on the grass among all the hailstones. The eyes of the members bulged. They think to this day that it came down from above — and had you known that storm, you might have believed it, too.

Brightly Fades the Don (Fingleton) pp61–2

SINGING IN THE RAIN

The weather also turned the pitch into a bowler's dream. Ian Johnson recalled that Bradman was delighted by the opportunity to avenge past indignities.

He was in the highest spirits, chuckling and laughing as the rain cascaded down. I remarked that surely he was not concerned about the rain when we had more than 600 runs on the board.

He replied: 'Ian, the first time I played against England in 1928, they scored 521, caught us on a wet wicket and got us out for 120. With a lead of over 400 they batted a second time and left us over 700 to make in the last innings.

'Then they invented Bodyline for my special benefit and, the last time I played against them in England, England made over 900 before Hammond declared and I broke my ankle while bowling and couldn't bat. Just this once we have them in trouble. Do you really blame me for being so happy?'

I must confess, I didn't blame him one bit.

Cricket at the Crossroads (Johnson) pp6–7

Keith Miller, however, found Bradman's attitude boorish. It contributed to a mutual distrust.

When I started cricket with Australia after the war everyone was happy to be alive. We went to Brisbane for the First Test in 1946. It was a mud heap for England. I was bowling on the worst sticky ever and I was frightened of hurting someone. I got seven wickets or something in the first innings. 'Blind Freddie' could have got wickets on that track.

I remember hitting Bill Edrich and Wally Hammond. Edrich, a chunky, gutsy little chap with a DFC was getting battered from pillar to bloody post. Hammond and Edrich held us up for a little while. Bradman came over to me and said: 'Bowl faster, bowl faster. Get them out.' He told me later, when you play Test cricket you don't give these Englishmen an inch, play it tough, flat out the whole way. 'Grind them into the dust' were his words.

I thought to myself that a war had just gone and a lot of Test cricketers and future Test cricketers had been killed and here we are just after the war, everyone is happy and now we have to grind them into the dust. So I thought: 'Bugger me. If that's Test cricket then they can stick it up their … ' Don kept up this incessant will-to-win which just wasn't my way of playing cricket.

Howzat! (Butler) p54

TWIN 234s

Bradman showed that his powers were fully restored with an innings of 234 in the Second Test at the SCG, which was ended by exhaustion rather than any bowler.

When he fell lbw, swinging at Yardley, with Australia 564, he limped into the dressing-room to tell his team: 'There's runs to be had out there — if only a man had legs.'

From the Boundary (Robinson) p243

Bradman's dig was bookended by a far slower but symmetrical innings from Sid Barnes. Whatever disappointment Barnes experienced in getting out was salved by the idea of Wisden *bracketing him with the Don.*

After that innings Barnes returned to the dressing-room with a huge grin and bathed in perspiration. As he unbuckled his pads he said happily, referring to Bradman: 'Well at last I'm in the record book with the little chap.'

Straight Hit (Miller) p33

KEEPING THE SPONSOR HAPPY

Though corporate cricket backers and man-of-the-match awards were decades away, wealthy patrons were by no means uncommon. In making his maiden Test century at the MCG, for instance, Colin McCool benefited from the largesse of punting plutocrat John Wren.

Jack Wren, one of the wealthiest businessmen in Australia, watched that innings. He liked his cricket and he suffered fiercely when things went against Australia. Certainly things weren't too good that day, because when I went in we were 6–192, and in his anguish he turned to a friend and said: 'I'll give this fellow a pound for every run he makes.'

Next day a cheque for £104 arrived at the dressing-room.

Cricket is a Game (McCool) pp25-6

A GENERATION GAP

Though Australia won the series 4–0, Bradman's failure to press for victory at Adelaide in the Fourth Test upset many watchers. Herbie Collins, then writing for a newspaper in Sydney, was particularly aggrieved.

Collins didn't like the 'feeling' that crept into cricket in the time of Jardine and Bradman. His own men, he admitted, played the game pretty hard, but there was always good feeling with the opposition. He thought little of Bradman's captaincy after the war and was sure he needled the Englishmen unnecessarily.

He saw Bradman behind the pavilion after that poor Test match of 1946–47 when the Australians so obviously played for a draw.

'I've written an article for my Sydney newspaper about you,' Collins said.

Bradman nodded.

'In case they don't print it in full,' said Collins, 'I'll tell you the theme of it. I've suggested that cricket would be a better game now if you got out of it.'

From one Australian captain to another, this was stringent criticism. Bradman passed on.

Masters of Cricket (Fingleton) pp107–8

CHUTZPAH

Keith Miller moved to NSW before the start of the 1947–48 season, which offered him some respite from public acclaim in Victoria … at least until he and Dick Whitington went to lunch at the NSW Cricketers' Club.

Said Miller: 'Dick, it's wonderful that nobody recognises you here. You can relax thoroughly when walking along the street.'

At the corner of Pitt Street, Miller stopped to buy a magazine. 'It's no use your getting it, Mr Miller,' grinned the newsboy. 'Your photo's not in this week.'

Miller laughed and handed the lad an extra-large tip.

Cricket Capers (Goldman) p12

721 IN A DAY

The 1948 Australians that Bradman led are widely considered the best touring team we have sent abroad. Essex managed to dismiss them within a day at Southend, which was unusual. The Australians made 721, which was freakish. As ever, Bradman was top scorer with a two-hour innings of 187 in which he demonstrated all his majesty.

The first three balls of one over were pitched on a good length on the off-stump. He smote them all past cover-point to the boundary.

'Can't you hit them anywhere else?' humorously asked the Essex wicketkeeper F. Rist. Without a word Don picked up the next three, all pitched on the same spot, and pulled them to the mid-wicket boundary. 'How's that?' he enquired turning to Rist at the end of the over.

Flying Stumps (Lindwall) p173

Not everyone could permit themselves to participate in this wholesale slaughter.
Amid the run-gluttony, Keith Miller lost his appetite.

Bradman, Saggers, Loxton and Brown all made centuries, their distinguishing feature being their rate of progress which varied from just under a run a minute to a run in a minute and a half. Miller came in to bat when the score was 2–364; he took guard perfunctorily and to the very first ball that was bowled to him he lifted his bat, flung his hair back and was walking back to the pavilion before the bails hit the ground.

If ever a situation could be said to epitomise the man, then this was it. Runs were there to be had, the Australians were to score another 357, but the idea had no appeal for him. As he walked towards the pavilion Bradman, the non-striker, whose instincts must have been outraged by the gesture, said to Trevor Bailey, the bowler: 'He'll learn.' Miller as we shall see, didn't.

Keith Miller (Bose) pp 56–7

The Maker's Name

When roused, however, Miller was fearsome. During the First Test at
Nottingham, the all-rounder reminded his regular rival Len Hutton that
provoking him was unwise.

The worst mistake a batsman could make against him was to hit him for four. He accepted 1s, 2s and 3s but boundaries were an indignity he did not cheerfully tolerate, and invariably the next ball would be an absolute fizzer. At Trent Bridge in 1948, he was trundling away with medium-pace off-breaks when I took two successive boundaries and 14 in the over. That was too much for Keith, but what else can a batsman do with half-volleys?

I knew what to expect, and in eight balls I had five bouncers, one of which left the manufacturer's imprint on my left shoulder. Two others leapt at my throat from just short of a length as if they had been bowled from no more than 10 yards away with a tennis ball.

Fifty Years in Cricket (Hutton) p51

First innings centuries by Bradman and Hassett, and 63 not out in the second innings from Barnes saw Australia home by eight wickets in that First Test, although the latter's taste for memorabilia caused some strife for him on the last day.

A strange interlude occurred when Barnes glanced a ball to the leg boundary and imagined he had scored the winning runs. He turned and commandeered the leg stump and made off for the pavilion in haste. Seeing him check out, the English fieldsmen and the umpires began to move towards the Stand, but they were greeted with howls of derision from the gallery who realised that there was still one run to be scored before Australia could claim victory.

Everyone returned to the wickets; Barnes who had disappeared into the dressing room seemed loath to re-enter the playing field. He finally appeared, preceded by the stump which he hurled out onto the field, and on picking it up he proceeded to the wicket and shaped up with it as he handed his bat to the umpire to place in the ground.

With Barnes it was more likely to have been a mathematical inaccuracy than excitement that this incident occurred. It fell to Hassett to make the winning hit and Barnes, running through to make the single, failed to souvenir a stump after all — much to his disgust.

Cricket Conquest (O'Reilly) pp53–4

A Dreadful Ribbing

Barnes made 141 as the Australians won the Second Test at Lord's with ease, but was quelled when they were held to a draw in the Third at Old Trafford. Fielding at short-leg, he took the full force of a lusty pull shot from England tail-ender Dick Pollard. Umpire Frank Chester was an eyewitness.

Barnes had no chance of evading the ball and he collapsed writhing in pain as it struck him like a bullet in the ribs. As four policemen carried him off the ground, and an ambulance rushed him to Manchester Royal Infirmary, everyone was convinced he had received a grave internal injury.

But on the Saturday morning he got out of his hospital bed and, with typical Barnes bravery, insisted he was going to bat. During a trial at the nets he joked with Press photographers but after a while grew so weak that he had to rest on the running-board of a car.

Yet no one could restrain him from going out to the wicket. After a sympathetic reception from the crowd and a somewhat theatrical hand-shake from Dick Pollard, he stayed at the wicket for nearly half an hour, then sank to the ground with a cry of pain. He took no further part in the game.

How's That! (Chester) p36

Recalling the incident some months later, Sid said: 'I had some Minties in my pocket when I got hit but I haven't seen them since those policemen carried me off.'

Slasher Opens Up (Mackay) p167

Barnes also revelled in presenting the injury as footage in his own films.

When the film showed him writhing on the ground in pain after Pollard's hit injured him, he commented drily: 'It would have killed any ordinary man.'

From the Boundary (Robinson) p197

HAT TRICK

The other fielding casualty of the Old Trafford Test was vice-captain Lindsay Hassett, who responded characteristically when he twice missed century-maker Cyril Washbrook on the deep fine-leg boundary.

After dropping two catches (and this in a Test) Hassett borrowed a helmet from a policeman and stood ready for the third time. No catch came then, but Washbrook sent Hassett along a bottle of champagne after play that day. That was one catch Hassett didn't miss!

Four Chukkas to Australia (Fingleton) p124

SPIKES

Hassett's dead-pan humour was in evidence when Australia played Oxford University.

When the pitch was to be rolled at one stage, Pawson asked Hassett what type of roller he would like. Hassett has a splendid poker face.

'What have you got?' he asked Pawson.

'There is heavy, the medium and the light,' answered Pawson.

'Haven't you got a spiked one?' asked Hassett without a glimmer in his eyes.

Pawson looked hard. 'I don't think so,' he answered very seriously. 'But I'll make sure.' And he went away to ask. Tony was known as 'Spike' Pawson after that.

Brightly Fades the Don (Fingleton) p71

STARTING OUT

Victorian teenager Neil Harvey played his first Test match in England at Headingley, and joined Keith Miller at a pivotal point: Australia 3–68 in reply to England's 496. It was to Miller and his later partner Sam Loxton that he owed much of his innings of 112.

The first three balls I played at and missed. Then Keith Miller who was batting at the other end, came down the pitch to have a few words with me and settle me down. But the best encouragement Keith gave me was when English spinner Jim Laker came on. I still hadn't scored at that point. Keith said to me: 'Let me take him for a while.'

Next thing I knew Keith played one of his lusty drives and hit Laker straight over my head and over the fence for six runs. Three balls later he did it again — another six. I thought to myself: 'Well this is not such a tough game after all.' Thanks to Keith my nerves vanished. We put on 110 runs in quick time to turn the Test round.

When Keith got out, my mate Sam Loxton came and hit seven sixes in his 93 runs. Meanwhile my game came good. I found myself hooking and cutting, pulling and driving round the wicket. I made 112.

Winning (Writer) p55

RADIO DAZE

When Loxton himself missed out on his first Test century, being dismissed seven short, he spared a thought for the folks at home.

Returning disconsolately to the dressing room, Loxton flung his bat into the corner and cried: 'There goes the old man's axe through the radio.'

Cricket Capers (Goldman) p72

That Winning Feeling

England set Australia a record 404 to win on the last day but Arthur Morris, with Don Bradman in tow, made a brilliant 182 to win the game. Harvey completed a memorable Ashes debut by hitting the winning boundary off Jim Laker.

I was at the crease with Bradman at the end and hit the winning run. I wasn't used to hitting winning runs in Test matches and was totally unprepared when the crowd invaded the pitch at the end. As Bradman hared past me to avoid their clutches I cried out: 'What do I do now?'

He replied: 'Son, we get out of here.'

Winning (Writer) p55

Tallon's Talent

England collapsed disastrously in the Fifth Test at the Oval, Lindwall taking 6–20 in their all out 52. The fast bowler's last wicket was Hutton, first in and last out for 30, victim of a famous catch by Don Tallon (here described by Keith Miller).

Lindwall, bowling to Hutton, was delicately turned off in the direction of fine leg. Everyone on the ground including the fieldsmen peered toward the fine leg fence expecting to hear the crash of the ball on the wooden fence.

Instead there was a raucous: 'Howzat!' Tallon slithering through the mud and sawdust, had the ball wedged firmly in his left hand. Hutton was out. I was standing in slips and, to this day, I cannot imagine how Tallon moved to take the catch.

Sporting Life, November 1950 p10

His Last Bow

In what he had foreshadowed as his last Test, Don Bradman went to the wicket needing four runs in order to become the only batsman in Test history to average a hundred every time he was dismissed. Warwickshire leg-spinner Eric Hollies was the bowler, Rex Alston and John Arlott the BBC commentators.

Alston: The crowd settle down again — they've got forty minutes — forty minutes more left to play and Bradman is now taking guard, Hollies is going to bowl to him and John Arlott shall describe the first ball, so come in John.

Arlott: Well I don't think I'm as deadly as you are Rex, I don't expect to get a wicket. But it's rather good to be here when Don Bradman comes in to bat in his last Test.

And now, here's Hollies to bowl to him from the Vauxhall End. He bowls, Bradman goes back across his wicket and pushes the ball gently in the direction of the Houses of Parliament which are out beyond mid-off.

It doesn't go that far, it merely goes to Watkins at silly mid-off. No run, still 117 for one. Two slips, a silly mid-off, and a forward short-leg close to him as Hollies pitches the ball up slowly (voice rises) and (sudden applause) he's bowled. (Applause continues. Several comments off-mike. Applause dies.)

(Slowly and distinctly) Bradman, bowled Hollies, nought. Bowled Hollies, nought. And — what do you say under those circumstances? I wonder if you see the ball very clearly in your last Test in England on a ground where you've played some of the biggest cricket of your life, and where the opposing team have just stood round you and given you three cheers and the crowd has clapped you all the way to the wicket. I wonder if you really see the ball at all.

Arlott (Allen) p136

On the Australian balcony, during all this, was Barnes. He had gone into the dressing-room, whipped up his camera before taking his pads off, and from the balcony filmed the last Test innings of his captain. There is no more enthusiastic photographer than Barnes. Adjusting his camera, he entered the dressing-room, unbuckled his pads with his skipper and told him he had got all his innings!

Brightly Fades the Don (Fingleton) p187

DON'T MENTION THE DON

Bradman's greatness, henceforward, would be a subject of curiosity and conjecture. 1948 tourist Colin McCool, when playing later for Somerset, had this response for the inquisitive.

Avinish Desai, who turned out for the Cricket Club of India in the mid-fifties, also played league cricket in England. He once found himself standing in the loo, next to the Australian Colin McCool, during the tea-break of McCool's benefit match, both being surrounded by several Englishmen.

Desai conversationally asked: 'McCool: Tell me, how good was this guy Don Bradman?'

McCool looked round, gestured to Desai to be quiet and said: 'Ssssh! Not so loud, you silly chap! If any of these Englishmen hear you, they'll pee in their pants.'

Darshak Mehta in *Willow Tales: The Lighter Side of Indian Cricket*
edited by Fredun De Vitre p56

MEETING WITH GIANTS

Alan Davidson, a left-arm paceman from Gosford, came down to Northern District to play in the Sydney Grade Competition in 1948–49. One of his first opponents was St George, captained by Bill O'Reilly.

The ball beat me hopelessly, the keeper too, and I scuttled out of harm's way for a bye. I said to O'Reilly with a sigh: 'Gosh, I'm glad I didn't have to face you 20 years ago.' He glowered down at me and said gruffly: 'Listen son, you're out here to bat, not to talk.'

Fifteen Paces (Davidson) p47

The St George attack was led by Ray Lindwall, whom Davidson had also idolised from afar.

To this day I can't remember taking block; I think I was mesmerised. Somehow the ball hit the bat — I didn't hit it. But the shock of the impact, I dropped the bat. The fieldsman nearby reached over and handed it to me. 'I believe this is yours son,' he said. That was my first meeting with Ray Lindwall.

I remember playing against him a year or two later. Ray came on to bowl from the Northern End and bowled this ball I thought was hittable. I went straight into it and it went like a 2-iron shot straight back past him — actually hit the sight screen on the full. Needless to say Ray didn't say anything except for a bit of a mumble which was his normal way. I never heard him swear, never heard him carry on. Back he went to his mark, turned around and I think my bat was going back not coming forward when the ball hit the stumps and skittles all round. Stumps went everywhere.

Ray Lindwall: Cricket Legend (Ringwood) p67

When Davidson was selected for the NSW state squad, he then encountered Lindwall's partner in pace Keith Miller.

Once at the SCG nets I was bowling to Miller and slipped in a shortish faster ball which caught him sharply in the ribs. He glared down the wicket: 'Have you had a bat yet?'

I replied: 'Yes, thank goodness.'

I think my reply would have been the same had I not batted. Miller is no man to tangle with in that mood.

Fifteen Paces (Davidson) p67

'We're Going To Win And You'd Better Say So'

Lindsay Hassett led Australia to South Africa in 1949–50 and they were at once in trouble in the First Test at Durban. He could not prevent South Africa reaching 311, or staunch an Australian collapse on a wet wicket for 75. But, despite an apparently hopeless position, Keith Miller was buoyant when he met writer Dick Whitington on the stoep of the Edward Hotel.

'I hope you haven't been stupid enough to write off our chances in your story to Australia?' he exclaimed, running his fingers through his hair.

'I haven't cabled it yet,' I replied. 'It's the most difficult story of a Test day's play I've ever had to write … '

'I'm sorry for Dudley Nourse,' Keith said. 'He's going to have the whole nation down on him like a ton of bricks when South Africa lose.'

'When they lose. If they lose, you mean. You're still 236 behind.'

'We're going to win and you'd better say so. You'll probably be the only press man who does. Just think of the feather that will be in your cap.'

'You must be joking?'

'I'm dead serious. Want to bet?'

Keith's luck as a punter was too well known for me to accept that £5 wager, but I modified my story — quoting the optimism of the Australian team.

The Golden Nugget (Whitington) p185

The Durban Dodge

South Africa's captain Dud Nourse was torn over whether to enforce the follow-on. He decided against it, expecting further rain, and fell into a brilliant ruse conceived by Hassett.

Hassett had other ideas. He was absolutely certain that the wicket would take spin on the Monday and he wanted his batsmen to have no part in it. In other words he wanted to keep the South Africans at the wicket without them scoring so quickly that they would declare, without them realising that the pitch was turning, and yet without them playing so badly that they realised something was up.

That's as sweet a little problem as you can get in a cricket match!

Hassett sorted it out like this: he decided he would use only three bowlers — Miller, Bill Johnston and Ian Johnson. These three, he reckoned, could keep the attack going indefinitely, for Miller was rich in stamina, Johnston was a two-purpose bowler (slow or quick) and Johnson thrived on long spells.

Having selected his bowlers, he called them together and briefed them. Under no circumstances were they to drop the ball short, or to try spinning it, he said ... the half-volley was to be the stock ball, with full-tosses accepted. The first man to drop the ball short would be pushed quietly overboard on the way back to Australia!

His plan outlined, he then warned each of the three to be silent about it. He wanted nobody else, not even in the Australian team, to know what he was up to. The fewer in on the secret the more likely it was to remain a secret.

It first started to come home to me that something was cooking when I saw this fruity length everyone was bowling. I wouldn't have minded a taste of some of that stuff myself. I got steadily more suspicious when, from my resident spot at first slip, I saw that not once throughout his spell had Bill Johnston tried to spin the ball.

I read bowlers' hands like a gipsy fortune teller, and Bill wasn't trying to do anything but put the ball there. At the end of an over I went up to him and asked: 'What's on? Why aren't you trying to spin?'

Bill, who would starve to death if he had to earn his living as an actor or a Secret Service agent said, Chicago-style out of the corner of his mouth: 'The skipper told me not to.'

I reasoned that for a moment, and then saw all. From then on that Springbok innings became the most intriguing in my life. They batted all day without Nourse attempting to declare. The fielding was fabulous, fantastic, magnificent, any superlative you like to put on it. The South African batsmen spent the whole time belting half-volleys into the covers, yet got so few through that their tally for the best part of a day's cricket was 99!

We held our catches, too. We had to, to make our case look good. It was a great feeling being an Australian that day ... I have never seen eleven men so dedicated to the task of just stopping a cricket ball.

One South African did spot what was going on. He was Cyril Vincent, a former player and selector. He knew the wicket was bad and went and pleaded with Nourse to declare. But Dudley stuck to his plan and did not declare until the last session.

Cricket is a Game (McCool) p47–9

On the last day, Neil Harvey played a brilliant innings of 151 not out and won the match for Australia by five wickets, with the benefit of a narrow squeeze.

I remember one ball their spinner 'Tufty' Mann bowled me. It did me like a dinner. It was beautifully pitched just outside off stump spinning into me. I pushed forward and missed and I froze waiting for that horrible rattle behind as it hit the stumps. No sound ... I was 40 at the time and had I got out then the game would have been gone.

Winning (Writer) p55

THE FREAK

While a gunner in Pom Pom Park at Port Moresby, Jack Iverson had experimented during games of French cricket with a homespun method of spinning the ball by extending a folded middle finger. He was toying with using it in competition on his return when he took a walk across Jolimont Park near the MCG with his wife Jean.

Playing on a pitch in the centre of the park with a wicker ball, that they could only trace because it rang a bell as its bounced, were two cricket sides from Melbourne's School for the Blind. The courage and persevering determination of those blind players began a train of thought and resolve working in Iverson's mind. 'If those chaps with all their handicap can do as well as that, I'm going to give my bowling discovery a go,' muttered Jack, more to the nearest oak tree and the summer air than to his wife.

'And Johnny, if you take it up, I know you well enough to be certain you will finish in there,' said Jean Iverson, pointing to the adjoining MCG.

R. S. Whitington, *Sporting Life*, October 1950 p47

Iverson was in New Zealand with an Australia B team led by Bill Brown while Hassett's men were in South Africa, where his 21 wickets at 13 suggested that his prehensile fingers held in them the power to perplex batsmen … and umpires.

At Invercargill a Southland batsman groped forward, overbalanced and sprawled full-length on the pitch. The ball had deflected from the inside edge of his bat and travelled to [Phil] Ridings in the slips cordon. Ridings grinned and smartly slipped the ball into his pocket. The batsman got up, brushed himself down, then looked around for the ball.

'You're out,' we chorused.

'How am I out?' he asked mystified.

'Caught,' we replied.

'Who caught me then?' he queried doggedly.

Ridings promptly produced the ball from his pocket.

The batsman looked at him for a moment then replied: 'Well I didn't see you catch it so I'm staying here.'

The batsman had the last laugh, too, because Iverson's guile and Ridings' sleight of hand had deceived the umpire who gave him not out.

Fifteen Paces (Davidson) p57–8

Considerable interest surrounded Iverson when first he encountered Freddie Brown's English team of 1950–51 while playing for Victoria.

Hutton, as practical as ever, sought Iverson out when the MCC team arrived in Victoria and were given a reception.

'I don't suppose,' said Hutton jocularly, 'that you'd like to show me how you hold the ball.'

Iverson smiled the invitation off.

Brown and Company (Fingleton) p50

Iverson took 21 wickets at 15 for Hassett's Australians, but disappeared almost as quickly as he arose. Miller and Morris manhandled him so badly in the Sheffield Shield a year later that his fragile confidence ebbed away.

Iverson returned to the Victorian side in the 1952–53 season, but batsmen were handling him with comparative ease. When he shared a cabin of the train with Ian Johnson after an interstate trip, they opened a couple of beers, and the Freak's first words were: 'I'm going out to graze, back to Melbourne fourths.'

Johnson asked why. 'I've lost it,' said Iverson. 'They're playing me easily.'

By His Own Hand (Frith) p36

NATURAL CAUSES

When during the MCC's match against Queensland the distance of the press-box from the players' enclosure at the Gabba handicapped the cricket writers, Arthur Mailey and Charles Bray of the Daily Herald *took matters into their own hands. MCC manager Brigadier M. A. Green recounts.*

At Brisbane the members of the press could not get hold of me, and when Denis Compton came off the field it was essential for them to know what had happened to him.

The Press Box was about twenty yards from where I was sitting, talking to the Governor, when a telegram was handed to me. it read: 'Please say why Compton left field. Mailey Bray' ...

I went down to see Denis Compton, as I always did when a player came off, and found that he had forgotten to put the bandage on his knee. However, I felt that the Mailey–Bray joke should not fade for such a mundane reason so I sent a telegram back reading, 'Mailey–Bray ref to wire re Compton natural causes. Green.'

Sporting Campaigner (Green) p149

WARR CASUALTY

Freddie Brown's Englishmen were a popular team, though the young Cambridge fast bowler John Warr became target of the time-honoured Australian hospitality.

When the boat carrying the English team berthed at the Sydney dock, a wharfie yelled out as J.J. came down the gang-plank: 'Hey Warr, you've got as much chance of taking a test wicket on this tour as I have of pushing a pound of butter up a parrot's arse with a hot needle.'

Long Hops and Larrikins (Chappell & Rigby) p33

CARDUS STUMPED

The great English cricket writer Neville Cardus was also stopped in his tracks by Sid Barnes who, unwanted by Australia's selectors, had turned his hand to press work during the series.

'Look here Neville,' said Sid, 'I've got an idea. What about me slipping a carbon paper into my copy today for you and you can do the same for me tomorrow. We both write the same sort of stuff.'

I think it true to say that that was the only time I have seen Cardus stumped for a word.

Brown and Company (Fingleton) pp72–3

MORRIS TRIUMPH

Out in the middle, Barnes's old partner Arthur Morris was having a devilish job in his long-running contest with England's Alec Bedser.

The turning point came finally when Bedser famously presented Morris with a present of Lindsay Hassett's *Better Cricket* before the Adelaide Test, with batting passages underlined. Morris was able to return it when, giving away his wicket rather than sit in for a splash of red ink, he was last out throwing the bat for 206.

One Summer, Every Summer (Haigh) p135

PLAYING THE GAME

The end of Morris's 206 was typical of the friendly, selfless spirit in which the first post-Bradman Ashes series was transacted. Keith Miller described the Australian ethic during the Fourth Test in Adelaide.

Morris opened with Ken Archer, batted right through the innings and with only Jack Iverson remaining, unselfishly threw his wicket away in an endeavour to score runs for his team. He could have joined the four Australians to have batted right through a Test innings. With Neil Harvey, Morris ranks today as one of the most unselfish batsmen playing ...

Ian Johnson gave an exhibition of sportsmanship that could not have occurred during the bitterness of pre-war battles. Given not out in the Fourth Test at Adelaide after a unanimous appeal for a catch behind off John Warr, Johnson nodded his head to the umpire and walked out. The umpire had no alternative but to give him out.

Johnson said Warr had not obtained a wicket throughout the Test series and thought he thoroughly deserved his wicket. Warr finished the tour with a bowling average of one for 261.

Had Johnson decided to abide by the umpire's decision, Warr would not have taken a wicket in the series.

Johnson's remark as he walked in was typical of the new way of thinking. He said: 'Warr worked hard enough to take 50 wickets and when he gets one it's taken away from him. Fancy walking out in a Test match when an umpire gives you not out. I must be crazy!' But, like his mates, Johnson was playing the game as a game.

Straight Hit (Miller) p35

CUT DOWN TO THIGHS

Journalist Ron Roberts organised a farewell on a motor boat going round Sydney Harbour. Cricket collector Eric Hill describes the way Lindsay Hassett discharged his leadership duties.

I was in conversation with Bill and Lindsay when a lady, for want of a different word, butted in rudely. She was approaching 45, as Groucho once put it, from the wrong side and was dressed outrageously in a bikini and rainbow-coloured half jacket which would have delighted on a slender young gazelle.

This person gushed: 'Are you the great Mr Hassett?' The elfin admission came a little sourly but improved as the next question arrived: 'My two little boys would love your autograph.'

'Have you got a pen?' he asked lovingly.

All saccharin and treacle she produced the pen, as Hassett invited her to sit alongside him with an interested and growing group gathering round.

Timing his moves to absolute perfection Lindsay signed his autograph twice — on the inside of each fat, sun-burned, overgenerous thigh of that very surprised Australian lady.

Wisden Cricket Monthly, December 1980 p16

'COME ON THE TIGERS!'

Australia was 9–222 on the last day of the Fourth Test against the West Indies at the MCG in January 1952 needing 38 to win, and few had much faith in the adhesive qualities of last man Bill Johnston when he joined teammate Doug Ring.

Bill Johnston, as amiable a fellow as ever pulled on a pad, emerged in his usual cheery manner while the crowd of 30,000 chirruped in anticipation. Bill's angular batting, with his feet moving back and his bat moving forward, was always good for a wholesome laugh. But it wasn't good enough to endure this crisis. Anyway, that was what the crowd thought. That was also the idea of the local constabulary for Johnston had gone only a few yards through the gate when a dozen men in blue solemnly moved out after him to encircle the ground and prevent spectators from visiting the pitch at the end of the match.

Ramadhin and Valentine were in conference as Johnston approached the wicket. So were Goddard and Stollmeyer. They set the field together, carefully and precisely. Ring paced about, obviously ill at ease.

Johnston prodded his bat both backwards and forwards and, to the amusement of the crowd, missed the ball. From the depths of the grandstand rose a cry: 'Come on the Tigers! The Tigers can do it!' But in fact no-one believed that the two Tigers (both Ring and Johnston came from Melbourne's Richmond club, known as the Tigers) could pull the match off. What the batsmen thought on the point was known only to themselves.

Masters of Cricket (Fingleton) pp 162–3

In fact, as the West Indians dissolved under the pressure, the Tigers did it in barely 35 minutes. Set up by Ring's bold hitting (32 not out), Johnston (7 not out) hit the winning run from Worrell.

Late that evening Bill Johnston's throaty laugh was still echoing in the dressing room. 'Actually,' said Bill (with tongue in cheek) 'the issue was never in doubt! I had with me my favourite bat. Not a mark on it. And Doug Ring and I understand each other. I was only sorry we weren't chasing another 50! I was just settling down to the job. But can anybody explain to me why that pack of policemen followed me on to the field?'

Masters of Cricket (Fingleton) p166

AIM TO PLEASE

Jackie Cheetham's Springboks of 1952–53 surprised the Australians by holding them to a 2–2 draw. Their fielding was exceptional, and the discipline their captain imposed extended even to his autograph practices.

Most young boys in Australia forget to use such words as 'please' and 'thank you' in their autograph quests and, as I refused to sign unless approached decently, I often heard them say: 'Here's Cheetham, don't forget the "please".'

Caught by the Springboks (Cheetham) p118

'NEVER OPEN THE DOOR'

The Australians led by Lindsay Hassett were a rather more informal ensemble. When Richie Benaud was inducted into its ways as 12th man during the First Test at the Gabba, he was given a stern lecture by vice-captain Arthur Morris about the nocturnal habits of his captain.

'Just remember this,' he said. 'Under no circumstances are you to open that door to anyone during the night, particularly if it's the captain who comes along.'

'Why is that?' I asked innocently.

'Well,' he said. 'The captain is a great chap, but at times he has an impish sense of humour and if he decides he'd like to wake someone up in the middle of the evening before the rest day it's not a good thing to be part of. I'm telling you again, under no circumstances open the door to anyone.'

At 2am there was a knock on the door, a knock repeated quite loudly a dozen times. But after I had half woken up suddenly I thought, ah, remember what Arthur said: ' ... under no circumstances open the door to anyone'. I dozed off, full of self-congratulation that I had remembered the instructions. Then the telephone rang and instinctively I reached out and picked it up, whilst at the same moment someone began hammering on the door.

I said, 'Hello' into the mouthpiece and a voice in my ear stated: 'Someone is knocking on your door.'

'Gosh, thanks very much,' I said.

I got out of bed, opened the door and Hassett pushed past me and walked toward Morris's bed — Arthur was now well awake and glaring past Hassett at me. 'I thought I bloody well told you not to open the door,' he remonstrated. Hassett sat on the edge of the bed, held out his hand and said to Arthur: 'Do you have a match? I'd like to talk to you about my golf swing!'

After our skipper had left, an hour later, Morris was kind enough only
to say, 'Mark it down in your book of experience, son, and never open
the door to Hassett at 2am.'

On Reflection (Benaud) p21

BARNES BARRED

Discipline was never Sid Barnes's strong suit, and a last blot on his escutcheon
when acting as 12th man for NSW against South Australia in November 1952
ensured he would never again play for Australia.

At drinks time he went out with a steward, and 9000 spectators saw Barnes
in a grey suit carrying a wireless set, a box of cigars, a mirror, clothes
brush and deodorant spray. He stopped in the outfield and raised his hand
to the crowd on one side of the ground and then the other, then proceeded
to the middle where he turned on the radio and began to look after the
NSW fieldsmen. He combed the long, dark hair of his old pal Keith Miller,
then skippering NSW, and held the mirror up to his face. His offer of
cigars all round was declined. Then the deodorant was squirted over
certain players.

By now the steward had left the field and the players were returning
to their places. The crowd, having enjoyed the joke, now wanted to see
some cricket, over five minutes having elapsed already. There was silence
broken by the odd cry of 'Get him off!'

There was rather too much for Barnes to carry off at once, what with
all the special equipment and a few jugs the steward hadn't managed to
carry off. Barnes walked off to an embarrassed silence and eventually
the field was clear for play to resume. Young Dean Trowse was out almost
immediately, his concentration probably disturbed. The locals didn't like
that.

Nor did the SACA, whose president wrote a letter of protest to the
NSWCA. Sid was in the doghouse again.

By His Own Hand (Frith) pp41–2

Barnes would remain part of the summer scene, however, as pundit,
propagandist and frequently patron to young cricketers. Alan Davidson
discovered this side of Barnes's nature when selected to tour England with
Hassett's 1953 team.

Before we left he turned up at my home and presented me with his cricket
bag. It was a handsome present, especially as I had little money to spend

on such a costly item. It was with some pride that I rubbed off the name S.G. Barnes and substituted A.K. Davidson. I reflected then that I hoped my own tour would bring just half as much success as Sid attained on his 1948 visit to England.

After the 1953 tour had ended, the Commonwealth Bank arranged for me to spend some months in its London office so I remained on. I went down to see the boys depart from Tilbury and returned to my hotel suffering from an acute bout of homesickness. The phone rang and Sid Barnes, who had covered the tour as a pressman said: 'You must be feeling a bit lonely. Come and have a meal.' We did and talked on until the early hours of the morning. After that I was ready to tackle London.

Fifteen Paces (Davidson) pp70–1

'POINT TAKEN'

Many roads led to England in 1953, an Ashes year and the year of Elizabeth II's coronation, and Prime Minister Robert Menzies was keen to make the most of his scheduled visit.

When Sir Anthony Eden cabled us about a conference in January I replied: 'No. What about June? Isn't there anybody on your staff who reads cricket fixtures?'

Eden's reply: 'Point taken. Conference confirmed for day after Lord's test.'

Lord's Taverners lunch quoted in *Cricketer*, October 1980 p22

DEBUT BLUES

Not everyone was enjoying the tour by the time that Lord's Test came about. The teenager Ian Craig admitted to the new monarch that he was finding conditions rather difficult to adapt to.

When teams were introduced to her in front of the Lord's pavilion, the Queen spoke longest to the freckle-faced boy with greenish eyes. Among the things she said was: 'I understand this is your first visit to England.'

Ian: 'Yes, Your Majesty, and unless my batting improves it will be my last.'

On Top Down Under (Robinson) p192

145

Dry Humour

Lindsay Hassett proved a popular captain in England. His puckish humour is shown to good advantage in this well-known story of an evening at London's Park Lane Hotel.

One evening when the dining room was even more crowded than usual, a waiter dashing around at great speed, dropped an ice cream. It fell on Lindsay's jacket. Profuse with apologies, the confused man first tried to wipe the ice cream off then said that, if Lindsay would remove his jacket, he would have it sent away for cleaning immediately. Without a word, Lindsay took off his jacket and handed it to the waiter who hurried off.

Then Lindsay noticed that the ice-cream had trickled onto his trousers. In an instant he whipped them off also and, from under the table, with scores of eyes from all corners of the room almost popping out of their sockets, threw them to the retreating waiter, saying: 'Here, take these as well.'

Lindsay then sat down in shirt and underpants to resume his dinner. Only by the faintest twinkle in his eye did he offer any facial clue that he had done anything unusual.

Flying Stumps (Lindwall) p143

Woolloomooloo — Wagga Wagga

An Australian could still feel pretty much at home in the England of 1953, although Jack Fingleton found a few contrivances after he signed the hotel register for his stay at Bristol somewhat puzzling.

I am then given a second book to sign — the Aliens book! This seems a little hard. An Australian an alien! So I sign below an American and a Turk and I have to say when I was born (not why, I notice), am I a male or female, how old I am, where did I come from, where do I go from here. I come, I wrote, from Woolloomooloo and I go to Wagga Wagga. Now let them check on that! Let the English equivalent of the FBI work that one out.

The Ashes Crown the Year (Fingleton) p160

Stiff Upper Lip

Young Richie Benaud had little reason to remember his English Test debut in the First Test at Trent Bridge, but he retained an indelible impression of the party held during it at the home of Bert Edwards, a Nottingham lace manufacturer.

I had made 3 that day, knocked over by Alec Bedser. Hassett was drinking a scotch. I was having orange juice. Hassett turned to me and said: 'Why are you drinking that stuff? Have a scotch.'

I told him I couldn't do that because there was a Test Match on. He again told me I should drink something harder so I asked him to let me try his scotch. I tasted it and said to him I didn't know how he could drink the stuff because it had no taste.

Hassett turned to the bartender and said: 'Give Mr Benaud a double scotch. He thinks this one is a bit tasteless.' I had eleven doubles and a treble and, when I got back to the hotel, the bed dumped me on the floor. I had a rugged night.

I got up the next morning to go to the Duke of Portland's place. I walked into the bus and sat down next to the driver so I could quickly ask him to stop if I wasn't feeling exactly 100 per cent.

Just then I heard a voice from the back of the bus say: 'Good morning Richie.' It was the Don sitting next to Lady Bradman. So I sat on that bus for 18 miles with my teeth clenched. It was the most agonising trip I've ever gone through.

Howzat! (Butler) pp113–4

Hearses For Courses

Hassett, Morris and manager George Davies returned to London after the Test while Miller took the rest of the Australians north to play Yorkshire at Bramall Lane. And therein lies a tale, related by English cricket writer Basil Easterbrook.

The match started on a Saturday. That evening Miller organised a party: 'Right boys, enjoy yourselves' …

Monday morning, as Basil Easterbrook recalls, dawned lovely and bright. He was on the point of leaving for the match when the manageress informed him that both Mr Miller and Mr Lindwall were still in their rooms. Easterbrook hurried there. Miller and Lindwall were throwing clothes on, the alarm had not rung, the rest of the team were already on their way to the match and there wasn't a great deal of time left. Grindleford, where the Australians were staying, was a picturesque Swiss style village overlooking a valley; there was no question of cabs.

In 1953 a Yorkshire match was almost like a Sixth Test. Bramall Lane would be packed. With the Australians fielding, Miller would be expected to lead the side out and nobody had yet kept Bramall Lane waiting.

Then Easterbrook recalled that a local funeral parlour had a black limousine. The funeral parlour was willing; the limousine was procured. By the time it arrived at the ground there were only a few minutes before the start of play and the 30,000 crowd were expectantly looking at their watches. Miller jumped out of the limo and, still getting his clothes together, shouted to Easterbrook: 'Pay the cab Bas, and collect it from Davies!' He rushed inside the pavilion and changed just in time to lead the Australians out.

The fare came to £2 but George Davies refused to entertain the claim. He suggested that Easterbrook write to the Australian Cricket Board. Though £2 was a fair bit of money in 1953, Easterbrook reluctantly decided to forget the whole thing.

Almost 20 years later, the 1972 Australians were playing at Old Trafford. There was rain and, as is Easterbrook's habit, he was quietly reading a book. Lindwall came up to him and thrust £5 into his pocket. 'That's for Grindleford, Bas.'

Keith Miller (Bose) pp104–5

FRED AND FRANK

The Australians encountered two young English quicks on tour who'd prove future rivals. The first was Fred Trueman who, while 12th man at Manchester, sought out Ray Lindwall for advice.

Lindwall happily accompanied the younger man to the nets. 'He asked me how to bowl the slower one and unfortunately I told him how to bowl it. He said: 'Thanks very much. I'll be the best bowler in the world now.' And as it turned out, he was.'

Ray Lindwall: Cricket Legend (Ringwood) p95

The other was Frank Tyson, then playing only intermittently with Northamptonshire while studying at Durham University, who briefly caused mayhem when Arthur Morris took the Australians to play the county. He recalls the delighted response of Freddie Brown to Tyson's astonishing speed.

I stopped with Freddie the night before and we had a few grogs, and next morning he wins the toss and says: 'You can bat, Arthur.' And I said: 'Well Freddie, thanks, that's very good of you.' Such a lovely man, of course.

Colin [McDonald] took strike and I wasn't really paying attention — probably a few too many the night before — but the slips were back twenty yards. I'm expecting the usual easy county medium-pacer and all of a sudden something goes past, and there's Col lying on the ground holding his knee. I thought: 'Shit!'

Col gets out, and Graeme Hole comes in, lays into his favourite square cut and it goes down to fine leg for four before you can blink, then this bloke we'd never heard of knocks him over. Tyson, he was just like a rocket. He was running a helluva long way but it was really his action: he was such a powerful man, got all his pace in the last couple of strides.

Jimmy de Courcy comes in at 2–6 and I'm saying: 'Where's bloody Neil [Harvey]? He wasn't ready or he hadn't arrived or something, 'cos we'd only been going five minutes, and Jimmy gets out. Well Neil comes in finally at 3–10 and we battle through it [they added 175 in two hours], but it was a bloody quick wicket. And every time I'm hit on the thigh or the hip, there's Freddie at short leg laughing: 'I've been waiting for this for years!'

One Summer, Every Summer (Haigh) pp136–7

TOSSED BY PITCHER

The Australians lost the Ashes when, after four draws, they were defeated at the Oval in a tense struggle decided by the bowling of Jim Laker and Tony Lock. The latter's bent arm caused considerable comment, not least from Lindsay Hassett on the field.

There were widespread doubts concerning Tony Lock's action — not all the time but particularly when he bowled his faster ball. When facing Lock, Hassett would often call down the pitch: 'Strike 1', 'Strike 2' and so on.

Arthur Morris: An Elegant Genius (McHarg) p125

A Boy And His Bat

Hassett retired after the 1953 tour, although he remained a mainstay of the Prime Minister's XI matches inaugurated by Robert Menzies. These created a fund of their own stories, perhaps the most famous of which involves the 1959 game where Hassett, on being dismissed, presented his bat to a boy.

The spectators thought this a typical Hassett act of generosity. They applauded warmly — all excepting Morris, who owned the bat.

Poor Arthur. 'You didn't give that bat away?' said the aghast Morris who, an hour before, had been hitting the bowling all over the ground with it. 'Why, that is the sweetest piece of willow I have ever known.'

'Arthur,' said Hassett, 'if you had seen the unbelievable look of bliss on the face of that small boy, I am sure you would never begrudge it.'

Four Chukkas to Australia (Fingleton) pp123–4

No More Coasting

Hassett also became a successful broadcaster and was capable in his quiet way of being a powerful motivator. Ian Johnson recalled an example from the 1953–54 season when, having taken 1–119 in two matches, he met Hassett at a New Year's Eve party before the Victoria-South Australia match.

At 2.30am Lindsay backed me into a corner and gave me the works. We had had a few beers and many statements were made. Lindsay leading off with: 'You know you're not getting stuck into it. You're just coasting.'

I got a bit annoyed with that and said he was talking through his hat but he came back with: 'If you've got any brains at all you'll get stuck right in. If you do you'll captain Australia next year.'

I told him not to be so damn silly. 'Well,' he said, 'there's no one else who could do the job as well if you get into it and show some form.'

Whilst I didn't take him all that seriously I was needled by his charge that I was not giving it everything and told him to wait and see. We had been close friends for many years and he stung me.

Every time I bowled from then on, his words were a spur, and in the next five matches I took 36 wickets … it finished up as my best season of all because of Hassett and I began to think I could get back into the Australian side. I set myself a tough training regime through winter and, to my amazement, was made captain of Australia for the series against Len Hutton's team in 1954–55.

Howzat! (Butler) pp97–8

150

THE COMING OF THE TYPHOON

Australia won the First Test against England in 1954–55 at the Gabba after being sent in by Len Hutton and, when it acquired a first innings lead of 74 in the Second Test at the SCG, the series had all the hallmarks of normality. Lindwall, however, had inadvertently stirred speed from the young Frank Tyson by hitting him in the back of the head. Hutton recounts how his team suddenly discovered a matchwinner in their midst.

The previous day he had turned his back on a bumper from Lindwall and took a fearful crack. We watched horrified as he went down like felled timber and lay inert and still. There was a hush around the ground and it took quite a time to get him to his feet and back into our dressing room, where he was stretched out on the massage table surrounded by medics and anxious teammates.

When he came out of his concussed state I swear there was a new light in his eyes as if a spark had been kindled deep down inside him. I am not given to fanciful imagination and the fact is that when he resumed bowling the next day he was a yard, maybe a yard and a half quicker than before …

His pace on that decisive and extraordinary day in Sydney was nothing short of frightening. After one ball Evans and the slips exchanged significant glances and moved back several paces. I never saw Evans so far back, and I'm told exactly the same retreat was made when Frank bowled his first over for Northamptonshire. Soon after the English fielders were saying: 'If we can get Ray to nut Frank again, there'll be no holding him.'

Fifty Years in Cricket (Hutton) p117–8

THE PIEMAN'S LAMENT

Tyson was even more menacing in the Third Test at the MCG when, as the effects of illicit Sunday watering wore off, a cracked pitch became unreliable in the New Year Test 1955. His breathtaking spell of 7–27 to end the match was, however, deplored by at least one local entrepreneur.

In the last innings Australia needed 239 to escape defeat, but England's speedmen Frank Tyson and Brian Statham dismayed the batsmen by making some balls shoot and others kick. They ripped through the last seven wickets in two hours, dismissing Australia for 111 when wicketkeeper Evans caught last man Johnston off Tyson — the last ball before lunch.

A crowd of 50 000 drifted away — and nothing looks so empty as the vast MCG without onlookers. In the umpires' room Mel McInnes and Colin Hoy were changing when a sad-looking character came in and asked: 'Who was the chap who gave Bill Johnston out?'

'I was,' said Mel.

'Well, I'm the caterer and that decision of yours cost me 10 000 bloody pies.'

Cricket's Fun (Robinson) p4

THE CLAW

The 1954–55 series were the first home Tests for the left-handed all-rounder Alan Davidson and, although his performances were moderate, his fielding caught the eye. Len Hutton recalled Davidson catching him for 80 at Adelaide Oval with a remarkable sleight-of-hand.

I hooked a long-hop right in the middle of the bat, but Alan at forward short-leg half turned his back and shot out his hands in an instinctive gesture of self-protection. Somehow the ball stuck in those massive fists and 'The Claw' had made another miraculous catch. At Sydney he also caught me so superbly that I forgot my disappointment in admiration.

Fifty Years in Cricket (Hutton) p133

MILLER V JOHNSON

On a happy, high-scoring and successful tour of the West Indies won 4–0, Australia was frustrated only at Bridgetown. Miller, having made 137 in their 668, had knocked over Weekes and Collie Smith to reduce the home side to 6–147, but his removal from the attack allowed Denis Atkinson and Clairmonte Depeiza to get started on a stand of 348. Miller was ropeable, and all Johnson's skills were needed to placate him … diplomatic and otherwise.

After play that evening in the Australian dressing-room, Miller called to his captain and his teammates, 'Come over here. You can all hear this.' Confronting Johnson and the grouped team, Keith said: 'I've bowled my heart out for you time and again in the sun and the heat on this tour Johnno, and today when I take two wickets in two overs, two vital wickets, you take me off. Don't expect me to keep slaving out there when the going's tough from now on.'

'Is that all you have to say?' retorted Johnson.

'Yes.'

'Meeting's closed then, except Keith that I'd like you to come back with me in my car to the hotel.'

Later on board the SS *Rangitane* during our voyage from Jamaica to New Zealand, I asked Johnson what occurred during the ride back to John Goddard's Hotel.

'I just told him I'd knock his bloody block off if he spoke to me like that again in front of the team.'

'What did he say?'

'Nothing.'

'He's got a pretty good reach, rather like Jack Johnson's. Weren't you taking a big risk?'

'No. I did quite a bit of fighting with professionals as a youngster and Keith knew. He'd also cooled down.'

I checked up on Johnson's account of the incident with Keith later on the voyage. He just grinned.

The Golden Nugget (Whitington) pp276–7

'HOW DID THAT HAPPEN?'

Only the prodigious Clyde Walcott confounded the Australians consistently, making 827 runs including braces of centuries at Port-of-Spain and Kingston. On 59 during his Jamaican 155, however, he also raised the ire of Keith Miller.

As I ran up at the start of my follow through I saw him tread on his wicket and I said to myself: 'You beaut', realising I'd got him out. I appealed to the umpire at my end and he said: 'Not out'.

Walcott was covering the wicket with his body but I had run off to one side and could see perfectly well what had happened even if the umpire could not. None of the fielders saw it happen because they were watching the stroke. I turned to the square leg umpire, pointed at the broken wicket, with the stump lying back at an angle of 45 degrees like the joystick in a fighter aeroplane, the bails lying on the ground.

He shook his head and said: 'I couldn't see. I was watching the ball go to the fence.'

'What the hell are you paid for?' I snapped at him. 'You are there to watch if the batsman is out not to watch him hit it to the boundary.'

Walcott bent down, knocked the stumps straight with his bat and replaced the bails.

'How did that happen then?' I asked him, hardly able to believe he would continue his innings. He replied that his foot had slipped after playing the shot.

The incident was over as far as cricket history was concerned, but I gave myself the satisfaction of saying: 'If that's how you want to play cricket, it's all right with me.'

Cricket Crossfire (Miller) pp72–3

'JUST CRACK AT EVERYTHING'

The Australians avenged any miscarriage of justice by replying to the West Indies' 357 with an innings including five individual centuries. The last by Richie Benaud was specially violent for, just prior to his turn in the centre, he'd received a cable from Sydney informing him that his wife was gravely ill.

For 15 minutes he played like a man in a dream. When his partner Ray Lindwall was caught by Depeiza from the bowling of King, Ian Johnson came in to bat. Benaud walked up to say: 'Just before I came in I got news that Marcia is very ill. I'm afraid I won't be here with you long. I can't seem to concentrate.'

'Don't worry. Just crack at everything,' replied Johnson

Sixty-three minutes later Benaud had finished blasting his way to the second fastest century ever scored by an Australian in Test cricket ...

Fours Galore (Whitington) p89

DUCKS DELUXE

Not only were the West Indians relieved when Johnson declared at 8–758. Opener Les Favell had managed a duck at the start of the innings.

For three days I had been sitting watching everyone joining in the avalanche of runs while the scoreboard had a big round 0 against my name. It was quite a relief when the innings was closed and the 0 was taken down.

By Hook or by Cut (Favell) p60

Keith Miller took the captaincy of NSW in 1953–54, commencing a period in which it would win the Sheffield Shield in nine consecutive seasons. He suggested at once a captain of remarkable intuition, and left a profound impression on the up-and-coming Richie Benaud. Benaud recalled, in his very first match under Miller's leadership at the Gabba, his shock at being thrown the ball for the sixth over.

'Nugget,' I said. 'The ball's still new.'

'Don't worry about that,' he replied. 'It'll soon be old. Just think about the field you want. Now we'll have a slip, a gully and a silly-point … '

At this stage he must have caught sight of my face and he said: 'It's all right, it'll spin like a top for an hour. We've got a great chance to bowl them out.' I took 5–17 before lunch and we would have had the whole side out before lunch if a catch at the wicket and a stumping had not gone to ground.

On Reflection (Benaud) p20

The astonishing story behind Keith Miller's best bowling figures has rarely been told as well as by Peter Philpott, who had the unusual vantage point of being the Nugget's travelling partner that day.

It all happened on Saturday, 19 November 1955, NSW was playing SA in a Shield game at the SCG. As usual in such circumstances, Keith was to give me a lift to the SCG, as my home in Balgowlah was en route to Sydney from Keith's home in Newport. As usual I waited at the corner of Sydney Road and Hill Street at about 9.30am.

Keith is a wonderfully kind and generous man: he has done many things for me and never let me down in any way. But on this day I thought he had. For at 10am he had not arrived. By 10.30am my concern had turned to despair, as the game was due to begin at 11am, and I was on the other side of the city. It was now too late for a cab to save me, and I began to contemplate the effect on my youthful career of a failure to turn up at a Shield game.

I need not have worried, for suddenly, up Sydney Road from the direction of Manly, a car came speeding. It screeched to a halt beside me, Keith apologised for the delay and off we went. His wartime airforce experience came in good stead that day, as we flew very low and landed inside the SCG gates just after 11am. Mid-flight he explained to me that his fourth son had been born the previous evening, and that he had come straight from the arrival and subsequent celebration. Sleep had not found a spot on the agenda, but I could tell the rum had.

We raced into the NSW dressing room to find the situation rather confused. Richie Benaud had assumed the captaincy and had the team ready to take the field but was one short. Fortunately rain had delayed the start briefly, and with a rush we could just make it and join the team.

Keith had no trouble, he was used to last minute changes. He kept on his white dress shirt, simply discarding the tie, pulled on creams over normal underwear, ripped on a pair of socks, donned his boots as yet with untied laces and was ready to go.

'Come on, let's get going,' he said, totally unconcerned, as I scrambled less successfully into my gear.

We went.

The ground was a little damp and the wicket appeared to have sweated under the covers, though it was not rain-affected. There was no doubt that Keith, now stooped tying up his laces in the middle of the wicket, had had no sleep that night and was, to a certain extent, hung over.

He went through the normal Miller routine, well-known to most of us, but always memorable for newcomers.

'Right, who bowls in this team?' he said, looking round and smiling. 'Oh, you bowl a bit, Pat. You take that end.' And so tall, lean and very pacy Pat Crawford measured out his approach from the southern or Randwick end. He had a blustering sou-easter behind him, humming over the scoreboard hill, the skies were overcast with scudding clouds, and humidity was high. A not unusual Sydney day.

Les Favell and Dave Harris resumed for SA with the score at 0–2. They had batted for 10 minutes on the Friday evening, after Miller had declared the NSW innings closed at 8–215. Crawford steamed in. As usual, the wicket was quick: there was bounce and seam, and the ball was swinging round, but as yet nothing extraordinary was there to view.

With the over completed, Miller looked round again. 'Who else bowls?' he said. 'Davo, you can bowl a bit. You have a go.'

So Alan Davidson began to measure what were to be his fifteen famous paces from the Noble Stand end, but before he had completed this, the Miller mind had changed.

'No I'll bowl. Give us the ball.' And walking back about 10 yards with no measurement of his run-up, he was ready to fire. He looked round, placed his field as he often did ('Scatter!'), waited until the fieldsmen had scattered efficiently, and bowled.

I was at second slip, and I can still recall that first delivery clearly. The seam was perfectly upright, the rotation perfectly even, about half-pace — which, with Miller, was still fairly brisk. It hit just outside off-stump, cut back from the off, and whistled over Favell's middle-stump, almost cutting him in half. Every player on the field shook his head and stared, particularly the batsman, and Miller himself. What did we have here?

Miller proceeded to bend his back. He was really quick, but that was not the major problem. It was the searing lift combined with the seam and cut which whisked the ball feet either way. Much of what he bowled that day was unplayable, and he only needed to bowl another 6.3 overs in order to get the rest he was after.

A Spinner's Yarn (Philpott) pp101–4

SA were batting again by lunch which, as Richie Benaud recalled, puzzled two South Australian supporters who arrived late.

They arrived at the SCG with one over to be bowled before lunch on the second day when openers Les Favell and David Harris had the SA second innings score 0–13.

'That's good,' one said to the other, no wickets down. 'But jeez mate, it's a bit slow isn't it?'

Inside Edge, December 1992 p23

THE RACE THAT STOPS A NATION

Brian Booth was Miller's drinks waiter at the Gabba against Queensland later that year, and watched Ken Mackay come off the worse for a brush with the Blues machine. It enhanced Booth's admiration for him.

He had a miserable match. In the first innings he failed to score. In the outfield he dropped three catches. When he went into bat in the second innings it was Melbourne Cup day and it was agreed to take drinks early to allow for the public broadcast of the race. A wicket fell conveniently. Slasher walked to the wicket facing the dreaded 'pair'. Drinks were taken. The race was delayed. Twenty-five minutes later Mackay faced a ball. He did not get off the mark.

'The longest duck I've ever made', was his only comment when he came back to the pavilion munching thoughtfully on his chewing gum. He did not throw his bat or kick down his stumps; nor did he blame the umpire or the pitch. It was worth being off the field to see that sort of self-control in facing uncomfortable failure.

At the SCG in the return match as Mackay came through the gate, Keith Miller said: 'Look out fellas, here comes Slasher. I have a feeling we won't get him for a pair in this match.' We didn't. Ken Mackay scored 203.

Booth to Bat (Booth) p102

'GOOD DON. HOW'S YOURS?'

Australia's selectors were still chary of selecting Miller for the 1956 tour of England, fearful that he might not at 35 be capable of opening Australia's attack. They were, of course, more worried than he was.

Later at a cocktail party on the night of the Centenary match between NSW and Victoria I was talking to Arthur Mailey when Bradman came up and said: 'Ah Nugget, how's your back?'

'Good Don. How's yours?' I replied.

'When are you going to see the doctor?'

'I'm not going to see any doctor. I'm finished with doctors.'

'When are you going to practise again?'

'I'm not practising. I've finished with cricket this season.'

'But we have to pick the team for England in a couple of days.'

'OK Don. You pick it on this season's performance. If I remember rightly I was top of the batting and bowling averages.'

Cricket Crossfire (Miller) p44

PYTHAGORAS

Miller was selected, as was John Rutherford, a West Australian scientist who was his state's first born and bred Testman. And the latter left quite an impression on the former, Miller recalling a day when the pair were standing in slips as a Hawker Hunter jet fighter flew overhead.

'What speed is that doing Keith?' he asked.

'About 700mph,' I replied out the corner of my mouth.

Silence for two or three more deliveries. Then Pythagoras said: 'That's a thousand feet a second, Keith.'

'Blimey!' was all I said but I am sure John did not realise that the exclamation was directed at his mental arithmetic.

A few overs later as we bent down he said: 'Have you ever seen a square hole drilled in a bottle by supersonic sound?'

'What the hell has this got to do with cricket?' I thought, but it showed me Rutherford's learning and trend of mind. Apparently he had seen this demonstrated a few days earlier. Some of the boys got to hear about it and pulled his leg. Rutherford, being a thorough man, went off and came back with the bottle.

Cricket Crossfire (Miller) pp158–9

Rutherford also earned a sort of fame when he and Ken Mackay, playing in their first match at Lord's against MCC, became lost opening the innings.

We walked proudly down the steps from the dressing room, the complete cricketers, determined to do something worthy of this famous ground; if only we could get onto it. Not knowing the route through the Long Room we wandered long corridors poking our heads through any door that suggested an exit.

'There must be some way out of here,' John muttered. 'The other mob's been out there for ages.'

We finally stumbled through a door and found ourselves facing the oval all right, but as we discovered later about thirty yards upfield from the players' gate. If those venerable members at Lord's thought we were playing a frivolous schoolboys' joke on their revered ground I assure them it was all done in innocence. We negotiated the fence and strode as unconcernedly as possible to the wicket.

I did not stay long and knowing no other way back to the dressing room, returned the way I came. Neil Harvey was first drop and as I had not passed him on his way to the wicket and he was not in the dressing room I enquired anxiously: 'Where's Ninna?' When told he was batting I 'woke' and after discreet enquiries found the correct route.

Slasher Opens Up (Mackay) p39

LAKERED

Having drawn a tense First Test, Australia won the Second Test at Lord's thanks to a prodigious 70-over, 10-wicket performance by Keith Miller. But three huge thrashings followed, the first at Headingley.

After six Australians had tumbled for 81 one afternoon, he tried pep talk, but pushed it too far by asserting: 'Here's where we make 500.'

One of the not out batsmen, Miller looking up from unbuckling his pads offered: 'Six to four we don't.'

On Top Down Under (Robinson) p178

Then there was 'Laker's match' at Old Trafford: en route to 46 series wickets at 9.5, the off-spinner took 19–90, and Ian Johnson's efforts to inspire a rearguard were unavailing.

You couldn't [recalled Ray Lindwall] use your feet because the ball was spinning so much and it was stopping and turning and kicking. One would spin from the off and the other from leg.

I went in to bat in the second innings and said to Godfrey Evans, 'What's going on Godfrey?' And he said, 'Nothing. It's not spinning.'

And I got three balls that spun so far he couldn't stop them and they went for byes. Two went down leg side and through the leg slips and one went down the off side through slips and it was the same type of ball … and I said to Godfrey: 'Thanks Godfrey. Not turning much, is it?'

Ray Lindwall: Cricket Legend (Ringwood) pp115–6

IAN CRAIG VERSUS GODZILLA

Australia was about to get its first experience of cricket on the sub-continent. It lost its first Test in Pakistan, won its first in India, and brought home a few colourful stories.

Ian [Craig], busy with his thoughts, was standing in the deep waiting for the ball to come his way when a huge goanna trotted past much to the merriment of spectators. Craig turned a ghastly shade of white and within no time was fielding 30 yards closer to the bat. He resolutely refused to retreat back to his position at deep third man until an understanding spectator had clobbered the offender with a stick and carried him from the arena.

My World of Cricket (Harvey) p126

'THE OLD TRAP'

Notwithstanding a modest Test record, twenty-two-year-old Craig was appointed to lead Australia to South Africa in 1957–58. Among his stars were Davidson and Benaud, who enjoyed their first sustained Test success. As Benaud plotted the demise of John Waite during Australia's handsome Second Test win at Newlands, he also observed Davidson's predisposition to complain of injuries.

Alan had been limping back to bowl and then boring in at the batsman and moving the ball late, either into or away from them. Then he would limp back and Craig would ask him if he were all right — he would say 'no' and get a sympathetic pat on the shoulder and then bore in again with yet another magnificent delivery.

The Cape Town pitch was very slow and I asked Craig if I could come up three yards at gully for the one that flew off the thick edge and wouldn't normally carry. Davo limped back for the next ball and Waite square drove it like a bullet. I caught the red blur, body parallel to the ground, and was just rolling over the second time when Davo arrived alongside me saying excitedly: 'It was the old trap, you know, the old trap.' It had taken him just two seconds to get down and the boys thought it was fastest he'd moved all day.

This was the match where, so much was he on the massage table, that we had a copper plaque engraved and nailed to the massage table and inscribed: 'The A. K. Davidson Autograph Massage Table'.

Willow Patterns (Benaud) p73

A RIBBING GONE WRONG

Harvey also showed his support for the new captain by scoring 759 tour runs at 50. And, although optometrist Jack Noriskin established that — like Bill Ponsford — he was severely myopic, this presented more problems off the field than on.

Neil's astigmatism once brought him embarrassment in East London. He was wearing sun glasses walking down a hotel corridor when he picked a burly figure approaching as Barry Jarman, the husky South Australian wicketkeeper. He waited until they were level and jabbed his elbow hard into what he thought was Jarman's ribs.

The big fellow gasped then glared in astonishment at Ninna who, after flipping his sun-glasses off his nose and seeing an unfamiliar face, dashed without a word down the corridor. The chap was a professional wrestler, staying in the same hotel. Neil gave him a wide berth for the rest of our stay there.

Slasher Opens Up (Mackay) p64

Angles On Elbows

England's tour of 1958–59 was bedevilled by allegations that Australian bowlers Ian Meckiff, Gordon Rorke and Keith Slater among others 'chucked'. The Fleet Street retinue covered this development with their usual impartiality.

An English afternoon newspaperman, a good friend of mine, came to me the next morning and asked whether I thought Slater threw. I began to wax technical on the point but he cut it short. 'Just say he doesn't,' said my friend. 'My opposition are saying he does and I want to be different.'

Four Chukkas to Australia (Fingleton) p11

Grout On Benaud

When Ian Craig contracted hepatitis, Neil Harvey was again overlooked as captain. But Richie Benaud at once emerged as a shrewd tactician and a 'player's man'. Wally Grout recalled this example of Benaud's no-nonsense approach during the First Test at the Gabba.

Jimmy Burke was batting to Peter Loader, who switched from bowling over to round the wicket. Burkie requested that the sightboard be moved to a position which would have obscured the view of some of the ground members sitting under the marquee. But to crusty officialdom this was unpardonable and the sightboard attendant was instructed not to comply.

Burkie, after some fruitless waving, gave it away and settled down to pick Peter as well as the conditions allowed. But he fell to the next ball from Loader which he lost in the backdrop of the crowd. Richie knew nothing of the sightboard incident until Jim's outburst in the dressing room. He leapt from his seat, face black as thunder and charged over to the members' area. I don't know what was said and probably never will but when the next request came to move the board in front of the members, it was moved.

My Country's Keeper (Grout) pp44–5

Benaud On Grout

As Benaud gathered a fine XI round him, Grout was one of his key players: a fine gloveman, a stubborn batsman and, as his captain recalled, never short of a word.

Wally Grout was keeping wicket when Ted Dexter made his debut in Sydney in 1958 and asked for, what to Wal sounded like 'Two laigs please'. Gloved hand to mouth, Wally murmured to the slips: 'Blue-blooded ones, of course.'

He was quite prepared to accept anyone having a shot at him as well, but the game was never quiet when Walter was keeping wicket. A weak throw from Don Seccombe that bounced seven times and ended resting at his feet in a Sheffield Shield game at the Gabba brought a wave and a cheery: 'Thanks Frankie'.

'Frankie … why are you calling me Frankie?' asked a perplexed Seccombe. 'My name's Don.'

'No,' came the reply over the shoulder, 'You're Frankie Sinatra aren't you? The Man with the Golden Arm.'

Willow Patterns (Benaud) pp184–5

TIME DIFFERENCE

Jack Fingleton described the Gabba Test as 'The Battle of the Snooze' after Englishman Trevor Bailey's entrenchment of 68 in 458 minutes. He recalled an exchange during this marathon.

At five to three somebody in the magnificent Brisbane pressbox … asked how long it was since Bailey had scored.

'At twenty past two,' answered George Duckworth.

'Today or yesterday?' yawned somebody.

Four Chukkas to Australia (Fingleton) p56

ALWAYS A HERO

For the decisive Fourth Test at the Adelaide Oval, Australia recalled Ray Lindwall for the injured Ian Meckiff. Lindwall had been an idol to Alan Davidson, and the left-armer found it almost sad when given first over and choice of ends ahead of his hero.

In the early days to bowl at the other end to Lindwall, especially uphill and into the wind, was really something. I found probably the hardest thing I ever did, when Ray came into the side in Adelaide in 1959, was to be bowling with the wind and downhill and seeing Ray coming uphill and into the wind. When you have a hero, you only see him as a hero.

And I always had it in my mind that he was the greatest and it was silly for me to be over him.

Ray Lindwall: Cricket Legend (Ringwood) pp123–3

'ALWAYS A FIRST TIME'

Australia recaptured the Ashes after five and a half years at the Adelaide Oval, then Benaud defied all cricket precedent by inserting the visitors in the match at the MCG.

Just before the captains left the dressing-room to toss, Bradman walked over to Benaud and said: 'It's never been done before did you know?'

Benaud answered with another question: 'What hasn't?'

'No captain has ever sent England in to bat in Australia and won the match,' replied the Don.

'Well,' said Richie, with a broad grin on his face to match Sir Donald's, 'There's always a first time, you know.'

A few minutes later we knew Benaud was not bluffing. 'We are in the field,' he snapped, 'so let's get into 'em.' We did. The gamble paid off, and England scored only 205.

Ins and Outs (O'Neill) p38

STORIES FROM THE SILVERWARE

National allegiances were forgotten in the business of the Sheffield Shield. Ian Meckiff remembered the intensity of the traditional Victoria–NSW match in 1958–59.

I opened the bowling against Jimmy Burke, and I didn't know he'd been clocked on the ribs by Frank Tyson and was pretty tender. He didn't want to get hurt and lose his Test place and was keen to get runs without any more bruising.

I remember coming in to bowl and really letting a few go. One ball nearly cleaned up Jimmy. He walked up the pitch and said: 'Mecka, you hit me anywhere on the body and you'll get this wrapped round your neck.'

All I said was: 'Look, if you get hit, you'll stay hit, so keep yourself nice.'

We were in the middle of a Test series and I remember going to lunch when both teams shared the same eating room. There was no mingling, you just went up and grabbed your own pie and peas with the NSW players on one side of the room and the opposition on the other.

We came out of that lunch. Jimmy Burke was waiting for me with the words: 'Don't forget you've got to bat and when I've got the ball I'm going to ping it straight at you.' This sort of thing went on for the whole game.

Howzat! (Butler) p248

Law 38

On other occasions, the Sheffield Shield had a lighter side. Playing at the MCG against South Australia, for instance, Victorian spinner Lindsay Kline explored a few potentialities of the run-out law, without discovering the right one. Bill Lawry was an eyewitness.

Lindsay Kline kicked the bails off as he bowled and the batsman hit the ball to third man, but there was a mix-up and both batsmen were at the same end. Lindsay got the ball and didn't know what to do — so he pulled a stump out of the ground and put the ball against it. Col Egar said: 'Not out.'

So he pulled out a second stump, and a third stump and put the ball against them, and two more times Egar said: 'Not out.' So then Lindsay got down on his hands and knees — the batsmen were still up at the other end — and started rubbing the ball in the stump holes. By the time he got to the third 'Howzat', everyone was on their hands and knees with tears running down their faces.

Inside Sport, February 1994 p117

Law 87

Les Favell, captain of South Australia, made against NSW an unforgettable contribution to Australians' superstitious dread of the score 87.

Our captain Les Favell had reached this score when O'Neill fielding in the covers casually remarked: 'Seen the scoreboard, Favell?'

'Yeah I seen it,' came the reply, and the captain promptly holed out next ball amid much mirth.

When Favell opened the second innings O'Neill called out: 'You're still on it Les.'

His attempted hook off the first ball from Gordon Rorke finished in the safe hands of Barry Bates at mid-on and triggered off some stifled laughter.

Bowled Over (Hawke) p36–7

TOSHER'S TOPPY

As he became a mainstay of Queensland's Sheffield Shield team, Ken Mackay had a great ear for a yarn.

Ern Toshack … beat me with a top-spinner and appealed loudly for an lbw decision to Queensland umpire Ron Weitemeyer. Ron turned it down and Ern very aggrieved said: 'But ump, that was my toppy.'

Weitemeyer, gentle as an understanding parent, said: 'Now Ern, you can't always expect a wicket with your toppy.'

Slasher Opens Up (Mackay) p197

YE OF LITTLE FAITH

When Ray Lindwall moved to Queensland in 1954–55, though, he discovered in his first outing against his old state that, at that stage, Queenslanders felt an inferiority toward southern opponents.

Personally Lindwall never suffered from any losers' complex. He'd come from a winning side and expected to keep on winning. But sometimes you had to wonder didn't you. Like his first game against his old side, New South Wales. He'd left the field that day with five scalps in his bag and, after he'd showered and come back to the dressing room, he found five batsmen lined up in their pads and gloves waiting for the call.

He asked Kenny Archer if the batting order hadn't been finalised or something. No it just turned out that they had five men lined up ready to go into bat. Lindwall had never seen anything like it. He suggested three of them should get their gear off and show a little faith.

'You know,' Lindwall says, years later, 'it's uncomfortable sitting in your pads. Not so much physically uncomfortable — more a case of sitting on a knife edge waiting to go out to bat. In those early days there was a feeling that we weren't good enough to beat the southern teams. I guess our team felt we weren't quite up to the job.'

John Birmingham, Inside Sport, November 1994 p62

ON THE MAT

When Benaud's side toured the sub-continent in 1959–60, they had the novel experience of a Test match on mats at Dacca. Benaud deputised Lindsay Kline as his supervisor: his task was to visit the ground each day before play commenced to ensure the mats were as tight as possible.

There was nothing physically demanding about this but his instructions were clear. By the time we arrived at the ground to start play, that mat had to be tight as a drum, both lengthways and widthways, and the morning we were batting in our first innings there was no doubt Lindsay had taken his duties quite literally and very much to heart.

'Pull, you bastards, pull,' was ringing out across the ground as we walked through the gate and no one in the centre was sweating more than L. F. Kline … That mat was so tight you could have strummed a tune on it.

On Reflection (Benaud) pp76–7

KILL THE UMPIRE

Umpiring, not for the last time, became a sore point on the tour. The Australians generally kept a lid on frustrations as they beat Pakistan 2–0 but, as Ian Meckiff recalled, just occasionally they did peep out.

Sam Loxton our manager was sitting in the stand with all the Pakistan Army brass — brigadiers galore — there being martial law in the country. There were all these kites you see in India and Pakistan flying all over the ground.

Sam, never stuck for a comment, looked up at the kites and quipped: 'See those bloody vultures up there? They're waiting for the umpire — he's gotta be dead.'

Howzat! (Butler) p244

Australia beat India 2–1, but Neil Harvey recalled the following occurrence from the final drawn Test.

I remember an incident involving our Colin McDonald at Calcutta. We had this Indian batsman lbw at least three times, but the Indian umpire would not give him out. Then Alan Davidson bowled a ball which knocked his off stump right back. Col ran all the way from fine leg, kicked the other two stumps right out of the ground and said to the umpire: 'That must have been close!'

Winning (Writer) p98

Dicky Knee

As well as two princely centuries on tour, Harvey claimed at Kanpur what Alan Davidson later judged the most remarkable catch he'd witnessed. The victim was Indian opener Nari Contractor for 74.

This is how it happened. I bowled a shortish ball to Contractor who immediately stepped back to hook. Harvey fielding at short-leg hurriedly ducked and turned his back in self-protection. Contractor hooked the ball alright but it stuck in the crook of Harvey's bent knee. Neil calmly reached down and plucked the ball to complete the most remarkable 'catch' I think I have seen.

Fifteen Paces (Davidson) pp126–7

'I'm Very Glad To Hear It'

In the First Test against the West Indies at Brisbane in 1960–61, Australia was 6–92 at tea on the last day, and Richie Benaud (6 not out) and Alan Davidson (16 not out) were joined in the players' section by Sir Donald Bradman.

He said what a wonderful game it had been over the four days and that today was building up to a great last session.

Then he added: 'What are you going for, Richie — a win or a draw?'

'We're going for a win, of course,' I replied.

His answer was direct: 'I'm very glad to hear it.'

Tale of Two Tests (Benaud) p32

A Single Too Far

Just before the final over, after Benaud and Davidson had added 134, West Indian Joe Solomon placed his first indelible mark on the match.

Now was the time for ice-cool judgement and, perhaps for the first time in his career, I thought Richie became flustered in a crisis. We'd stolen singles before but now could afford to pick the right ball to collect that last handful of runs. Instead, Richie turned a ball to Solomon at square leg and bolted off for a suicidal single. With a deft unerring throw Solomon knocked down the wicket and I was out by feet.

I had made 80 and our stand had been worth 134. With 11 wickets into the bargain I had had my greatest ever Test ... But as I walked back to the pavilion I sensed that victory, so invitingly close, yet might elude us. I sympathised with our tailenders, Wally Grout, Ian Meckiff and Lindsay Kline, for they had sat for several hours in the dressing-room and must have been in a high state of nerves. Wally had smoked his way through a packet of cigarettes and when suddenly his turn came to bat, he could not find his gloves. He was sitting on them!

Fifteen Paces (Davidson) p130

A SURPRISE BOUNCER

When Hall bowled the first ball of the final over, Grout ran a leg-bye. Benaud was on strike and optimistic of his team's chances.

Five to win and seven balls to go ... I thought. One four will do it, just one four ... concentrate ... concentrate.

Next ball ... it was a bumper. Surely no-one in their right mind would bowl a bumper at that stage of the match ... but it was a bumper delivered with every bit of speed and power the big fella could muster. I tried to hook ... trying for the four runs that would have all but won the game. The only result was a sharp touch on the gloves and Gerry Alexander's victory shout as he caught me.

Have your ever tried so hard to do something ... concentrated so desperately that everything else was pushed out from your mind ... and then seen it disappear in a fraction of a second? Then you'll have some idea of how I felt as I passed Grout at the other end and said: 'All yours Wal ... '

He merely lifted his eyes and muttered: 'Thanks very much!'

Tale of Two Tests (Benaud) p36

'THE GOOD LORD'S GONE AND LEFT US'

Meckiff defended his first ball, and Grout regained the strike when he called for a bye from the next. Wes Hall takes up the story.

I knew that Wally, the hook specialist would be hoping for a bouncer to finish the game off with one stroke. Fair enough I would let him think it was Christmas and he was going to get a present. I must have disguised it well enough for when it dropped on a length Wally was already into his stroke and the ball soared toward square leg. Any catch in this vicinity should be the wicketkeeper's and I could see Alexander standing stock-still. Suddenly I realised I had to get there and, although following through on the off, twisted sharply and hared after the ball. I was under it when Kanhai's head struck my elbow, the ball spilled out of my hands and on to the turf. In anguish I could only blurt out, 'The Good Lord's gone and left us,' a remark which startled the square leg umpire. I cannot remember ever being so disappointed as I was at that moment. Frank came over, patted me on the back and told me to forget it.

The batsmen had crossed for a single and, with three balls left, Australia were only three runs short of victory. Meckiff cracked my next delivery away on the leg side and the boundary fence seemed to draw it on like a magnet. He and Grout ran one, then another and went for the all-important third as Hunte picked up the ball on the squre leg boundary. A glorious low throw flashed into Alexander who splattered the stumps with Grout skidding home on severely grazed elbows.

Everyone's eyes focused on umpire Hoy. He flung his right arm up high and we were saved.

The scores were level, the last man Kline was in and two balls remained.

As I walked back, tugging on my gold cross round my neck, Frank called out: 'Remember Wes, if you bowl a no-ball you'll never be able to go back to Barbados!'

The thought of me throwing the game away in one false move sent a shiver down my spine. I made sure my right foot was well behind the crease and banged down the ball plum on the middle stump. Kline turned it away to square leg and took off on the winning run.

He never made it. Solomon swooped like an eagle and, with only one stump to aim at, skittled the wickets. Everyone was delirious, but I was so tired I could not jump to the heavens. Most of us, including myself, thought we had won. We knew it could not be a draw with the last man out and the despondent Meckiff was heard to moan: 'Fancy losing like that.'

Pace Like Fire (Hall) pp67–8

Neil Harvey remembered the post-match dressing room scene.

All the West Indians came in, and players, officials, pressmen and umpires stood around slapping each other on the back in a frenzy of excitement. Sir Donald Bradman greeted the match as 'the greatest Test of all time'.

And Slasher Mackay walked up to Joe Solomon and stuck out his hand and said: 'Well thrown Joe but I thought your action was a bit suspect.'

My World of Cricket (Harvey) p108

'I'D LIKE YOU TO BE THERE AT 6PM'

Australia won the Second Test, the West Indies the Third. And the tourists were on the point of winning the Fourth at the Adelaide Oval when last man Lindsay Kline joined Ken Mackay.

Kline wasn't the greatest left-handed batsman Australia has ever produced but he was keen and had a sound defence. In order to get a sight of the ball, he had just been to the nets at the back of the ground to have some practice against Johnny Martin the left-hand spinner so that he could simulate batting against Sobers.

So many times was he beaten and dismissed by Martin in the nets that eventually he came upstairs again hoping that he would not be needed. And now as he passed me he said: 'What would you like?' I said: 'I'd like you to be there at 6pm.' And continued on to the shower without the slightest hope that the optimistic suggestion would be carried out.

Willow Patterns (Benaud) p96

SIX O'CLOCK SWILL

Mackay and Kline added 67, but more importantly batted right through the session and into the last over. Mackay faced Hall for those last eight balls.

Now Slash, if ever you've had a job to do, this is it. This is war and that big bloke pelting in is not going to beat you.

The first ball was a beauty and I jammed down on it at the last instant.

Boy that was quick, and into the wind too. There shouldn't be any bouncers on this wicket, but one might stay low; better get your nose down lower.

Hall's next two balls flashed by off stump. I knew I could safely let them go.

Five more of those Wes and I'll be happy.

The fourth had to be played. I cracked it firmly past point and could have had two runs. But what was the use?

No one bawling from the stands: 'Run yer mug'. That's good. They are with me.

The fifth I watched go by off-stump.

What's the matter, Wes? You're wasting them. Hullo, there's something cooking. Worrell's having a yarn to him. So he's going to bowl round the wicket. Trying a new angle, perhaps hoping for an lbw or to find something on the pitch. Well, it won't do any good.

Balls six and seven were screamers and dead straight.

Crikey they were good ones. One ball to go Wes. This is your last chance. All right let's get it over with. I've been here four hours, you're not going to shift me with your last ball.

In came Hall round the wicket. But he didn't bowl. He lost his step, raced over the bowling crease then bounced the ball on the wicket in front of him in disgust. I don't know if legally that constituted a delivery but I was not game to ask. It was a no-ball anyhow. Back went Hall and in again, this time over the wicket.

'No ball', called umpire Col Hoy. But the crowd didn't hear him.

A wave of cheering schoolboys swept onto the oval, racing towards the wicket. The police, aware that something was amiss, leapt into action. In different circumstances the sight of policemen lumbering in pursuit of schoolboys agile as monkeys would have looked riotous. But my nerves were stretched to the limit. All I could say was: 'Get 'em off, get 'em off.' It was as well this match didn't happen in India. The match would never have ended.

When the boys were herded back to the boundary, Wes made his third attempt to bowl the last ball. He trudged back to his bowling mark. Onto the field toddled a small boy, autograph book in hand.

The crowd roared. This was too much. I'd soon have to appeal against the light.

I know Wes loves kids but the look he gave that little bloke should scare him off a cricket field for life. Police again cleared the area, and Wes steamed to the wicket for the 10th time in this over. Again every ounce of concentration was needed.

Come on, let's get this game over. What are you going to dish up Wes? If it's not on the stumps there's no way I'm going to play it. It'll be a short one for sure. Here it comes. It's short! Let it hit you. Ouch! That hurt. Watch it doesn't roll onto the wicket. Good! We made it.

Slasher Opens Up (Mackay) pp103–5

Old McDonald

Australia's 356 in response to the West Indians' 292 in the last Test at the MCG was underwritten by Colin McDonald's brave 91, during which he bore numerous body blows from Hall.

On one occasion he took a real snorter which sent him to his knees clutching his side. I went down the wicket to help him and said: 'I'm sorry Colin.'

'That's all right,' he winced. 'It was my fault.'

Let me just add that, despite all the buffetings, Col sought me out at the end of the tour to give me an Australian sweater. It was a fine gesture from a great sportsman and friend.

Pace Like Fire (Hall) p65

A Grouse From Grout

As the West Indies made 321 in their second innings, Col Egar turned down a caught behind shout against their top scorer Gerry Alexander that Grout reminded him of in characteristic fashion.

We were riding back into town from the cricket ground in the same car. We stopped at some traffic lights and I said to Col: 'You get out here, don't you?'

Col looked out the window and said: 'No this isn't my hotel.'

I then read him a traffic sign attached to a post: 'Blind pedestrians cross here.'

Col took it as I knew he would — a good bloke Egar!

My Country's Keeper (Grout) p77

For Whom The Bail Falls

Grout had reason to be thankful that Egar's sight occasionally failed him. The Australian was batting on the last day when a famous incident occurred.

With three wickets in hand and four runs needed to win, Grout ran for a ball that had gone down behind the stumps. A photograph shows Grout some yards down the pitch with Alexander pointing to a stump with the bail off. Grout completed two runs and then the umpires conferred.

Egar at the bowler's end sought advice from Hoy, and was told that neither Alexander's hands nor Grout's bat had hit the stumps. As Egar said he was still undecided as to how the bail came off, he did what the rules entitled him to do — he gave Grout the benefit of the doubt.

It is easy to sit in judgement long after the event and come to a cool decision. The umpires have to act quickly, although the evidence strongly suggested that Grout was out; Alexander's hands were nowhere near the stumps, even if unseen by the umpire, the bail could have come off only in a legitimate way. A movie of the incident left no doubt that Grout cut the ball on to the stump.

The Greatest Test of All (Fingleton) pp83–4

'MY SCALP, MY NECK, MY BODY'

Grout got out next ball, but Mackay and Martin saw to it that Australia won by two wickets to take the series 2–1. And half an hour after the finish, a famous ceremony occurred where the popular West Indian captain Frank Worrell handed his cap, tie and blazer to Benaud.

Speaking to the thousands massed in front of the grandstand, Worrell said: 'I give Richie my scalp, my neck and my body — the legs are not worth having.'

Spontaneously the big crowd broke into: 'For he's a Jolly Good Fellow.'

As Benaud came to the microphone, a barracker tried to have the last word with him: 'Put Benaud on to bowl' he cried out.

Benaud accepting Worrell's tributes, said aptly: 'Frank has given me, so to speak, his scalp, neck and body — but he is in every Australian's cricket heart for evermore.'

The Greatest Test of All (Fingleton) p86

THE GAG

Although Richie Benaud led Australia against England in 1961, much of the opposition he encountered was from within his own camp. Manager Syd Webb was so anxious to rein in the charismatic captain that, after remarks he made about his injured shoulder were misquoted, Benaud was forbidden from further comment.

174

The next morning we were going down to Lord de Lisle's place. A car was supposed to pick me up at the London hotel, but there were a couple of friends of Syd who lived 15 miles out of London. The car which was to call for me picked them up and I was left behind.

I then made a hurried trip to Lord de Lisle's, arriving late. As soon as I got there, Tom Goodman from the *Sydney Morning Herald* came up and asked me how my shoulder was progressing and would I play in the First Test. I told Tom to go and ask the manager. It turned out to be a very famous quote.

An aftermath of this concerned Norman O'Neill's selection for the Test. He had damaged the knee in the Sussex game. We had to change trains on our way to Birmingham for the Test. The three selectors on tour were Neil Harvey, Col McDonald and myself. We were standing in the bar at Euston railway station. Syd Webb had a medical report on O'Neill. He said to us: 'Well he won't be playing in the Test.' I told him he couldn't say that at this moment and that we'd wait until he had a fitness test.

'Well I'm saying he won't be playing,' said Webb.

I then informed him that we three selectors would sit down and sort out whether or not O'Neill played. There was a long confrontation in the bar after which I told him he was to look after his side of things and manage the team while we looked after selection. I then said that if we thought O'Neill fit, he would play. And he did play — made about 70 or something like that.

Howzat! (Butler) p114

The Ridge Test

The Lord's Test was a gruelling encounter during which all batsmen suffered from inconsistent bounce allegedly from an underprepared pitch. Australia's match-winner was an unlikely character: a left-handed opener called Bill Lawry whose nickname, since a Victorian 2nd XI trip to Adelaide six years earlier, had been 'Phantom'.

It was a trip that didn't get me any runs, but it succeeded in getting me both a nickname and a tour 'initiation'. I arrived at the carriage armed with some magazines including some Phantom comics. The Victorian skipper Dick Maddocks looked over my purchases and said: 'I see we've got a Phantom fan. We'll call him the Phantom.'

Run-Digger (Lawry) p28

Lawry made 130 out of 340 in Australia's reply to England's 206 on the second day. And, when the Duke of Edinburgh came into the Australian dressing room after four days, the testimony to a bruising contest was Wally Grout's black eye.

'Look after that eye,' said the Duke. 'I suggest you put some steak on it.'

Wally, whom I have never known to be stuck for a word, came back with: 'We eat all our steak sir.'

Slasher Opens Up (Mackay) p118

Manchester Miracle

Australia led by only 150 runs with one wicket in hand on the final morning of an eventful Fourth Test at Old Trafford and were resigned to defeat. But, against the odds, Alan Davidson and twenty-year-old Graham McKenzie suddenly gave their captain runs to bowl at.

The game was firmly in England's grasp. At the wicket, Davidson was looking like 'an old, old man'. McKenzie, who had been receiving treatment from masseur Arthur James for his sore leg, was taken by surprise when the three wickets fell. He had to rush to get his pads on, but he knew the prospects of Australian victory had almost disappeared.

What followed was like a story from a Boy's Own Annual. Carefully keeping McKenzie away from the danger man David Allen, Davidson for one of the few occasions on tour revealed his undoubted batting ability. First he saw Statham out of the attack. Close his replacement tended to overpitch his off-breaks allowing Davidson and McKenzie to score fairly freely. Meanwhile Allen, after nine overs, had conceded only two runs, and Davidson decided to hit him out of the attack. Twenty runs came in a single over — 6, 4, 4, 6 — while McKenzie watched the ball sail over his head. England's captain Peter May took Allen off. By now McKenzie was batting confidently, fifty runs coming in 25 minutes, 85 in an hour, and England's grasp was weakening by the minute. Finally it was Flavell who managed to bowl McKenzie for 32, leaving Davidson 77 not out. Together they had added 98 runs in 102 minutes, stretching Australia's lead from 157 to 255.

Garth (Jaggard) p73

Davidson, breathless but triumphant as he tossed his bat into a corner proclaimed: 'We'll do these jokers, Rich.'

Tale of Two Tests (Benaud) p89

'STICK WITH ME, WAL'

Benaud agreed but, when Ted Dexter's majestic batting took England to 1–150, Wally Grout had doubts about his captain's optimism.

I sent a look of disgust down the wicket to Richie and reminded him at the end of the over that I had money on this match and if he kept bowling that stuff I was going to do my dough. Benaud, serene as ever, said: 'Stick with me, Wal, we're going to win this game.'

He sent Ted a similar ball in the next over and even Dexter must have had some compassion for Benaud as he slammed it to the fence. The next ball looked a 'dead ringer' for the other two and Ted again played the cut. But the ball carried top spin and skidded from the bat into my gloves.

I will never forget that moment. The way I clung to that ball it could have been gold bullion and Benaud's broad grin from half-way down the wicket said as plainly as if he had yelled out: 'I told yer!' I have never doubted the man since.

My Country's Keeper (Grout) p94

ROUGH CHANCE

England's captain Peter May, who had made a debonair 95 in the first innings, took strike … and Benaud decided to try bowling into the rough round leg stump.

It was no good trying to keep him quiet … we had to get him out and quickly. I reasoned that there was just a chance if I could land on those rough spots to him … that I could trap him …

The first ball didn't land in the rough at all but on the leg-stump and May played it back down the wicket.

'Get it out further, you idiot,' I said to myself.

The next ball did land in the rough and as May tried to sweep it, the ball dug into the turf and whipped back towards leg-stump. I saw all this from where I had run to the on-side of the wicket … there was that terrible fraction of a second as I waited for the ball to hit the leg-stump ... and then an unrestrained yell of joy.

Tale of Two Tests (Benaud) p93

THE MAN UPSTAIRS

Dexter came to challenge Benaud as England's captain in 1962–63 and his team won the Second Test. But Australia at once retaliated, winning the Third at the SCG thanks largely to some inspired bowling by Davidson (9–79). When bowling to the Rev David Sheppard, Davidson appeared to have called on heavenly guidance, through batsman and lay preacher Brian Booth.

In Sydney's Third Test I beat David with three consecutive outswingers. I scratched my head and walked back past Brian Booth on my way to my bowling mark saying to him: 'Didn't you say a prayer for me last night?'

Booth replied: 'You've got to do a bit yourself you know.'

I put up my hands and offered a silent prayer. The next ball Sheppard snicked and was caught at the wicket. Booth laughed and said: 'See, it pays off if you do it yourself. I hope that convinces all you other blokes, too.'

Fifteen Paces (Davidson) p169

THE JOY OF SOCKS

Not a praying man, Norm O'Neill needed some extra help when he came to play in the Fourth Test at the Adelaide Oval. His wife Gwen provided the remedy for a run of low scores.

On the first morning of the game I went down to the gate at the Adelaide Oval to leave some tickets for my wife, who had flown in from Sydney. Gwen had just arrived and had a small brown parcel in her hand. She gave it to me and said: 'Darl, I remember your mother used to take care of a pair of lemon socks for you as they are supposed to give you luck. So I've bought you a new pair in the hope they will do the same trick.'

I went straight back to the dressing room and just like that day ten years before put on the lemon socks under a pair of ordinary cricket socks. Not long afterwards I was batting. Australia had lost three wickets fairly cheaply. I got through a slow start and went on to play one of the finest innings of my career and certainly one that gave me immense satisfaction. I scored exactly 100, my first century at home against England.

Ins and Outs (O'Neill) p159

BACK IN TOWN

Wally Grout returned from injury in that match, and was also immediately his old self.

We had all missed his repartee which flashed again when I beat Dexter with one that got up quickly.

Dexter said: 'That was a good ball Wal.'

'Naw,' said The Griz as he flipped the ball to slips. 'You just made it look good.'

Slasher Opens Up (Mackay) p155–6

A MUG FROM MING

Comment was passed too when, at a dinner for both teams, Sir Robert Menzies called England's Fred Trueman to the top table to present him with a pewter mug for his 32nd birthday.

England's team manager the Duke of Norfolk turned to his host and said: 'That was very generous of you, Menzies, but I would like you to know you have undone the hard disciplinary work of the last six weeks.'

Ray Robinson, *Cricketer Close-Up* p16

LAST CHUCK

The throwing controversy was reignited in November 1963 when Ian Meckiff was recalled for Australia's First Test against South Africa at the Gabba. Square-leg umpire Col Egar's four piercing calls in Meckiff's first over effectively ended the bowler's Test career. Wally Grout recounted the reaction in the Australian slips cordon.

My immediate reaction to the call of no-ball was to think some idiot in the crowd was trying to be funny. No-balling from the grandstand may be considered a certain laugh riser among the moronic element at home but I have not yet heard it raise so much as a titter from genuine cricket watchers. I snatched a look at Richie in the gully to see how he reacted to this type of barracking and his eyes were fairly popping.

It was then I knew that the call came from square leg umpire Col Egar. Ian was called on the second ball, and again on his third, fifth and ninth deliveries. It was during this over that I remembered that a horse the team had backed had failed to get up and I mentioned it to Richie.

Richie's snapped reply: 'I've got enough to worry about' indicated just how deeply affected he was by Meck's plight.

My Country's Keeper (Grout) p113

There was at least one amusing sequel to the tragedy.

Benaud was sipping tea in the lunch-room when O'Neill told him masseur Jock Anderson was walking around muttering threats. Through a doorway a figure appeared, hat pulled down over sunglasses. The intruder displayed a *Sporting Globe* showing headlines asking why Benaud had not bowled Meckiff from the other end: 'Why didn't you?' rasped the semi-disguised Jock.

Lifting the paper he pointed a revolver at Benaud and fired. It was only a cap gun but, at that moment, Richie said, his past life flashed before him.

On Top Down Under (Robinson) p203

DIAMONDS

Having foreshadowed his retirement, Benaud did not captain Australia again. His successor Bob Simpson was acutely conscious of the shoes he was filling.

Benaud was the greatest bluffer in cricket. All the time he would be trying to outwit the opposing players and if he could not outwit them he would outbluff them. In the Commonwealth team tour of Hong Kong, Richie had been fiddling with the game in his usual fashion until it got to the stage we had to get six batsmen out for six runs or lose the match.

Richie slipped the word to Neil Adcock to get stuck into them. Sure enough Neil bowled over the six wickets for five runs and won the match.

The finish prompted the English bowler Harold Rhodes to exclaim: 'There's no doubt about you Benaud, if you put your head in a bucketful of garbage you'd come out with a mouthful of diamonds.' When I was elected captain Benaud sent me a telegram: 'Congratulations. Remember — diamonds are a skip's best friend.'

Captain's Story (Simpson) p40

CHRISTMAS CRACKER

The retirements of Neil Harvey, Alan Davidson and Ken Mackay also left a gaping hole, although the last discovered that his absence from Queensland's annual Christmas match against South Australia would not be mourned.

One Christmas morning when I was apparently boring the locals more than usual, a voice in the crowd yelled: 'Why don't you go home Mackay? You've been bumming Christmas dinners off us long enough.' I liked that.

Slasher Opens Up (Mackay) p13

'I THOUGHT THIS WAS A BLOODY TEST MATCH'

The First Test of the 1964 Ashes series opened dramatically when, responding to a call from newcomer Geoff Boycott, reserve opener Fred Titmus was bowled over by Australian medium-pacer Neil Hawke. A chivalrous gesture followed which, the bowler recalled, not all the tourists appreciated.

Simpson had reminded me that I had right of way to field a ball and it was the batsman's duty to avoid me. I remembered this when Boycott played me on the on-side and called for one. I darted after the ball and poor old Fred Titmus crossed my line on a collision course. He finished sprawled on the ground and Grahame Corling, fielding at mid-on, picked up the ball and lobbed it back to Wally Grout standing over the stumps. Wally made a sweep with the ball over the stumps without removing the bails and then lobbed the ball back to me.

From the covers came the startled cry: 'I thought this was a bloody Test match!' which suggested not everyone was in accord with Wally's gesture.

Bowled Over (Hawke) pp67–8

PETER SURGE

Australia was reeling at 7–178 in reply to England's 268 in the Third Test at Leeds, and Peter Burge was feeling his way painfully against spinners Titmus and Norman Gifford. But then, as Hawke joined him, the brawny Queenslander saw a way out.

Burge saw Dexter signal that he was about to take the new ball.

For Burge it looked like a reprieve, a release from the straitjacket imposed by the spinners. He walked down the wicket to Hawke. 'Ted's

181

taking the new ball. Let's make the most of it. The spinners will be back soon enough. We've just got to take it out on this new ball.'

Innings of a Lifetime (Barker) p46

Hooking and pulling with abandon, Burge added 105 with Hawke and a further 89 with Grout. The keeper remembered their stand.

Peter and I were leaving the dressing room to resume the innings when I heard Simmo say to somebody: 'The old feller will do it.' I might have some more hair on my head than Peter but I knew this hadn't fooled Simmo.

The faith of Bobby's inspired me to square cut Freddie Trueman's first ball to the fence and hook his next to the opposite boundary, which prompted Ted Dexter to bark at Freddie from backward square leg: 'Why are you dropping them short to this fellow?'

Later in the innings, when Freddie Titmus was dropping his deliveries on the proverbial postage stamp, Trueman the No 1 gamesman walked in from leg slip between overs, took a long look at the pitch and said to me: 'I wouldn't like to be you fellows batting on this in the second innings.'

I said: 'The way you are bowling Freddie, we won't have to,' one rare occasion when I had the last word with him.

My Country's Keeper (Grout) p143

Drawn And Quartered

Australia needed only 111 in their second innings and won by seven wickets, prompting Simpson to a batting endurathon at Old Trafford that ensured the Ashes' retention. His 311, his first Test century, was at 762 minutes the third longest innings in first-class cricket history. And one of the most exasperating a home crowd has ever had to sit through.

As he removed his pads with perspiration pouring down his face, a Lancashire member complete with cloth cap and pipe looked up at the players' balcony and yelled: 'Declare Simpson you bastard.'

Wally Grout leaning over the rail took a deep draw on his cigarette and enquired drily: 'What about the Oval 1938?'

Bowled Over (Hawke) pp 78–9

Off-spinner Tom Veivers bowled for so long, when England made 611 in reply to Australia's 8–656 declared, that when the last locals Fred Rumsey and John Price were at the crease he was within reach of a Test record held by Sonny

Ramadhin (the West Indian spinner had bowled 98 overs in an innings against England in 1957). Simpson thought Veivers deserved the record but, it transpired, the off-spinner did himself out of it while bowling to last man John Price.

We gave Price the drum about what was going on. It was a simple plan. Tom was to bowl wide of the stumps and Price wasn't to bother playing him at all unless Tom happened to make a mistake and put one on the stumps. If this happened Price was to do everything possible to keep the ball out of the wicket. Naturally we wouldn't appeal.

So much for the theory. Tom trundled up for the first ball of the over and bang it was right on the stumps. The same with the second and the third. Whatever he did he could not keep the ball away from the wicket. It was as if the wicket was a giant magnet and the ball was a lump of iron. The trouble was that Tom had been bowling for 55 overs straight on the same line. He had got into the groove so well that he could not get out of it. He could not bowl a bad ball. Finally in his efforts to bowl one out wide he lollypopped the ball up into a looping full toss which so surprised Price he missed it and was bowled. Tom had virtually mesmerised himself out of his record.

Captain's Story (Simpson) pp74–5

A Karachi Crawl

The Australians played in India on the way home, then drew a Test against Pakistan where they matched the locals in slowness of scoring on a low-bouncing Karachi wicket. Newcomer Ian Redpath was particularly culpable.

I know in my second dig I got about 40 not out in one of the slowest hands I ever played; I think it took me something like four hours to make them and, when I got back to the pavilion, Wally Grout picked up the bat and examined it closely: 'Strewth Redders,' he said, 'I could put this straight back in the sports shop and sell it as a new bat. It hasn't got a mark on it.'

Always Reddy (Redpath) p62

Altered States

As NSW's long run of success in the Sheffield Shield ebbed, other states had a chance to impose themselves. South Australia were led by the case-hardened

Les Favell, whose character impressed itself on whomever he played with. The young Ian Chappell recalled a day when his captain, having had unusual difficulty playing WA's Jim Hubble one day at the Adelaide Oval, demonstrated the art of strike monopoly.

When we resumed after lunch Les was facing Terry Jenner, who'd been brought on to bowl his leg-spinners. Les jumped down the track, hit his first delivery over mid-off's head and it raced to the boundary.

As we crossed for the first run Les was singing 'happy birthday'.

The ball had crossed the boundary rope meantime and we crossed at a walk. Les was still in a chirpy mood and called out: 'Don't think you're going to see any of this bowling young 'un.' He was as good as his word.

Long Hops and Larrikins (Chappell & Rigby) p47

Chappell also had an interesting experience in a country game for South Australia, when left-hander Lyn Marks conned his way into being allowed to keep wickets.

Test all-rounder Ian Chappell spun along a leg-break that left a batsman stranded four yards out of his crease. Grabbing at the ball, the self-appointed keeper fumbled his first attempt at stumping. Seeing this, the batsman stopped heading for the gate and tried to regain his ground. With one eye on the returning batsman, Lyn had only one eye left for the ball. While it juggled in and out of his one glove, his other glove knocked the bails off. Stumbling forward, he flattened two of the stumps.

As the batsman lunged for the crease Lyn at last grasped the ball and, with it, removed the remaining stump. The umpire signalled: 'Out'.

From amid the wreckage of stumps and bails, Lyn commented: 'A lesser keeper would have panicked.'

Cricket's Fun (Robinson) p8

Renowned for his fierce resolve and combative nature, WA's Barry Shepherd set about ridding his team of their inferiority complexes.

In one of his early matches for WA, John Inverarity recalls that early wickets fell. As he prepared to leave the dressing-room Shepherd's massive left hand seized him by the shirt front. An anxious Inverarity wondered what was coming next. 'If you get out before lunch,' his captain ground out between clenched teeth, 'don't bother coming back in here.' With Shepherd's threat ringing in his ears, Inverarity batted with genuine caution, even for him. Runs were irrelevant, survival everything. By one o'clock Inverarity had made it. Wicket intact, he strode off the ground ready to be acknowledged by his captain. Instead as he entered the dressing-room Shepherd's burly figure brushed past snarling and frowning at him.

A startled Inverarity suddenly thought, 'Did I get it wrong? Did he tell me to stick around till tea?'

Garth (Jaggard) pp155–6

Shepherd was succeeded by another uncompromising opponent in the former Surrey and Leicestershire left-arm spinner Tony Lock, who Ian Brayshaw recalled was never averse to an appeal or two.

For tense moments you couldn't go past two brave acts by Tony Lock. On the first occasion Lock appealed in all seriousness to a South Australian umpire after a young Greg Chappell had defended, then thumped the ball, which had stopped nearby, back down the wicket in Lock's direction.

Technically, I guess Chappell was out for hitting the ball twice. But the umpire thankfully refused to give a decision and the game continued.

That was in the 1967–68 season, and in Melbourne only a few weeks later Locky pulled out another unusual appeal — this time against another most promising young batsman in Paul Sheahan. A wicket had fallen about 10 minutes before stumps and I'll swear it was at least seven minutes before Sheahan made it to the crease … so Locky appealed.

The Victorian umpire preserved his own skin, plus that of the Old Fox, by also declining to give a decision.

Cricketer Magazine Annual 1976–77 p58

The weirdest dismissal of the period, however, befell John Inverarity while playing South Australia that season.

Conditions were ideal for batting that afternoon. The second-day wicket was flat and true and the light so clear one could almost distinguish each stitch on the ball. Greg Chappell was bowling tidily but unthreateningly to me at medium-pace. He had prevented me from scoring for the first 10 minutes of my innings and then, quite unexpectedly, bowled a wild delivery which looked certain to provide me with a gift boundary to open my account. I prepared to give it the full swing of the bat as it went past at waist high.

An instant later my stumps were scattered. I could not believe it. The ball looked so inviting before it vanished. Now I was out for a duck, clean bowled without even offering a shot, utterly baffled by the Chappell delivery. All the confidence and faith I had in my ability to bat drained from me. My eyesight and my judgement had deserted me. My cricket world was in tatters; it flashed through my mind that if I could make such an awful misjudgement and fail so badly I had best try no more. It would be impossible for me to continue if one shaped to square cut such an easy offering, lost it and simply stood ineffectually and allowed it to crash into the stumps. It was an intolerable humiliation; I felt finished as a cricketer.

As these thoughts rushed through my mind, I was unaware that anything extraordinary had happened; only that my judgement had been terribly astray. Within moments, however, the truth of what had happened to that freakish delivery became apparent.

I had taken but a step or two towards the pavilion when I heard Greg Chappell say that he'd killed two birds with one stone. Simultaneously Rex Blundell, the South Australian keeper, held up a dead swallow. 'You've killed the bird, you rotten swine,' he said jokingly.

Middle & Leg (Pollard) p143

'THE ELDERLY ONE'

Bob Simpson's men were surprised when they arrived in Montego Bay at the commencement of their 1965 Caribbean tour to find that locals already had an intimate knowledge of their records. Surprised — and not always rapt.

We were stretching our legs at the airport when an intended on-looker approached and gave what we soon learned was the standard greeting from practically every West Indian: 'What's your name, man?'

I told him and he said: 'Oh the elderly one.'

My Country's Keeper (Grout) p171

SABINA 65

The Australians were keen to take a look at the West Indian paceman Charlie Griffith and, after the First Test in Kingston, tended to agree with those who had already branded him a chucker. Simpson was bowled first ball by a no-ball, O'Neill's hand was broken, and Brian Booth had a near-death experience at the hands of the muscle-bound Bajan.

When I reached the crease the only fieldsman in front of the wicket was at cover. Griffith ambled in and bowled a ball of medium pace.

Surprised I tentatively played it wide of him. He reached out a long arm and fielded it. Next ball, similar action, I leaned forward and steered it to mid-on for two. My mind raced: 'Griffith is not fast. He must be holding himself back.'

What happened in the next two balls is almost beyond description. Again he ambled in for the third delivery. I saw his arm come up. The next thing I knew was that something grazed my nose and just touched the tip of my cap. An agonised shout came from the press box: 'He's got him!' I do not recall even seeing the ball leave his hand or even whipping past my face — but I felt it! Had it been a fraction closer it would have hit my head.

That delivery, I believe, got me out. He bowled again off his short casual run. My thoughts were: 'Short back lift here. Get well in behind it. It could be a yorker. It could be another bumper.' I doubt whether my bat really left the blockhole. My middle and off stumps were shattered by that screaming yorker. I have never been so comprehensively bowled.

Booth to Bat (Booth) pp114–5

HARD HEADS

An enthusiastic Australian cricket lover — Sydney solicitor Bruce Miles, president of the Cricket Supporters Association — air-freighted a batch of helmets to Trinidad before the Second Test. They arrived a decade or so early.

The West Indians thought this a great joke and the Australian skipper Bobby Simpson refused to collect the consignment which, to the best of my knowledge, still lies in a Port-of-Spain warehouse.

But it rather reflected the feelings of the side when one Australian player muttered: 'Well I'm not too proud to wear a helmet. I would very much like to get home with this head still on these shoulders.'

Run-Digger (Lawry) p85

WARN OUT

Although they lost the rubber 2–1, the Australians kept their heads and rewrote a few records on the way. Simpson and Lawry conspired at Kensington Oval in a record Australian opening alliance against the fiercest Griffith could offer.

Charlie had been sending down a few bumpers so I asked umpire Cecil Kippins what he thought constituted intimidatory bowling. Kippins told me he thought the bowling was OK at the moment.

Soon after this Griffith began sending down 3 or 4 bouncers an over. Kippins went over to him and gave him what pressmen called a friendly warning. It wasn't exactly a caution. Kippins merely put his arm round Charlie's shoulders and told him he'd better watch the way he was bowling. The warning made as much impression on Griffith as a mosquito buzzing round an angry lion. His next over to me he rocked down five bumpers out of six balls.

Captain's Story (Simpson) p160

DOCTOR LORD

As they added 382, Neil Hawke had been feeling dispirited by a neck injury. No available doctor could relieve it. But unorthodox relief was at hand.

I felt so low in fact that I was sitting alone in tears away from the pavilion. The tiny groundsman approached me in sympathy and when I explained he said: 'Mr Hawke, I will come for you at your hotel at 7.30 in the morning.'

I had nothing to lose and I was waiting at the door when he arrived at the Marine Hotel. He drove into Bridgetown to a small house in a ramshackle back-street area. There were about eight people sitting in the small waiting room and I felt terribly conspicuous being the only white man.

Eventually my turn came to see a Dr Lord and I entered a room bare of furniture apart from a bench-like table in the middle. I was told to strip to my underpants and lie face down on the table. Dr Lord took one look at the base of my back and jubilantly exclaimed: 'Ah, I see you have something out of place down here.'

He pressed both thumbs firmly down on either side of my backbone and raised each leg upwards as high as he could. He repeated the treatment and said: '$4 please, and if you have any more trouble please come back again.'

I couldn't believe how I felt. From the perpetual state of agony I'd been in to have complete relief was overwhelming. Under my tour agreement with the ACB I was only able to seek treatment authorised by the manager so I could tell no one about my miracle cure. It turned out I bowled 64 overs in the match and some curious eyes were cast at me.

Bowled Over (Hawke) p104

'I'M OUT'

Brian Booth, one of the most gentlemanly players to wear a baggy green, demonstrated his sense of decorum when he led the tourists against a Trinidad Colts side captained by Frank Worrell.

When on 15 I turned a ball to square leg. The fieldsman dived and leapt to his feet holding the ball aloft. I wasn't sure if he had caught it, so I asked: 'Did you catch it?'

Thinking he had said yes I walked briskly off toward the pavilion. As I went the Colts had a hurried conference with their captain. It appeared that Lynch had caught the ball off the ground. Unaware of the drama in the centre I passed Peter Philpott near the gate, wished him good luck, and kept walking to the dressing room. I started to take off my pads.

A few seconds later Peter came running in. In amazement I demanded: 'What are you doing? Don't tell me you're out already!' He spoke urgently: 'They won't let me go in. They want you to go back.'

'I can't do that, Peter. I'm out.'

'You're not. That's the point. They want you to go back. Worrell says he won't continue the game until you do.'

Sir Frank was a fine sportsman. It was up to me to play the game in the spirit in which he wished to play. I felt it would be ungracious and petulant not to do as he asked. There was a burst of applause as I walked back.

Booth to Bat (Booth) pp117–8

BEATLE CUT

When Australia's visit to Rhodesia and South Africa in 1966–67 started promisingly with Graeme 'Beatle' Watson starring in Bulawayo in a two-day friendly, journalist Bob Gray found it impossible to call through his copy unless he could pay for it with Rhodesian money. He enlisted Bob Cowper and Neil Hawke in the process.

Armed with confidence and 10 rand which he had borrowed, he joined Bob Cowper and me at the casino. I quickly exhausted my money on greedy poker machines and departed for our hotel leaving the pair at the roulette table full of as I could see it false optimism.

About 3am I was awakened by the pair — well the worse for drink — clutching a handful of notes and wearing huge grins. They had both cleaned up and Gray was now able to telephone Sydney with the story.

Lying back on the bed without one single note, Gray's headline began: 'The Beatle who gave the Matabeleland a hard day's night.' He then proceeded to give an accurate review of the day's play, so I am sure I saw a genius at work.

Bowled Over (Hawke) p120

GHOUL ON THE HILL

When South African wicketkeeper Denis Lindsay made a dashing 137 at Kingsmead, Hawke made himself popular with the crowd on Castle Hill by putting him down.

Early in his innings Lindsay hooked a delivery from Renneberg down to deep fine leg where I was fielding in front of a packed Castle Corner. I was a trifle slow picking up the trajectory of the ball against the backdrop of trees and was forced to make a desperate lunge. Although I got two hands to the ball the impact on my elbows dislodged it and a chance went begging. The crowd behind me enjoyed my discomfort and Lindsay's good fortune and as I returned to the fence I picked up an empty baby's cot hanging on a picket. I held it aloft as if to say: 'If I'd had this I would have caught it.' The crowd was delighted and from that moment I was adopted by the hillites.

When Renneberg replaced me after tea at fine leg, the crowd kicked up such a din that the game could not restart until Simpson returned me to my accustomed position, the hairs on my neck bristled and my face flushed as I jogged to my position amid tumultuous applause from my 'fan' club.

At the end of the game hundreds spilled onto the ground and took up a position outside of the pavilion chanting: 'We want Hawke.' Simpson said: 'You'd better get out here Ghoul or there's going to be a riot.' I was chaired shoulder-high to Castle Hill by a deliriously happy crowd who proceeded to ply me with cans of lager and had me sign everything from baby nappies to sun hats for the next 40 minutes before returning me in like fashion.

Bowled Over (Hawke) pp126–7

I Did Not See Her Passing By

Bill Lawry led Australia to England in 1968 with a side including a gangling off-spinner called Ashley Mallett. He recalled his trip for one notable faux pas during the Second Test at Lord's as players mingled with dignitaries.

I distinctly remember talking among a group of fellow players when I saw from a distance of about ten yards away, the figure of a rather elegant looking woman approaching.

My short-sightedness had never really embarrassed me before, but I really couldn't make out who the woman was, but called out, 'I say my dear, will you not join us here?'

By now you will have realised that it was none other than Queen Elizabeth.

Rowdy (Mallett) p37

Run Out Of Luck

Ian Redpath was a victim of Charlie Griffith when Australia played the West Indies at the Adelaide Oval in January 1969 ... though not after the fashion of the fast bowler's previous conquests.

Having watched Ian Redpath backing up too early from the bowling end, Charlie Griffith lopes in for his second delivery with an intention nobody suspects; for a batsman has not been run out at the bowler's end in Australia for 20 years. Bringing that long arm over, Griffith notices that Redpath is more than a yard out of his crease, and he knocks down the nearest stump with a circular swing of his arm ... Umpire Rowan unhesitatingly raises his arm and Redpath walks off without any sign of anger. If anything he looks bewildered.

Hooting, booing and jeering, however, follow the initial stunned silence. Every ball Charlie Griffith delivers now is greeted with boos. As they come in for tea, Griffith is hooted the whole way up the George Giffen Stand in an exhibition unlike any I have seen at the Adelaide Oval since Jardine positioned a Bodyline field immediately after Woodfull was struck down by one of Larwood's deliveries in January 1933.

Fours Galore (Whitington) pp200–1

HELL'S KITCHEN

Lawry's Australians tackled India on its own wickets in 1969–70 and won a vivid, violent series made all the more memorable by their experiences of local conditions and culture. Eight-wicket victory in the First Test at Bombay was achieved in spite of heat and hygiene, recalled by Ian Chappell.

The stadium-guesthouse where we stayed wasn't fit for a dog. One evening, some of the players were looking for toasted sandwiches at the stadium. They were told that the cook had gone but that there was some bread in the kitchen. Brian Taber went downstairs and came back with a loaf under his arm. 'If you want to eat another meal in this place, don't go down and look at the kitchen,' he said.

Being curious, a couple of us went to investigate and we found cats in the refrigerator, cats runnings over the uncovered food, green slime on the floor, barred windows with no glass, and a rubbish tip with an unbelievable stench outside the window.

Chappelli (Chappell) p65

RIOTOUS ASSEMBLY

The closing scenes of the match were punctuated by pitch invasions. A full-blooded riot occurred as Australia set off to make the winning runs, and Ashley Mallett watched as a large Indian bailed up Lawry and asked him if he intended playing on.

I must add that my admiration for our captain soared when he said he intended to stay on the ground. The Indian smiled and left with the ominous words, 'If those people break down the fence, grab a stump and take a few with you. Good luck.'

Rowdy (Mallett) pp43–4

GLEESONIA

Ultimately the only Australian casualty was unorthodox spinner John Gleeson, who received a bump on the head from a flying bottle. It was the start for him of a memorable tour: his appeal during the tourists' match at North Zone elicited the following notable arbitration.

After several exasperating overs, Gleeson found the elusive edge, Brian Taber took the catch and our appeal was unanimous. But you'd have sworn the umpire had been carved from stone. Nothing happened.

He stood there. We stood there … until a couple of guys started running from the covers to put the question again.

At last after what to us seemed an eternity, the finger was raised.

As we gathered around congratulating Gleeson and Taber, the umpire walked the length of the pitch, tapped Johnny on the shoulder and said: 'Oh Mr Gleeson, I'm very sorry to take so long over that decision but there was a strong wind blowing against me and it took a long time for the snick to carry to my end.'

Chappelli Has the Last Laugh (Chappell) p37

Gleeson proved persuasive also in Bangalore, where he came in to bat against South Zone with Australia 8–36 and struggling to avoid defeat against the off-spin of Erapalli Prasanna.

He walked out there waving his bat, windmill fashion, as real batsmen do to loosen up. He stopped at the bowler's end and started waving it helicopter fashion round the umpire's head. We had no way of knowing that Johnny was saying: 'Look you little bastard, if you give me out lbw, I'm going to wrap this thing right round your bloody neck. And if you or your mate give Bill Lawry, the bloke at the other end, out lbw then I'll wrap it round the neck of the bloke who gives him out!'

For the next hour and 50 minutes, Johnny and Bill merely padded the ball away. Bill would poke his right pad down the wicket, Johnny his left. There were lots of appeals from an Indian field long accustomed to a raised finger being a formality. And every time Johnny would give the umpire the mean eye, raise his bat a little and slip him a wink and a smile when the response was negative.

One for the Road (Walters) p98

'WHAT A GREAT BALL!'

Off-field entertainment for the players was scarce, with movie theatres one of the few available recreations. After Bill Lawry was bowled by Subroto Guha in the Third Test at Delhi, they became even more popular.

Whenever we went to the movies over the next four weeks there was always a newsreel showing the ball that had bowled Lawry. Phanto would say: 'Not again!' And we'd all clap and say: 'What a great ball!'

Not Just for Openers (Stackpole) p73

SELF-CENSORSHIP

Despite their 3–1 victory in India, Australia's energies were depleted by the time it arrived in South Africa for a four-Test series and it was duly trounced in every match. Ian Chappell made only 92 runs in eight innings … although he did pick up a habit that would last him the rest of his playing days.

I'd got a duck at the Wanderers in Johannesburg and, just to rub salt in the wounds, as I was walking off this prick grabbed the cap off my head and took off. From that time onwards I took off my cap as soon as I got out, and I'd have my gloves and cap in front of my mouth as I walked out so the TV cameras wouldn't catch me cursing myself for a stupid shot or whatever.

Bedside Book of Cricket Centuries (Smith) pp89–90

HIDE OUT

Lawry, in particular, was grieved by the umpiring of C. M. P. Coetzee, and could not accept his parting gift.

After the last Test he came into our dressing room with a prettily wrapped gift and tried to hand it to Bill.

'Look,' said Bill. 'I can't take it off you. I'm not a hypocrite.' Taken aback Coetzee gave the parcel to our manager Fred Bennett who handed it to Chappell. It turned out to be a plaque with a piece of lion's skin attached to it. Phanto might have been more interested in something containing Coetzee's skin.

Not Just for Openers (Stackpole) p85

RECORD KEEPING

At the Gabba, Australia ushered in its youngest wicketkeeper. Rod Marsh caught Boycott, Fletcher, Illingworth and Snow but — to his mortification — turfed another three chances. Doug Walters dispelled some of his depression.

After the match I was having a beer with Doug Walters, who quipped: 'Well Bacchus, if you'd caught them all you'd have got a world record there.' Tremendous!

You'll Keep (Marsh) p59

194

FROGGY

Fitzroy's Alan 'Froggy' Thomson bowled himself into the side for the Second Test, although his windmill action bowling off the wrong foot perplexed even his teammates.

His effort prompted Victorian wicketkeeper Ray Jordon to tell Froggy that Ray Lindwall must have had an incorrect action. 'The way you're bowling, Froggy, everybody else has been bowling the wrong way.'

The Doug Walters Story (Walters) p87

FOT

More classically-inclined, though still raw, was Perth's Dennis Lillee, who took 5–84 on his Test debut at Adelaide. Dick Whitington thought highly of his speed and his humility.

Lillee has pace, courage, tenacity and that late outswinger. With proper coaching and nursing he could become great. His whole attitude is admirable, especially when catches go astray. And he is fine in the field — determined and confident.

After the Seventh Test at Sydney he came across to the M. A. Noble Stand to ask Keith Miller for Ray Lindwall's address. 'He might be able to teach me how to bowl,' he said.

Captains Outrageous?: Cricket in the Seventies (Whitington) p195

'THEY'LL NEVER TAKE ME ALIVE,' SAID HE

With Australia one–nil down after six Tests, the Australian selectors, for the only time in our history, sacked a captain during a series. That Bill Lawry heard about his dumping second-hand on the radio made his successor Ian Chappell furious.

The night I was appointed captain of Australia, I said to my wife Kay, 'they'll never get me like that'.

Chappelli (Chappell) p1

THE ABOMINABLE SNOWMAN

Chappell led Australia into a tense and absorbing Seventh Test. In the process of securing a first-innings lead of 80, however, tailender Terry Jenner was submitted to a searching examination by English speedster John Snow. Ray Robinson describes the events.

As the first rose toward his ribs, Jenner gingerly fended it away with his bat. It ran around the corner for a single, giving Chappell the strike for four balls. Facing Snow again for the sixth ball, Jenner unhappily squirmed out of its way as it reared. Had he stood still, it would have struck him near the left armpit. The over count so far to Jenner: two short-pitched balls, at least one of which an umpire could have classed as intimidatory.

To follow up Jenner's apprehensive wriggle from the sixth ball, Snow's field-setting was changed by bringing Willis from mid-off to the on-side. This made four leg-trap fieldsmen: deep leg (Underwood), leg-gully (Hampshire), close short-leg (Illingworth) and mid-on (Willis). Stepping back, Jenner stared at the reshuffle like a bird transfixed by a snake's mesmerism. Like every cricketer watching, he recognised the field adjustment as preparation for catching a mishit off a bouncer to come. It came. Banged down short, it cut in as it reared toward Jenner's collarbone. As he tried to duck beneath it, the ball struck the left side of his head near the back and rebounded toward cover. Jenner's collapse on the pitch brought a thunderous hoot from the keyed-up crowd.

From close-leg, five yards away, Illingworth was first to the stunned Jenner. Hooting and abusive shouts from the Hill continued as the pallid tailender was lifted to his feet. Willis carried the dropped bat as masseur David McErlane and Lever helped Terry walk unsteadily off, blood oozing through his hair.

The Wildest Tests (Robinson) pp152–3

After Snow had an altercation with spectators on the boundary edge and suffered a bombardment of beer cans, Illingworth led his team from the field. While umpire Lou Rowan was trying to persuade him to return, the result of the match hung in the balance.

Sitting side by side broadcasting, ex-captains Benaud and Lawry had made a small diversionary bet on the match. Illingworth's disappearance through the gate reminded Lawry of this. Turning to Richie he said: 'It's a forfeit. Pay up, Benordy!'

The batsmen stayed at the wicket. Lillee, playing in his second Test, walked along to Chappell and asked: 'What do we do now?'

196

Greg: 'We stay here until we are told to do something differently.'

The Wildest Tests (Robinson) p155

When play resumed after a tense seven-minute hiatus, Lillee proved an obstinate partner for the younger Chappell. His innings, though, almost did not continue into the third day.

After play resumed I hung on till stumps and naturally was one of the first in the nets the following morning to practise my batting. However, to my surprise, Ian Chappell came up to me and told me he was grateful for the job I'd done filling in for Jenner when he was hurt, but that T.J. was ready to continue his innings now and I could drop back to my normal position in the order.

I thought this was a bit odd, but this was the Australian captain. So I didn't hurry back from the nets for the start of play, preferring to use the time there having a good workout. The umpires had gone onto the ground before Ian realised I had taken him seriously and the joke was backfiring. He had to send a runner to get me back to the dressing-room in a hurry to prepare to continue my innings. Boy was I gullible.

My *Life in Cricket* (Lillee) p21

Butler Did It

When a World XI led by Garry Sobers replaced South Africa as the tourists for the 1971–72 summer, emerging star Greg Chappell struggled to convert starts into scores. A bout of soul-searching was occasioned when he received a letter from father Martin containing an article by Keith Butler of the Adelaide Advertiser.

My father finished off the letter by saying: 'Son I don't believe what Butler is saying is true, but maybe it bears some thinking about.'

I sat there in my hotel room thinking about my cricket of the last 12 months or so and realised that I had been looking for the easy way out. I'd convinced myself I was sacrificing my wicket for the sake of the team. But really I didn't want to put the hard work in. I was cheating on myself.

A bunch of guys from the Rest of the World team rang asking me to go out with them for a drink but I was preoccupied with the letter and stayed in my room. In the darkness I thought of the article and my father's comments, I thought about my frame of mind and my career. Suddenly it came to me that on the days I scored runs my thinking was good and on the days I failed with the bat my thinking was not so good.

If I could get my thinking right regularly, it became obvious I would score runs regularly. I knew then that what happens in your mind is as important, probably more important, than the physical side of batting. I decided then and there to spend more time on my mental preparation than on my physical preparation.

Winning (Writer) p81

'DEAR DIARY ...'

Chappell scored an unbeaten 115 in the MCG international, then an unbeaten 197 in the SCG international. And, when selected for England, he had the dubious privilege of accompanying the team's most nervous flier on the first leg of their trip to England from Adelaide to Sydney. He later reported to colleagues the experience of travelling with Ashley Mallett.

According to Greg, Rowdy had in his pocket a diary which he soon produced in the airport lounge to note that at 7.25 he 'arrived at airport'. The moment they fastened their seat belts on board the plane, says Greg, Rowdy went through the usual routine. He stopped an air hostess and ordered a double scotch as soon as the bar opened; then he reached into his bag and fossicked around until he came out with a cigarette, which he placed between already trembling lips, matches at the ready for the instant the 'no smoking' light went out; then instead of sitting back in his seat with a customary firm grip on the arm rests he dived into his bag. Greg couldn't help noticing him pull out his diary and make a second entry: '7.45, taxied to leave for Sydney, from where we will go to England.' Back went the diary into the bag.

Greg later admitted to having been mightily impressed by all this and wondering how long it could last. Soon the aircraft was off the ground and again Rowdy plunged into his ghastly bag. Out came the diary and in went the third message: '7.49, plane took off for Sydney on way to England.'

Greg thought, that's terrific Rowd, you're really doing well. Off went the 'no smoking' light and the cigarette was lit in such a hurry that he dropped his matches into the open bag and set fire to some of the newspapers. Rowdy had stamped that out when the stiff scotch arrived. In the process of receiving that godsend he spilt most of it on himself.

As Greg reported to the team later, 'The nerves really had a grip on Rowd then. Next thing he was back into his bag, fossicking round for some time without coming up for air. I wasn't game to ask him what he was looking for, but after a while he became very agitated. Then he emerged with a grim look on his face, a pen in his hand and a corner of a charred newspaper, whereupon he wrote the following words: '8.09, lost diary.'

You'll Keep (Marsh) pp73–4

WALTERS AND STEELE

The mordant wit of Doug Walters was evident when Australia played Surrey.

Walters played a quick and handy innings, which came to an end with what one writer described as a 'wild village ya-hoo'. When good-humouredly challenged on this matter by manager Ray Steele, Walters answered without a smile: 'It was an attempted lofted drive forced on me by the ball dropping quickly in flight.'

Tigers Among the Lions (Chappell) p28

STEELE AND WALTERS

Steele was one of Australia's most popular managers. Walters himself remembered the Victorian's words at the team dinner the night before the Second Test at Lord's.

Ray is a nice bloke, but this night he was very angry. He ripped some newspaper clippings out of his pocket, and read a few of the headlines the Poms had written after the First Test.

'Aussies take it lying down,' he read, and then pulled off his glasses and said: 'Pig's arse they do.' It was a great piece of motivation and worked wonders for team morale.

The Doug Walters Story (Walters) p105

CAPTAIN HOOK

Ian Chappell himself had a lot on his mind before that Lord's Test. He had been falling frequently to his pet hook, and it wasn't until a meeting in the dressing-room that he chose to persevere with the stroke.

I had a stack of letters telling me to stop hooking including one from my grandmother — and she wasn't the greatest expert on the game. The day before the start of the Second Test I had a net and got Jeff Hammond to bowl short to help me decide what to do. I remember a guy behind the net saying to me: 'Even your mates are trying to bounce you out.'

I still hadn't made up my mind when I was padded up and waiting to go in after we'd bowled out England for 272. In came Kenny Barrington and, bugger me, even he told me to stop hooking. He told me to wait until I'd got fifty before I even thought about it. I thought: 'I know he's trying to help but the day I accept advice from an Englishman will be the first — so I'll hook. But will I?'

John Snow wanted to go from the Nursery End and he bowled Francis for a duck. Then Price got Stackpole caught by Gifford and we were seven for two — the crowd were in and the game was on when Greg came in to bat.

I knew I was going to get a few and, sure enough the first one hit me as I was caught in two minds. Then John Snow hit me and that decided me. I went for everything and I reckon about 40 of the 56 came from hooks. Looking back it was important for the other batsmen — especially Greg and Graeme Watson who had also got out hooking at Old Trafford. The more short stuff I got, the more I hooked because I was now sure it was the best way to establish a domination we badly needed after the way Snowy got after us in 1971.

The Innings of My Life (Bannister) p57

Fit For A Queen

When Greg Chappell's cultured hundred and Bob Massie's parabolic swing gained Australia an eight-wicket victory within three and a half days, the tourists celebrated with vigour. So much vigour, in fact, that the normally-abstinent Dennis Lillee had a memorable regal audience at the subsequent Buckingham Palace reception.

He went along very quietly that afternoon, with no-one taking much notice of what or how he was drinking. When he got to the palace, we had to line up in two groups. I had to introduce the Queen to the players, while Ray Steele did the same for the Duke. Everything went well until we got to John Gleeson. I said, 'Your Majesty, this is John Gleeson.'

Gleeson said 'How do you do ma'm,' in the correct manner.

Next in line was Lillee. 'Your majesty, this is Dennis Lillee,' I said.

'G'day,' said Dennis.

This was rather embarrassing to say the least, and I didn't know whether to laugh, cry or run out of the room. I'm sure the Queen didn't know what to do either, and the situation didn't improve when we moved on to Rod Marsh, the next in line, who found it hard to keep a straight face. We got through without further drama, however, and the Royal couple moved off.

I went over to Steele and said: 'You wouldn't want to know what Dennis Lillee said to the Queen.' Ray gritted his teeth, 'I suppose it was G'day, exactly the same as he said to the Duke.'

Chappelli (Chappell) p81

'NO APPLE!'

Lillee emerged as a fast-bowling force on tour with 31 Test wickets and also as a character. He enlivened the county match at Leicestershire by bowling a tennis ball at his old confrere Graham McKenzie, then pocketed an apple over lunch at Sussex and used it for his first delivery on resumption.

It landed on a good line and length, but broke up on hitting the hard turf. One piece hit the stunned Sussex batsman on the pad dead in front, while another careered on to hit the stumps. An international incident was avoided when a sharp-witted umpire threw out his right arm and called 'No apple!'

My Life in Cricket (Lillee) p26

'WE ARE THE GREATEST!'

A fraternal alliance of 201 between the Chappells and sublime speed bowling by Lillee gained Australia a winning position in the Fifth Test at the Oval, but the direction of the match was still in doubt when Rod Marsh joined Paul Sheahan with the tourists needing 71 for victory. As they got the better of the English attack, Ian Chappell remembered, it was local West Indians who provided the most vocal support.

With only four runs required to win a group of West Indian supporters who had yelled loyally for Australia the whole six days moved down to the boundary and I will never forget as long as I live the biggest of the group picking up the boundary flag, waving it round his head and calling out: 'We are the greatest.' Such are the liaisons of international cricket!!

Tigers Among the Lions (Chappell) p144

About Last Night ...

It fell to Marsh to score the winning runs, which tied up the series at 2–2, and to lead the subsequent celebration.

I was facing Tony Greig and poked one just behind square leg off my toes for the winning single. 'You little beauty,' I thought, and then went into an uncontrollable dance of victory. I kept on jumping and waving my bat, whooping it up like a child.

The rest of the day and the night was the same. I ran into Paul the following morning and he made some comment about how well we were knocking over the champagne the night before. As I don't drink champagne, I asked, 'What champagne?'

He laughed and replied: 'At dinner time, don't you remember we sat together at dinner?' It was news to me.

You'll Keep (Marsh) pp78–9

Fire Down Below

Richie Benaud's younger brother John was capped for the First Test against Pakistan that summer, and remembered his debut for his 'least successful shot'.

That came in the dressing room at the Adelaide Oval during a Test against Pakistan. In a nervous moment I lit a cigarette and carelessly waved out the match.

Like the arrow in the air, it fell I know not where until Dennis Lillee began shouting that his cricket bag was on fire; he was wrong, it was only his shirt and trousers.

Australian Cricket, December 1974 p30

A Bit Over The Top

Benaud's most successful shot came during a daring 142 in the Second Test at the MCG, although his skipper Ian Chappell was under pressure from Kerry O'Keeffe beforehand to send the batsman a placating message.

'He's playing so well I don't see how a message from me could help him,' I said.

'Well I've seen it all before and he'll throw his wicket away before he gets to a hundred,' Kerry maintained.

Just at that stage John Benaud seemed to changed tactics entirely, quietly pushing the ball away for singles instead of belting them to the boundary.

'There you are,' we said. 'He's settled down and is going to get to his hundred with safe singles.'

'No he's not,' Kerry argued. 'He's just going to push singles until he gets to 94, then he'll try to hit a six.'

Benaud duly pushed his way to 94, then unwound an enormous lofted drive that sailed high over the sightboard and disappeared into the dense Melbourne crowd, who roared their approval of this novel method of creeping to a first Test century.

Passing Tests (Chappell) p20

WOK

Novocastrian leg-spinner John Watkins, capped against Pakistan, was picked for Australia's tour of the West Indies and had a terrible time. Capable of bowling well in the nets, he could not find the cut strip in matches, despite encouragement from Doug Walters.

At Point-a-Pierre, for the match against Trinidad, I told him all he had to do was relax when he went out to bowl. Throughout the tour he'd been singing 'What shall we do with the drunken sailor?' on the buses. I said to him, 'Look, go out there and whistle that song when you bowl. It might help you to relax.'

I'll never forget the first couple of balls Wok bowled in Trindad's second innings. He came in to bowl the first ball whistling: 'What shall we do with the drunken sailor?' And sent down the biggest wide you've ever seen.

It didn't deter Wok. He came whistling in for the next ball and it was a wide just as far down the other side of the wicket. Looking back, I don't think the whistling would have worked even if Wok had been able to get the balls on the stumps. We were all laughing too much to field the ball.

The Doug Walters Story (Walters) p112

BOMBER'S BRAINSTORM

Ian Chappell was learning all the time as captain, not least from his own players. An example came in the First Test at Sabina Park when debutant Jeff Hammond decided that he'd like to bounce local star Alvin Kallicharran.

'Shit Mate,' I said. 'He's a good hooker and this is a pretty good track.'
    'I think I can bounce him out.'
    'Righto Bomber,' I said. 'At least you've told me. You've got two shots at it. I'll place the field to give you a bit of protection, and if it doesn't work we'll go back to my plan.'
    First bouncer a little glove from Kallicharran, Rodney Marsh caught it and he's out. You never know where your next idea is coming from. Maybe even from a kid in his first Test.

Bedside Book of Cricket Centuries (Smith) p88

COLD FEET

After two draws, Chappell also played a decisive innings in the Port-of-Spain Test despite the handicap of a tennis mishap incurred playing John Benaud.

In the West Indies in 1973 he was playing tennis against me and I wrong-footed him on one of those artificial courts and he sprained his ankle the day before the Test. He hopped round the court singing out: 'Go and get some ice from the bar.' So we choofed off to the bar and got the ice and he jammed his foot in the ice bucket and he didn't let up on the treatment all afternoon.
    The next day he went into the Test with the thing strapped. He could hardly walk. It was in Trinidad and they'd prepared the usual spinners' paradise for Lance Gibbs there and Chappelli got 97 in the second dig and played marvellously.

Extra Cover (Egan) p123

A LAST HURRAH

That effort notwithstanding, the home side needed only 66 to win at lunch on the final day with six wickets standing. The captain gave his XI a final hurrah before the afternoon session.

As the Australians prepared to file dolefully out of their lunch room to what seemed like certain defeat, Ian stopped at the door, turned and gave that hurrah. He said: 'You've been bowling and fielding like a lot of pricks. A quick wicket can change everything. We're going out there to win' ...

Max Walker opened the attack with a regulation, post-lunch warm up ball which Kallicharran cut at hugely only to find the gentlest of edges dolly to Marsh.

'You could feel the surge in the team,' said Greg. 'Coming so close on Ian's words. The West Indies just went to water.'

Greg Chappell (McGregor) p99–100

TANGLES

The manful bowling of Walker, a former VFL footballer with Melbourne, nicknamed 'Tangles' for his homespun action, was also fundamental to Australia's victory in the Fourth Test at Georgetown. As Alan McGilvray noted, the medium-pacer was soldiering on under considerable handicap.

On the morning of that match I was waiting for a cab to the ground. Max Walker arrived in the hotel foyer at the same time. He was barefoot walking on his tip toes. The backs of his legs were a mess. Blood vessels had burst. He was black and blue and generally in a dreadful state. It looked as if it would be impossible to get a boot on, let alone bowl in a Test match.

'Max,' I said. 'You can't possibly play in that condition. You'll do yourself terrible damage.' His reply was the story of the tour. 'Somebody has to do it mate,' he said.

The Game is Not the Same (McGilvray) p161

His captain remembered similar devotion to duty.

Walker was like a machine: just wind him up and he would bowl for hours and hours. I remember after he had bowled 37 overs in 85 degree heat one day during the Barbados Test, Max turned to me and said: 'I used to think Barassi was a hard man, he's got nothing on you.'

Chappelli (Chappell) p89

Whatever his motivations, some enticing inducements came Walker's way from one spectator as he patrolled the boundary fence.

On one of these little interludes, just after I'd taken Lawrence Rowe's wicket, he leaned over the fence and said: 'Hey Walker' (actually he made it sound like Wocker).

'Hey Walker,' he said. 'you bowl another ball like that and you can have my wife.' And I swear the guy was serious.

Tangles (Walker) p70

BLOOD ON THE PITCH

Mike Denness's English tourists of 1974–75 arrived at precisely the wrong time: just before Ian Chappell harnessed a formidable pair of fast bowlers in Dennis Lillee and the volatile, voluble Jeff Thomson. Tony Greig recalled how he, his colleague Keith Fletcher and his manager Bruce Francis first learned they might be in for something wickedly quick.

I shall never forget as long as I live wandering up King's Cross at midnight one night with Bruce Francis and Keith Fletcher to buy the Sunday papers. We took them back to the hotel and opened them in the coffee lounge — and sputtered over our cups. In one of the papers was a huge article by Thomson referring to blood on the pitch. Pommie blood, and the fact that it wouldn't bother him if he hurt a few batsmen. The seeds had been sown.

Wisden Cricket Monthly, December 1982 pp25–6

Greig made a valiant 110 in the First Test at the Gabba, including a partnership of 58 with tailender Derek Underwood for the eighth wicket that probably took a few years off the life of the latter.

I was bubbling over with adrenalin when Underwood came in to bat, walked up to me and said: 'Well what do you reckon mate?'

I told him: 'It's a straightforward question of fighting for your life.'

I will never forget the way he looked at me going slightly pale and said: 'Thanks a lot.'

One thing Underwood does correctly is to get his front elbow up. Well the first ball was an absolute flier from Thomson. It rose up off the pitch and passed through the crook of Underwood's arm between his elbow and his ear. How it didn't kill him I still don't know. There was a look of absolute death on Underwood's face as he came down the pitch and said to me: 'Mate you're spot on right.'

Ibid.

LILLEE V THOMSON

Lillee and Thomson swept Australia to victory at the Gabba and the WACA and in lore were linked ever after as a pair. Ironically their first meeting, a couple of years before in the Sheffield Shield when Thomson was bowling for NSW and Lillee batting for Western Australia, had not been harmonious.

Dennis comes strutting in, real mean bugger, you know, the King, sort of thing. I thought, I'll show him.

I wasn't going to bounce him. Doug [Walters] made sure of that. 'Don't bounce him, for Chrissake,' he said.

'Don't worry about him,' I said. 'I'll soon fix him up.'

Anyway, Dennis got a four off me. I think it was an edge. So I really let one go. It got up off a length and smashed him on the gloves. He let go of his bat and held his hand and ran a single, and when he got up to my end he said, 'I just hope you can hold a fucking blade, pal!'

I was grinning, and I said, 'Listen pal, you've got the bat at the moment. Just get up the other end and see how fucking good you are!' And Doug had turned white as a ghost. He must have been pooping himself.

Thommo (Frith) pp36–7

SIX AND OUT

Walters himself left the other indelible imprint on the Second Test at the WACA, with an innings of 103 including a century in a session. When he attained that landmark with a six from the last ball of the second day, he thought instinctively of the reception his colleagues would provide.

Ah yes, the dressing room. Now wouldn't that be a scene, I thought. The guys would mob me, say 'Bewdy Doug' and all that sort of stuff. They'd probably douse me with champagne. I'd be a hero among my peers. I rather fancied that.

Surprise! When I walked into the room I found it empty. Not a soul in sight. You bastards, I thought. Here's a man hitting a six off the day's last ball to complete a century in a session and you haven't got the decency to be there to hero-worship me when I get back. You probably didn't even watch the last over. Where are you, you sods?

Surprise number two was when Ian Chappell appeared from a toilet shower and gave me a blast: 'You dopey bastard!' he said. 'What do you mean by playing a totally irresponsible shot and getting out on the last ball of the day. Haven't you learned anything about team first, individual second?'

Jesus, that's lovely, I thought. Not only had he not seen the last over, but he'd stuffed up what happened anyway. Chappelli glared at me for a couple of seconds. Then he broke into a huge grin and gave me a hug — the pre-arranged signal for the rest of the guys to emerge from hiding in the showers.

Sure they'd seen it, and what a reception they gave me! Doug Walters didn't have to open his own beers that night.

One for the Road (Walters) p10

Up To The Minute

With the stimulus of a century, Walters was percolating with good humour as Thomson and Lillee rounded up the Englishmen on the last day.

There was one particularly cruel piece of wit as England captain Denness walked to the wicket in the second innings with a string of failures behind him on tour so far. Walters, standing at third slip, quipped to Greg Chappell at second: 'Don't tell me we have to put up with him for another minute!'

You'll Keep (Marsh) p112

The Receiving End

Denness himself recalled the way the pace bombardment gradually got the better of his batsmen, citing this exchange during the Third Test at the MCG after his openers Amiss and Lloyd had put on 115.

When David Lloyd came back into the dressing room after his dismissal as I was padding up, I said, 'Well played David.'

He replied: 'Bloody Hell, captain, you never get any balls in your own half.'

Any cricketer getting out in a Test match, or any other game, is obviously annoyed with himself. He may come in and throw his bat down or just sit in silence, inwardly cursing himself for getting out. But on this occasion, within seconds of his dismissal, Lloyd's body was quivering. His neck and the top half of his body in particular were shaking.

He was shellshocked, suffering from the effects of never having to move around so quickly in all his life. It was the reaction from his continual ducking and weaving to get out of the firing line.

I Declare (Denness) p111

St George v Dragon

It was the hostility of Australia's bowlers that also subdued the Englishmen. David Lloyd looked on during the Fourth Test at the SCG at a memorable exchange after Tony Greig had momentarily turned the tables on Lillee by hitting him with a bouncer.

Keith Fletcher fielding at gully shouted in that Eastenders accent: 'Well done Greigy, give 'im another.'

The atmosphere of the game suddenly changed. Lillee reared round and said: 'Who said that?'

'I did,' said Fletch.

We finished the day's play and retired to our hotel. We were all together in the team room watching the news when an interview with Dennis Lillee came onto the screen. Now, as England players, we were not able to give interviews during a game but it seemed that all the Aussie players had their own programmes …

After all the usual questions about the game in progress, Lillee was asked: 'How do you get on with the England team? What sort of blokes are they?'

'The Poms are good sorts,' he replied. 'I get on well with them all.' He then leaned forward and looking straight to camera continued: 'Except that little weasel, Fletcher. I know you are watching and I will sort you out tomorow.'

We all had a good laugh about it, but it was not funny if you happened to be Keith Fletcher.

The next day Australia made inroads into our batting and the moment of truth arrived when Fletch had to go out and bat. No helmet, no visor, just his MCC cap with St George on his horse as the badge. Lillee met him at the gate and escorted him to the middle: 'Now it's my turn you Pommy b------.'

It was as if all Australia had heard the interview. There was a tremendous crescendo of noise around the ground. Lillee threw the kitchen sink at him, but Fletch was very watchful and played superbly well.

Then it happened, that one false move that a batsman never wants to make. Lillee bowled another bouncer which did not get up as much as Fletch anticipated and it hit him straight on the head as he took his eye off the ball.

We had all been watching proceedings on the edge of our seats in the dressing room and I will never forget Geoff Arnold the former Surrey and England fast bowler jumping up and shouting: 'Blimey he's just knocked St George off his 'orse.'

G'day Ya Pommy B......! (Lloyd) pp18–20

An Unusual Congregation

Chappell's Australians were renowned for their pranks, Doug Walters frequently their instigator. Journalist Peter McFarline recalled this one from the night after Australia beat Pakistan in the opening match of the 1975 World Cup.

One fast bowler overindulged a trifle in his favourite drink and was kindly led to bed, non compos mentis, by some teammates.

This did not miss the attention of Mr Walters who was attending a party given by some local people. He promised them early morning fun, somehow found a lectern and a bible and set them up at the scene of the party.

In a superhuman effort, he half-coaxed, half-carried the inebriated fast bowler clad only in pyjama bottoms to the party and demanded he read from the bible. Half-way through this amazing performance the bowler's only piece of clothing slipped quietly to the floor to the amusement of the congregation. Our fast bowler stumbled on, blissfully unaware of his nakedness.

Cricketer, February 1980 p18

'Oh My God! I'm Going!'

More gruesome fun was had at the expense of the Sri Lankans, whom Australia met in their next World Cup match. When Anura Tennekoon's team showed unexpected resistance, Chappell gave Jeff Thomson carte blanche to retard their progress.

Anyway I hit this bloke Mendis on the head. They're only little fellas so you couldn't call it a bouncer exactly. He fell down face-first, and when they brought him round, his captain's saying: 'You'll be right', or something or other.

But Mendis just says: 'Oh my God! I'm going!' He went and he wasn't coming back! They took him to hospital.

But the real trouble came when I hit Wettimuny on the foot. He was waltzing around and he wanted to go too. That was enough for him. I'd already hit him in the chest. As I walked past him at the end of the over I said to him: 'Look it's not broken you weak bastard,' I said. 'I'll give you the tip … if you're down there next over it will be!'

His captain gives him the pep talk, you know, 'stick around, I'll look after you' sort of caper. Then the captain obligingly just blocked out Dennis to make sure he wasn't going to get down my end!

So this poor bastard was facing me again, and the ball landed in exactly the same spot and whacked him straight on the instep again. You should have seen him — jumping round he was.

This is where the plot went into action. The ball had come straight back up the pitch to me, and as I collected it, the boys are yelling out 'Throw down the stumps, Two-Up, throw down the stumps!'

I'm saying: 'No no no, I can't do that, no' — all in a split second. Then I thought 'bugger it!' and threw the ball and knocked the stumps over. I jumped up and shouted an appeal, but no other bastard's moved. They all sat or stood there with their arms folded! They'd done me stone cold on purpose.

Thommo (Frith) pp56–7

An All-Run 17

After the effect of the blazing bat of Clive Lloyd and the slick-heeled fielding of Viv Richards, Australia needed 59 to win the 1975 World Cup Final from their last pair. Umpire Dickie Bird recalled, however, the buoyancy of their approach.

When last man Dennis Lillee joined Jeff Thomson at 9–233, Lillee said jauntily, 'We'll get these Dickie.' Fifty-nine were needed. I couldn't see it myself. But slowly the runs started coming and the crowd became more and more excited.

Thomson skied a ball to Fredericks at mid-off. But it was a no-ball. The crowd, thinking the match was over, ran on in their hundreds. I was engulfed. My white cap went, Thomson's sweater, the spare ball and I felt a sharp blow on the head which left me dizzy. I could just hear Lillee shouting, 'Come on, we can run 17 off this and win the game.' He was running up and down.

Thomson was less enthusiastic. 'Don't be stupid,' he screamed. 'One of these so-and-so's could have the ball in his pocket.' Police were on the pitch trying to restore order. The fans were asked to go back to their seats because the match wasn't over. Reluctantly, they began to drift away.

Tommy Spencer came over. 'What the bloody hell is going on?' he said. 'How many did they run?' I said I didn't see what had happened to the ball. It had been swallowed up in the crowd though later it was thrown back. We decided to give the batting side four runs because Fredericks' overthrow had been stopped by a spectator.

The game restarted but at 274, with 18 needed off eight balls, Thomson was finally run out and the West Indies won. On came the crowd again like Genghis Khan and his army. I was surrounded by milling West Indians. Keith Boyce was yanked over and as he lay on the ground, fans took off his boots and made off with them as souvenirs. They stripped Thomson of his pads, his bat and his gloves. Police helmets were everywhere.

As we scrambled off, I said to Lillee, 'How many did you run?'

He said, 'Seventeen.'

Not Out (Bird) pp68–9

SPEEDING FINE

A win at Edgbaston, a draw at Lord's, and a Test match abandoned at Headingley because of a vandalised pitch guaranteed that the Ashes would remain in Australia. Hasty departure from Leeds, though, almost got the better of Jeff Thomson, when he drove Greg Chappell and Alan Turner to London in one of the team's British racing green Jaguar XJ12s.

Greg dozed in the front seat until after about half an hour he heard Thommo ask: 'What do you reckon I should do?'

'About what?' asked Greg.

'That blue light flashing in the rear vision mirror,' said Thommo.

How long had it been there?

'Oh about 20 minutes.'

Then he had better slow down and let it catch up. Thomson pulled into the second lane and a police Range Rover pulled them over in pouring rain.

POLICE: Do you know the speed limit on the motorway is 70mph?

THOMMO: Yeah.

POLICE: Do you realise that I've been following you for the past 15 minutes at 120mph and couldn't gain on you?

THOMMO: Yeah that'd be right.

POLICE: Do you realise that when the road's wet if you hit the brakes you're aquaplaning, your wheels aren't actually touching the surface of the road?

THOMMO: Yeah I've done that three times already.

POLICE: Bloody hell! I don't mind if you kill yourself but I've nearly killed myself twice trying to catch you!

After identifying the culprits the police radioed base and relayed their instructions: our jurisdiction runs out five miles down the motorway, be a bit sensible and get going.

Greg Chappell (McGregor) pp121–2

MASTER CLASS

Lillee took 21 wickets in the four Tests and returned from England further enhanced by the acquisition of a leg-cutter that he picked up after play one day from John Snow.

I went up to him and said: 'Can I have half an hour of your time?'

He said: 'Of course' and away we went together.

'I want you to show me how to bowl a leg-cutter,' I told him.

He simply took hold of an old ball and showed me exactly how it was done. I was 25 at the time, but I knew I'd need that ball one day.

My Life in Cricket (Lillee) p147

DROPPING THE TWEEDS

Ian Chappell stood down from the captaincy after the series, electing to continue for a season as a batsman. And, though he led South Australia to a Sheffield Shield, it proved a turbulent year. Chappell later explained to the Adelaide Advertiser's *Keith Butler the circumstances leading to him lowering his trousers to adjust his protective equipment.*

I was accused of dropping the tweeds during a match. I was also accused of pointing my backside towards the committee enclosure at the Adelaide Oval, sort of giving them the arse.

A picture was taken of the incident. It was probably good photography. It happened in the newspaper you work for Keith, and you wrote the story. It was on the front page. It must have been a bloody slow news day for that to be on the front page. Unfortunately the story and the picture went everywhere. But I'll tell you my side of the story.

Everyone goes on about slow over rates and I've always believed the batsman's duty is to be ready for the bowler when he's ready to bowl. There was no greater fiddler at the wicket than myself, but I always tried to go out of my way to be ready for the bowler. There were times when I even ran back to the crease to be ready …

At the stage when I dropped my daks it was the end of an over. One of my thigh pads had an attachment which had come undone and was sticking into my leg. I thought of calling half a dozen guys around while I fixed it. That's the usual thing to do. But I thought if I did it would waste a couple of minutes of time. I actually thought I could fix the attachment by just undoing my pants and leaving them loose while I fixed the straps. In doing so my tweeds slipped down further. Today I always get this 'dropping the tweeds' bit and it gives me the shits.

Howzat! (Butler) pp38–9

Later in the season, after a win over Victoria, Chappell took an Australian state side close to a strike over team selection for the next match against NSW. The boycott was called off after a meeting at Chappell's house on 24 February 1976, but the crowd at the subsequent game could not resist bringing it up again.

As I walked out to the crease after the loss of our first wicket, a wag on the SCG Hill called out: 'I thought it was one out, all out for your mob.' I'm quite fond of the Sydney Hill. At least they have a sense of humour.

Chappelli (Chappell) p132

MANY A SLIP

Greg Chappell was making his way as his brother's successor, compiling a brace of centuries in his first match as captain at the Gabba against Clive Lloyd's West Indians. Chappell later admitted that his career did not begin auspiciously.

The First Test in Brisbane Greg tossed with his 1932 King's Head penny, won, as he did five times out of six that series, and sent the West Indies in.

Greg opened up with five slips, a gully, a bat pad, fine leg, third man and keeper. It took two or three balls before he realised he did not have a cover. 'There were times Ian must have bitten his tongue and thought: "He's got to find out for himself",' said Greg.

Greg Chappell (McGregor) p127

ACCIDENTS IN ADELAIDE

Terry Jenner sustained an unusual injury when WA met SA at the Adelaide Oval for their first Sheffield Shield match of the 1976–77 season: he pulled out of his delivery stride during a spell of 4–73, and wiped from his mouth the deposit just left there by a passing gull.

The players who were rolling on the ground in their mirth as T.J. cleaned up, almost missed a moment of rare humility from their leggie.

'Quite appropriate I suppose,' he said, pointing to his mouth. 'There's been quite a bit of the same coming out over the years,'

The Wit of Cricket (Brayshaw) p30

A month later, Jeff Thomson sustained a far more serious injury during the First Test against Pakistan. Dashing for a caught-and-bowled, he collided with short-leg Alan Turner and dislocated his shoulder. The fast bowler recalled the immediate aftermath.

I didn't feel a lot of pain — until I tried to use the arm to get up! I thought: 'Shit, my arm won't move, you know?' I remember getting up, and seeing Turner still down there, dead as a maggot. I felt like laying the boot into him! I got up and I was cursing. If I could have bowled then I would have bowled the quickest in my life!

I said to the other blokes: 'Hang on a minute. I'll see if I can get my arm over.' But the arm was just torn away. If the collarbone had broken it would have been fairly easy, but the ligaments were all torn away, and the shoulder was just hanging.

We went up to the dressing room, I remember, and the bloke had to cut my shirt off … I said to the physio, 'What can you do with this? I've got to get out there and bowl.'

He looked at it and said, 'We'd better get a doctor!'

Being quite pig-headed I said, 'Don't get a doctor; just get a bloke to put this back in and I'll get on back out there.'

He was a quiet bloke, and I'm sometimes a rowdy bloke, so it was quite a scene. Then this little bloke comes in and says in a soft voice, 'Can I have a look?'

'What d'ya reckon?' I said. And he said he'd probably have to operate on it and put a pin in it and all that.

I said; 'Pig's arse! And anyway, mate,' I said, 'who are you? What would you know about it? I'm waiting for the doctor to come in.'

You guessed it: he was the doctor.

Thommo (Frith) pp75–6

THE ILLITERATI

Left the fast-bowling duties on his own, Lillee bowled at his best. In fifteen first-class matches in 1976–77, he took 93 wickets. Against Pakistan he employed as stimulus the eccentric pronouncements of their manager Shuja-ud-Din, who had branded the Australian players 'illiterate'.

Dennis was sufficiently put out to have a go at Colonel Shuja the next time they met … Shuja walked up and in his most pleasant tone enquired after Dennis's health. There were quite a few people in the room at the time and I reckon that each one was holding his breath. So when Dennis's reply came, it was all the more impressive because of the background of silence. Putting on his most vacant stare, Dennis emitted something that could only be described as a guttural grunt.

Looking somewhat bemused, the Colonel repeated his question. 'How are you Dennis, all right?' At which Dennis repeated his grunt, only louder and deeper than before.

Obviously alarmed at this unexpected reaction, the Colonel hastily stepped back a pace and in a slightly more timid voice ventured to enquire if Dennis wasn't feeling well.

'How the hell should I know?' growled Dennis, putting on his most intimidatory scowl. 'I'm bloody illiterate aren't I?'

Cricketer at the Crossroads (Walker) pp18–19

WORKING FOR THE MAN

Lingering discontent over rates of pay for Test cricketers came to a head that summer, when media proprietor Kerry Packer — in search of the TV rights to cricket for his Channel Nine network — responded favourably to plans for a breakaway cricket spectacular mooted by comedian John Cornell and manager Austin Robertson. Ian Chappell was earmarked to lead the Australians, and remembered his first meeting with his new boss vividly.

Packer was in good humour when Robertson summoned Chappell to CPH for a first meeting late on a Friday evening. Stockinged feet on his desk, Packer studied Chappell's Western-style boots with cheery dubiousness. 'Cowboy, are you?' he said, before offering the former Australian skipper a seat. 'Now, who do you want in this fucking team of yours?' When Chappell pointed out that his brother now led Australia, Packer retorted: 'You think this is a fucking democracy, do you?'

The Cricket War (Haigh) p37

A NICE LITTLE EARNER

When Robertson and Cornell moved among the Australian team on a tour of New Zealand seeking expressions of interest, they asked Lillee whether players could be stimulated by improved financial reward. The former enlisted the fast bowler in an experiment for the Second Test at Eden Park.

'I'll tell you what,' he said, 'I'll pay you $50 for every run you make over 20 when you bat in this innings.' I was due in soon and when I did get out there I worked awfully hard to get 23 not out — and boy, was I upset when Max Walker got out.

When I came off the field Austin told me they had to leave for the airport in forty minutes and they'd pay me $200 for every wicket I took before they left. By the time they'd gone I had four wickets. Not a bad way to earn $950!

My Life in Cricket (Lillee) p91

DOWN FOR THE COUNT

When not counting his cash, Walters was busy amusing himself in New Zealand by counting crowds.

'How many people here today, Doug?'

Kim Hughes at first slip reckoned a thousand.

Walters at second said: 'Well in a matter like this I want to be accurate. Hang on a minute … '

As the bowler began his run, Doug started counting heads: 'One, two, three, four … '

And this went on for two hours! When the counting stopped, Marsh asked the verdict.

'Don't know,' said Doug, 'since I started a few more have come in. One, two, three, four … '

Chappelli Has the Last Laugh (Chappell) p11

100 Years Young

Good fellowship abounded during the Centenary Test at the MCG on 12–17 March, celebrating the first hundred years of Test cricket, even when cross words were exchanged on field. So discovered blond South Australian batsman David Hookes, who brought the crowd to its feet by hitting five consecutive fours from England captain Tony Greig's 13th over just before getting out.

As I was walking off Greig said: 'Piss off.'

I half-stopped and turned round, spat the dummy and said: 'At least I'm an Australian playing this game and not a fucking pommy import.' …

No one was more surprised than me when I saw Tony Greig walking into our room [at close of play], carrying a long-necked bottle of beer and two glasses. 'Mind if I sit with you son?' he said.

'Please do,' I replied.

And he said: 'Well played.'

Hookesy (Hookes) pp30–1

Spotted

When Greg Chappell's 1977 team went to England without the injured Lillee, they found in Thomson's schoolboy friend Len Pascoe a willing and pacy replacement. He was also a master of the malapropism, as Rod Marsh recalled when Australia met Yorkshire, and the quick bowlers were under instructions not to bounce Geoff Boycott.

Thommo, though, has always been a creature of habit and promptly let Boycott have a couple of short ones. Greg was furious and made his feelings quite plain.

'Oh well,' said Lennie, with wisdom beyond his years. 'Ya can't expect a leopard to change its stripes!'

The Gloves of Irony (Marsh) p109

BOYCOTTED

As controversy spread after the announcement of Packer's World Series Cricket, however, it was Boycott who exploited Australia's disintegrating morale. The critical reprieve during the Third Test at Trent Bridge that freed the Yorkshireman to compile 442 runs in three Tests at 147 is recalled here by umpire Dickie Bird.

When he was 20, Boycott got an outside edge to a delivery from Jeff Thomson and the ball went straight in, and straight out of, Rick McCosker's hands at third slip. Thomson was again at my end. He bowled that one from wide of the crease, which he often does, and Boycott had no need to play it. But he was getting impatient. Greg Chappell standing next to McCosker, went down on his knees in frustration. 'Oh no,' he said. By Test match standards, it was a very catchable catch.

At the end of the over Chappell walked past and I said: 'That could cost you the series.'

And he replied: 'You're right.'

Not Out (Bird) p127

LIGHTS OUT

All the Packer signatories suffered the disdain of former colleagues and were approached with caution by friends. Max Walker, for instance, underwent a curious late night meeting with his mate Jim Higgs.

Max Walker's wife Tina answered the door at their Doncaster home in mid-September 1977 to find Victorian leg spinner Jim Higgs cloaked in darkness. The medium pacer cum architect had been expecting Higgs, who wanted to examine some technical drawings for his civil engineering class, and turned on the porch light. 'Oh, right, go for it,' he said. 'Look at whatever you want.'

Higgs was clearly uncomfortable. 'Look mate,' he said. 'Can you turn out the light? I've been told I'm not supposed to be here. The VCA reckons we shouldn't talk to you blokes.'

The Cricket War (Haigh) pp108–111

There was, however, no avoiding the contracts they had signed. When David Hookes took his accountant to Sydney and explained he was under pressure from the Australian Cricket Board to quit his contract, Packer quickly stiffened his sinews.

He said: 'You'd better come with me.'

And we went down to a video room where he had an operator screen all the Channel Nine commercials for WSC. I seemed to be in most of them, either featuring up front or merely in the background, presumably because I was the youngest player and WSC needed young players.

Packer looked at me, looked at the accountant and said: 'If David pulls out, I'll sue the board for inducing breach of contract and David will spend the rest of his life paying me back what I sue him for. You've got two minutes to think about it.'

And he walked out of the room.

The accountant turned to me and said: 'You're going to enjoy playing World Series Cricket.'

Hookesy (Hookes) p45

Hookes would become one of the most successful and conspicuous figures in World Series Cricket. His innings in the Second Supertest at the Sydney Showground in December 1977, retrieving an Australian batting collapse against the West Indies, is remembered clearly for its denouement.

From 5–89, however, the Australians rallied. Roxanne Hookes began watching her husband and, with 7200 spectators, to swing along with his strokes. The marauding Garner dropped short and was poached for 17 runs in an over. Holding, slower on his second breath, went for five intoxicating fours in his first over when recalled. Even Roberts seemed negotiable when Lloyd roused him and, so sweetly was Hookes harmonising with Marsh just after tea, that the Antiguan seemed reluctant to continue. 'I've had enough,' he told Lloyd.

'Just three overs Andy, fast,' the captain asked. His bowler shrugged.

'Did you hear that?' said Hookes to this partner. 'If we can see Andy off, we'll be right. Just concentrate on seeing Andy off.'

As the South Australian recalls with the clarity of a road accident victim, the slow bouncer arrived. 'Andy bowled me a "lolly gobble bliss bomb" first up and I got that away all right,' he says. 'But the next one made a mess of me.'

A couple of feet shorter, several yards faster, it caught the hooking Hookes *in medias res* despite his two hours, 81 runs and 14 fours. His head resounded, his body completing a full circle that ended in a semi-balletic swoon. 'And,' intoned Benaud gravely, 'he's in trouble.'

Murray was first to reach him, Hookes recoiling from his touch as he spat blood. Fielders were magnetised and Marsh charged from the non-striker's end. Only Roberts, chasing the ball from his follow-through, remained locked in his private thoughts.

As manager Rudi Webster bustled from the West Indian rooms, Packer himself was hastening to the Australian dugout. He was waiting among them when the bloodied, bare-headed Hookes was lowered gently on Doc McErlane's treatment table. Roxanne Hookes held her breath.

The newcomer Laird, a Supertestman just three years out of Perth club cricket, was transfixed. 'I'd never seen a broken jaw before,' he says. 'And I can still remember the splinters of bone through the blood on the floor of the dressing-room when Hookesy was brought in. They were like little bits of glass.'

Packer was the twenty-two-year-old's ambulance driver, his Jaguar ignoring traffic lights, for the one-mile journey to St Vincent's private hospital. A double fracture of the jaw and cheekbone was diagnosed, a five-week fracture in Hookes' season prescribed.

The Cricket War (Haigh) pp129–30

NIGHT MOVES

Crowds were poor during the first season of World Series Cricket, the only exceptions being night matches Packer inaugurated at VFL Park. One game ended unforgettably at 11.48pm on 24 January 1978 with West Indian No. 11 Wayne Daniel hitting a six from the last ball off Mick Malone to defeat the Australians by one wicket.

As the crowd bubbled, umpire Duperouzel hared to the sightscreen to repel children already storming the playing arena, then reprieved Malone from a palpable leg-side wide to Garner. Garner's swipe to Greg Chappell at long on finally pitted Malone against Daniel for the penultimate delivery. Cameras swivelled round the ground like prison-yard searchlights, capturing Ian Chappell's urgent dialogue with Malone, a mid-pitch conference of terrified tuition, and a West Indian dressing-room full of curiously camera-shy Australian women.

'I'd probably bowled at Daniel before,' Malone recalls. 'But I just thought: "I'll pitch it up and see what happens". It was a bad ball, it was too short, it was too wide, I gave him too much room.' Seeing the ball veer to leg, Daniel's eyes shut with the effort of connection. So did Malone's. The invading crowd lost sight as the ball vanished over mid wicket. Only Ian Chappell was silent. 'Ian didn't say a word and he didn't need to,' says Malone. 'I didn't need a "bad luck Mick", because I knew it had been a bad ball. And I didn't need "You're a bastard" either. Ian's silence was deafening. But I think I did play the next game somewhere like Toowoomba!'

The Cricket War (Haigh) p154

NEW KIDS ON THE BLOCKHOLE

Test cricket, meantime, was continuing. Bob Simpson had returned from retirement to lead Australia in a five-Test series against India that introduced to the big time a bevy of youthful new faces ... and, as writer John Lapsley discovered when he visited the side during the Third Test at the MCG, their nicknames.

Dice (Dyson) is taking guard and the Jaffa (the redhead Cosier) is at the other end.

'I see Dice got the first strike. They both like to. Must be taking turns,' says Simpson. 'Bill Lawry and I used to take turns. We'd even remember at the beginning of the new season whose turn it was.'

The rest of the batting order reads: Rags, Bilko, Simmo, Rats, Rocket, Stumper, Dunny, Two-Up and Sammy-Rat. Clag is drink waiter. Not quite the way it is on the scoreboard. Ogilvie, Serjeant, Simpson, Toohey, Mann, Wayne Clark (WC of course equals dunny), Thomson, Gannon plus Hughes ...

'How old are you now?' Steve Rixon asks Jeff Thomson in a quiet moment.

'Twenty-seven,' replies the third-oldest member of the side.

'Yeah? That old?' says Rixon in vague disbelief.

Australian, 7 January 1978

LOSING THE WAR

World Series Cricket gained access to the Sydney Cricket Ground for the summer of 1978–79, and the move was at once vindicated by the crowd of more than 50 000 at its first day–night encounter on Tuesday, 28 November 1978. As Packer's push then went from strength to strength, the official Australian side led by Graham Yallop lost its Ashes series 5–1. A new hero was paceman Rodney Hogg — who took 41 wickets in the series — but the dwindling attraction of traditional Tests was shown by poor attendances in Sydney.

In the course of the over a voice boomed out from the Hill, demanding 'Put on the other channel!'

With its obvious reference to World Series Cricket, this was a not too subtle complaint about the slow scoring, and one with which most of the spectators would have been in sympathy.

From the Outer (Meyer) p80

AEROGARD AND SPAGHETTI

When Hogg was largely neutralised by pitches inimical to his pace when Australia toured India in September 1979, colleagues Yallop and Davenall Whatmore looked on in bemusement at some of his cricketing habits.

Yallop: When Hoggie first arrived he brought with him a supply of food he called his 'Test match rations'. They included cans of spaghetti and baked beans. The first day we arrived he was into his Test match rations, well before any of the Tests started. He took some stick from the boys over that.

Whatmore: At the Second Test in Bangalore we were all given cans of Aerogard supplied by the masseur Frank Hennessy. At the pub we were staying at all the rooms had mosquito nets. Of course, Hoggy had to spray all of the net, his bed and everything. He finished his can of Aerogard within a week. They were meant to last a bit longer than that. So we gave him lots of advice about what he could do with his Aerogard and spaghetti.

Cricketer, October 1980 p26

THE TIN BAT

The first season of rapprochement between Packer and the board resulted in a tricornered Test and one-day competition between Australia, England and the West Indies that bristled with controversies. The most infamous was Dennis Lillee's use of an aluminium bat during the First Test against England at the WACA, which Greg Chappell anticipated when he saw the instrument at practice the day before the match.

Greg picked it up for a trial. 'It was a real tinny thing, hollow, just didn't go,' said Greg. 'It went BOINGG, BOINGG, jarred and you just couldn't hit the ball off the square with it.' Greg had a mild shot at Lillee. He wasn't going to use that, was he?

Lillee whipped around: 'What do you mean?'

Greg's evil mind chimed: here was a way to get the boy stirred up.

In retrospect Greg believed that had he told Lillee that in the interests of the team he should use his normal bat, Lillee may, or may not have used his favourite Duncan Fearnley. Greg did not know that bat was cracked. Greg did know that Lillee at number nine would be bowling soon.

He intended to let Lillee bat for an over, take the bat off him, and fire Lillee to fury when bowling. Events went awry. Rodney Hogg took the cracked bat out to Lillee who rejected it. Lillee came in for a new one and Greg sat like a sphinx knowing that one blink from him would set Lillee off.

Rodney Marsh saved him the trouble. 'It's not like you to let people tell you what bat you can use,' he said deadpan.

Lillee stopped. Marsh was bloody right. Out he went with the metal bat again. 'Thanks for your help Bacchus,' said Greg, exasperated.

He looked round for Rodney Hogg to take another bat out, but Hogg would not have a bar of it. He told Greg later: 'I could see myself, on national television, before a packed ground, and Dennis hitting me between the eyes with his aluminium bat.'

Greg then had the tiger by the tail himself. Fortunately Brearley had involved himself at the crease. When Greg arrived with the new bat Lillee heave-hoed the aluminium so, to Greg's relief, the Poms became the cause of it all.

Greg Chappell (McGregor) pp179–80

NEW AGE UMPIRING

The umpire without a sense of humour in the relentless summer was doomed. And Dick French could still hear the lighter side of an exchange with Len Pascoe in a 1979–80 World Series Cup match between Australia and England.

Boycott was facing up to Pascoe — there's a good pair — and Boycott was nought. Pascoe put one down the leg side and Boycott tried to turn him. It hit the pad and it deflected through to Marshy.

Well, they all went up for the caught behind. Marshy threw the ball into the air. Pascoe jumped the stumps and set off to embrace him. And I'm the umpire. I was convinced Boycott hadn't hit it. I thought: 'This is going to be fun. Anyway here goes.' And I said 'Not out'.

Lennie stopped in his tracks. He looked at me. He glared at Boycott. Then he called out to Marshy: 'Hey Bacchus, before you chuck the ball back, will you take that splinter out of it?'

Extra Cover (Egan) p113

Umpire Robin Bailhache remembered also a candid admission from Dennis Lillee during a hard day bowling to the West Indies in the First Test at the Gabba.

It was hot, frustrating toil for a bowler of Lillee's type, recalls Bailhache, and after a while the champion became a little worn and dejected. At the end of one over a dejected Lillee stood halfway down the pitch and Bailhache moved to save him the walk back to get his hat.

As he handed it over a rather haggard-looking Lillee said: 'Jeez it's hard being a fast-bowler and I ought to know ... I used to be one!'

The Wit of Cricket (Brayshaw) p50

CRYING IN THE CHAPPELL

Ian Chappell played his last first-class cricket in 1979–80, disappearing with little fanfare but with an unequalled reputation as a taskmaster. South Australian apprentice seamer Ross McLellan had this rueful reminiscence of his first match for South Australia against the Englishmen in November 1979.

I had a really good game. I played under the captaincy of Ian Chappell, failed to take a wicket and dropped Geoff Boycott. That was like dropping Jesus while playing under God.

Cricketer, February 1981 p15

When Australia toured Pakistan at summer's end, its pebbly pitches confounded many of the visitors. Lillee went for weeks without a wicket and Hookes weeks without a run.

He [Lillee] wrote to his wife Helen in Perth and said: 'I finally got a wicket today — my first in Pakistan. But it was only in the nets and it was only Hookesy.'

Hookesy (Hookes) p68

UNDERHANDED?

Repercussions from the conclusion of the second World Series Cup Final in January 1981 at the MCG between Australia and Geoff Howarth's New Zealanders were endless. This is author Adrian McGregor's account of the infamous 'underarm' that Trevor Chappell bowled to deny the visitors' last man Brian McKechnie a chance of tying the match.

Greg reached Trevor who was spinning the ball from hand to hand grimacing. Trevor had just spoken to Rod Marsh who advised him: 'Try to bowl exactly what you've been bowling.' The previous ball that had dismissed Smith hit the stumps only 30cms from the ground. It seemed excellent advice. But Greg could go one better.

'What are you like at bowling your underarms?' Greg asked Trevor.

'Oh I don't know, why?'

'Well you're about to find out.'

Trevor looked surprised, then impressed. He thought: 'That sounds like a pretty good idea. That'll make it pretty hard to hit a six.' Greg turned to umpire Don Weser and told him to instruct the batsman the delivery would be underarm. Weser rolled his eyes in amazement. McKechnie looked up to take block and saw Weser heading for square leg umpire Peter Cronin. He thought they were checking it was definitely the last ball.

Greg and Trevor, both in Australia's colours of wattle with green panels, stood together for about 10 seconds, Greg in a white washing hat, Trevor bareheaded, if his wild curly mop could ever be called that. Greg set his field and demonstrated to Trevor the delivery, swinging his right arm slightly back as though to bowl underarm. Then he headed back to deep mid-on.

Umpire Weser told McKechnie leaning on his bat of the proposed underarm. McKechnie replied, 'You've got to be joking' and dropped his bat in astonishment.

Watching television in Adelaide Martin Chappell turned to Jeanne and predicted the underarm. Sam Trimble in Brisbane actually said aloud to himself minutes before: 'Bowl an underarm.' Old captains think ahead forever. The Channel Nine commentary hiatus was finally broken. Bill Lawry: 'It looks to me like they're going to bowl an underarm off the last ball ... this is possibly a little disappointing ... let's make sure ... would you ever have believed it?'

Greg watched Trevor wave Rodney Marsh back from the stumps. Marsh shook his head and mouthed back: 'No mate don't do it.' Trevor shrugged his shoulders and nodded towards Greg.

Greg Chappell (McGregor) pp199–200

1981 BLUES

Greg Chappell's decision demonstrated his fatigue at the end of an arduous summer, and he declined the 1981 Ashes tour. West Australian Kim Hughes led an inexperienced but game squad that looked during the Third Test at Leeds to be on the brink of a 2–0 lead. Having made 9–401 on a pitch sure to deteriorate, Australia bowled England out for 174. The tactical decision about whether to send England in again was not, however, cut and dried, because neither was the pitch. Australian coach Peter Philpott was actually sitting in the BBC Test Match Special box when Hughes needed to make his decision.

Eventually Trevor Bailey put the question to me: 'Peter will you enforce the follow-on?'

I paused and felt sorry for Kim Hughes whose final decision this would be and who would live with the responsibility. My reply was something like this: 'Trevor, the English batting is so shattered with confidence so low that I don't think Australia can ignore the psychological advantage of enforcing the follow-on. But I wouldn't like to be batting last on that wicket with more than 100 to 120 to get.'

A Spinner's Yarn (Philpott) p178

Long Odds

Not that it seemed to matter when England slid to 7–135 in their second innings and odds of 500–1 were quoted by Ladbroke's against an English victory. But it is a funny game.

I went round the others, asking if any of them wanted to have a bit, but there were no takers. I got to Marshy and said: 'Look, you're silly if you don't … put ten on.' He said he wouldn't, so I suggested five, 'just to be with me'. However I just couldn't talk him into it because he was convinced, like the others, that there was no way England could win.

So I decided to go it alone and asked our bus driver Peter to go and put the ten on for me. As we were walking down the stairs out on to the field Marshy saw Peter going round to the betting tent and yelled out: 'Pete!' When Peter turned round Marshy showed him five fingers, indicating a five-pound bet.

My Life in Cricket (Lillee) p169

Ian Botham played a brilliant innings of 149 not out and, set 130 to win, Australia was then rounded up for 111 by Bob Willis. Not since 1894–95 had a team been beaten after enforcing the follow-on (John Blackham's Australians against Andrew Stoddart's Englishmen at the SCG).

England had, amid national rejoicing, committed what *The Cricketer* called 'daylight robbery'. At 2.20, Australia had required 169 minutes for an innings which should have won them the game, although a bewildered Hughes thought his side 'didn't do much wrong except lose'.

Test Eleven (Whimpress) p231

Hughes Views

Australia lost the Fourth Test at Edgbaston from a similarly unassailable position, and England's gnomic captain Mike Brearley felt a sympathy for Hughes when the Australian wondered how his team would be received at home.

Kim kept saying, 'I suppose me mum'll speak to me.' Pause. 'Reckon me dad. And me wife.' Pause. 'But who else?'

Phoenix from the Ashes (Brearley) p108

Two Debuts

A few Australians did enjoy the 1981 series. Michael Whitney, a left-arm paceman from NSW, was called up while playing minor cricket for Fleetwood as a reserve for the injured Lawson and Hogg in the Fifth Test at Old Trafford. Whitney described how the call-up was communicated to him while he was involved in a midweek game as a guest of Gloucestershire against Hampshire.

Fred Bennett [the manager] had just rung. I was to get off the field and speak to him. I was to report to Old Trafford immediately.

I was elated to have been considered but when Geoff Lawson had broken down, Hoggy the same, Carl Rackemann also injured, Thommo had gone home and Len Pascoe was recovering from a knee injury I really was the only one available.

I made the trip up to Old Trafford and was met by Fred Bennett. Upon arriving at the dressing-room we were joined by Kim Hughes. He congratulated me and told me what he wanted me to do tomorrow — bowl line and length.

I said: 'What do you mean?'

He said: 'Haven't they told you? You're playing in the Test tomorrow!'

I couldn't believe it, having played just seven first-class games and a few John Player League games. It didn't hit me until the third day of the Test. Another thing that was amazing was that Ray Bright had moved out of his room so I was going to room with Dennis Lillee.

They gave me my cap and jumper and we left for the ground. It was a great thrill to walk onto the ground in the company of Marsh, Lillee and company.

After Lillee and Alderman had bowled about 15 overs, Kim Hughes said this was it. I did all the stretches and limbering up for the cameras. Waved to my mum in Australia. Kim said: 'Bowl line and length and don't be nervous.'

I really hadn't time to be nervous. I bowled my first ball and Chris Tavare played it out to square leg, and down came the rain! All that exercising for one ball! Peter Philpott came over and said: 'That was a great ball.'

Speech to the Australian Cricket Society reprinted in
Wisden Cricket Monthly, January 1982 pp8–9

Despite the carnage wrought by Ian Botham, Whitney took four wickets. The other Australian to derive something from England 1981 was NSW batsman Dirk Wellham, who acquired a century in his first outing when capped for the Sixth Test at the Oval and remembered ever afterward Botham's chivalrous attitude.

After I had been on 99 for 15 minutes, the drinks break came and brought some relief from the seemingly endless tension. I drank, chatted about nothing and returned to pick up my bat and began to pull on my gloves.

As I composed myself to continue, a voice from nearby said: 'You've done all the hard work, don't throw it all away now.'

Disbelieving I looked up as Ian Botham walked past. Botham, the nemesis of Australia's batsmen and the man who had been trying harder than anyone to dismiss me in my first Test for 99!

... Ten minutes after the resumption, my instincts took over and I punched a shortish delivery through to the cover boundary. It was hard to believe that I had scored a century in my first Test. It was 'Boy's Own' stuff and I didn't know what to do or where to look. The first man to shake my hand was Botham, saying simply: 'Well played.'

To return the compliment, in his next over I played back to a good-length ball and was lbw (Botham) for 103. There was definitely no pain involved, though.

Solid Knocks and Second Thoughts (Wellham) pp41–2

TROUBLES IN TRANSLATION

When Javed Miandad brought a Pakistan team here in 1981–82, one laborious business was obtaining a consensus among writers of what to call one of its members. Phil Wilkins described this bon mot by the West Australian's Ken Casellas.

Then we came to the delicate business of the name of young all-rounder Ejaz Faqih. So conscious to the danger involved was team management that when the side was released to play WA the full names were all written out except one, and he was written Ejaz F. On the official team sheet he was down as Ejaz K.

'How is it?' enquired the doyen of the Perth press box. 'That when I write f you see k?'

Cricketer, December 1981 p12

Look Back In Anger

There followed in the First Test at the WACA the more sinister phenomenon of the so-called Lillee–Miandad incident, where umpire Tony Crafter had to interpose himself between two cricketers apparently on the point of coming to blows. This is Lillee's account.

I was bowling from the Northern End when Miandad played one away through the on-side and took off for a single. He could see there was going to be an easy one in it and had slowed to a walk about two-thirds of the way down the wicket. I had stopped in my follow-through and also had noticed there wasn't going to be much of a continuation of the action and so turned to go back to my mark. I had just made the turn when I felt a sharp blow in my side, ribcage area. I recoiled and realised that it had been Miandad striking me with what I presumed had been his bat.

He then continued on down to the crease at the bowler's end. I followed him down the wicket and just by the stumps tapped him on the pad with my boot as if to say: 'What do you think you're doing? You can't get away with that.' It was not, as described in the media, a vicious kick, it was no more than a tap with my boot.

That doesn't mean I should have done what I did. I should not have retaliated in any way. The incident was unfortunate and I'm certainly not proud to have been part of it. However, I am upset that the fellow who actually caused the whole thing has escaped untarnished and unpunished.

My Life in Cricket (Lillee) p181

Home Comforts

Australia then visited Pakistan in September 1982 and suffered a 3–0 towelling that made players think fond thoughts of home comforts.

The only legal place you could buy an alcoholic drink in the country was in the permit room of the large international hotels. To complete the simple transaction of having a beer required the possession of a 'permit'. This was a document roughly the size of a credit card and we were issued with these by the Australian Embassy. On each it noted that the bearer was a certified alcoholic. Rod Marsh thought that fair enough — but it seemed pretty funny to me, considering I didn't drink at all. Notwithstanding I was still certified.

Rod got sick of drinking spirits and local beer so he enquired at the Embassy how they got their supplies and what's more could they send some to the team. Two days later a large styrofoam esky arrived in our hotel marked: 'Vaccinations. Keep refrigerated. Handle with care.' Team manager Freddy Bennett was a bit confused by this as he knew nothing of any further injections the team might need. On opening the box it was discovered that the whole team could swallow these vaccines — five dozen ice-cold cans of Swan Lager!

Henry (Lawson) p46–7

LAST MEN STANDING

Australian hopes in the Fourth Test of the 1982–83 Ashes series at the MCG ended up hingeing on a last-wicket alliance of tailender Jeff Thomson and Allan Border, whose form to that stage had been wretched. But the former stuck round and Border's form steadily returned when England's skipper Bob Willis decided to concede him singles.

Counselling his colleague through the day's last 45 minutes, Border began relishing England's misdirection: 'When the partnership had started the Poms had been full of the joy of living. By stumps they were showing a little strain.' ...

The sight of 10 000 queuing for a day that could end in a ball cheered Border and Thomson next morning — 44 and 8 respectively — as they performed ritual nets.

Willis' plan remained to defend against Border but, as the scoreboard flashed the run requirement at thirty-second intervals and a second new ball was survived, confused fielders began colliding.

With the crowd 20 000 just after noon and the target reduced to a single stroke, Willis bowled his fiercest and most frugal over with Border on 60. The left-hander glanced a couple to deep fine leg but could not appropriate the strike for Botham's 26th over. Mid-pitch conferences at 12.20pm confirmed the air of imminent decision and Thomson took fresh guard pondering the possibility of a boundary.

Border recalled the next few seconds and the uncanny collaboration of Botham and slipsmen Tavare and Miller with clarity. 'When he [Thomson] hit it, my initial reaction was that it was going over the top and for four. Then I thought: "It's in Tavare's hands and we're gone". And when it bounced out of his hands I thought: 'Beauty we're back in it'. Then all of a sudden, Miller was there.' England had won by three runs.

Border recalled Marsh's dressing room prowl — peering beneath kits, behind doors and in lockers — and its explanation: 'I'm looking for four runs.' The atmosphere next door was no better. Wrote Allan Lamb: 'I know callers expected to witness scenes of absolute mayhem with England cricketers dancing with delight knocking back champagne as if Australia was going to run out of the stuff at any moment. Instead, even half an hour after the match had finished they found the room like a morgue ... Most of us just sat around staring into space hardly saying a word. Now and again one would make a move toward the shower and get changed.'

The Border Years (Haigh) pp54–6

AN EARLY NIGHT

Victorian Dean Jones was selected to make his first Australian tour with Kim Hughes' team visiting the West Indies in February 1984, and was quickly reminded of his junior status as the First Test approached.

Three days before the Test I was rooming with Geoff Lawson who had sinus trouble or something. It was 8pm and we were watching TV when, stuff me, he gets up and switches off the set. Not a word. When I asked him what was going on he said: 'I've got a Test match to play in a couple of days so I'm going to have some sleep.'

I'll always go along with professionalism but it was 14 hours before we had to turn up for training. But that was it; kicked out. I had to go and find another room.

Deano — My Call (Jones) p38

'HE'S PASSED AWAY'

Hughes found the various humours of Rodney Hogg problematical, notably when he found 12th man Carl Rackemann fielding in a tour match apparently substituting for the South Australian.

'Hoggy's gone off,' said Rackemann.

'What do you mean gone off?' asked Hughes. 'He didn't tell me. Go and find out where he is.'

Big Carl returned to the field soon after, smiling, and said: 'He told me to tell you, captain, that he's passed away.'

This wasn't good enough for Kim naturally and he sent Carl off again to retrieve Hogg. When Rackemann returned Hughes again asked after Hogg's whereabouts and Rackemann said: 'He told me to tell you he's gone for a drive.'

This was understandably too much for Hughes who promptly found his errant fast bowler in the dressing room and ordered him back on the field quickly.

Hookesy (Hookes) p116

GREG'S GIFT

It was West Indian pacemen who posed most Australians problems, however, and Allan Border kept a lonely watch for Australian batsmanship on that tour. Someone at Castries picked up a useful souvenir while Border, leading the team against Windward Islands, was watching the game with the local Prime Minister.

As Greg [Ritchie] was walking off with the army of kids, he magnanimously presented his bat to one of them. The Prime Minister was amazed. What a superb gesture, he said, typical of Greg's lovely personality and character.

I was pretty surprised, too; Fat Cat had just given away my bloody bat! It's the last time I'll lend him something as valuable as that.

Allan Border (Border) p124

HEIR CUT

The West Indies began to make similarly short work of Australia when they visited that country six months later. Defeat at the WACA in the First Test saw several Australians backpedalling, and Rod Hogg felt the humiliation.

Hoggy rang his wife and said: 'Are you videoing the cricket like I told you to?'

'Yes.'

'Did you just video my dismissal?'

'Er ... Yes.'

'Well erase the tape, I don't want my son growing up thinking his father's a coward.'

Allan Border, Inside Edge, April 1995 p10

Making The Grade

Although the Australians were comfortably defeated, the series introduced two players who would become fixtures in future XIs. The first was Tasmanian David Boon, who made a flinty 51 when capped in the Second Test at the Gabba.

I had made a few runs but after a while Marshall, who was bowling fairly 'sharpish', trotted those extra few steps down from his follow-through and said: 'Boonie, I know this is your first Test match, but are you going to do the right thing and get out? Or do I have to come round the wicket and kill you?'

Being a shy young man at the time, I didn't say a word back — in fact I'm not sure if I even looked at him …

I was still in when Hogg came to the wicket. 'Babs,' he said, 'this is the perfect opportunity for you to start your career with a good average by a not out because I don't think I'm going to hang around too long!' But Hoggie did hang around and batted extremely well for a tail-order paceman.

It was during an over which Marshall bowled menacingly around the wicket that I hit the ball perfectly, hooking to the boundary. Hogg came storming down the wicket towards me in what I thought was experienced player–young player congratulation mode. However, instead of a pat on the back I was expecting, Hoggie shrieked: 'What are you trying to do — get us all killed?'

In the Firing Line (Boon) pp78–9

The other novitiate was Queensland's teenage fast bowler Craig McDermott, who was called up for the Fourth Test at the MCG and took five good wickets. The first, though, was not one for the scrapbooks.

I did not deserve the first one. I bowled a throat-high beamer to Richie Richardson, who fended at it and deflected the ball down onto his stumps. It was an accident — the ball slipped from my fingers — but Richardson did not look too pleased, either. The first thought that came into my head was: 'What a lousy way to take your first Test wicket!' Graeme Wood ran in from covers to congratulate me. 'Don't worry about it,' he said. 'Another seven of those and we'll have 'em all out.'

McDermott: Strike Bowler (McDermott) p59

Remember Your Roots!

The backdrop to what was Allan Border's first series as captain was clandestine work by agents of South African cricket, who were working to inveigle a team of Australians to visit the veldt as a 'rebel XI'. Rising star Dean Jones, then on the periphery of the Test team, was dissuaded by his father Barney's peroration.

I told Dad I was definitely going and the manure hit the fan. We had a blue that lasted for days. He would drag me into his study and roast me, belittle me, do everything he could think of just to change my mind. 'If you go over there you'll never play for Australia again,' he roared. 'You'll never play for your state again. And do you realise they'll probably stop you playing for Carlton!' I don't think anybody else in the world would have brought up Carlton in that particular debate but Dad had to whack it in.

Deano — My Call (Jones) p47

SHEFFIELD STEEL

Having won the Sheffield Shield in 1971–72, Western Australia became the dominant state for most of the decade and into the early 80s. Opponents needed all means at their disposal when the home team batted at the WACA, as player Ian Brayshaw recalls of a high-scoring encounter with Queensland in 1979–80.

The Queensland bowlers were just about on their knees by afternoon tea but thought during the break that Tony Mann simply must declare the WA innings closed at that juncture. However as the interval wore on it became obvious to the weary Queenslanders that there was to be no respite.

Their captain, burly Gary Cosier, decided it was time to make a point to his opposite number. As he led his team out for another session in the field he stopped at the door of the WA dressing room, poked his head and called to Mann. 'Hey Tony, do you think we could borrow the WACA's bowling machine?'

The Wit of Cricket (Brayshaw) p102

South Australia became a force again when David Hookes succeeded John Inverarity as captain in June 1981. Harnessing a world-class opening attack in West Indian Joel Garner and Rodney Hogg to win the Shield in 1982–83, he dealt with the latter's mercurial streak and strange reluctance to bowl bouncers.

From our gully and slip position Garner and I tried to encourage Hogg to bowl bouncers at Yallop. Finally he did bowl one, though it was undoubtedly one of the worst he ever let go.

Undeterred Garner and I both tried to ensure some more by saying: 'Well bowled Hoggy.'

Hogg stopped, glared at me and said: 'You know it was shit.' And he glared at Garner and said: 'You know it was shit.' And he glared at Yallop and said: 'And he knows it was shit. So just let me get back and bowl.'

Hookesy (Hookes) p95

NSW then rose again for the first time since the early 1960s, drawing on a group of young players regimented by Rick McCosker and Geoff Lawson that included the idiosyncratic off-spinner Greg Matthews.

Walking in Dennis Lillee's shoes is never easy. But NSW and new Test all-rounder Greg Matthews has done it already and with success. Noticing that Matthews was having foot trouble during the NSW–WA Shield Match, Lillee offered the youngster his cricket shoes. They proved a perfect fit and Matthews scored 86 and took 3–41 against Pakistan in the tour game at the SCG.

Cricketer, February 1984 p22

FLIPPER

Injuries are not normally contagious, but one that befell South Australia's batsman-wicketkeeper Wayne Phillips also floored his wife and doctor.

Sturt and State batsman Wayne Phillips — and his wife Janine — were the centre of events in a recent district game against Glenelg. Phillips attempted to hook a ball from Brian Vincent which bounced off his bat, onto his nose and rebounded back to Vincent: he was out caught and bowled for 31.

Phillips was assisted to the dressing room and lay on the bench receiving ice treatment on his bloodied nose when his wife came in, took one look, and promptly fainted. She knocked her head in the fall and received a cut lip and forehead.

The couple received attention during the tea interval by another Sturt batsman, Pat Flynn, a doctor, who must have been upset by the whole affair, being dismissed for a duck shortly after.

Neil Blundell, Cricketer, February 1982 p31

'Flipper' Phillips was actually one of the most gifted natural players of his era, and one of the most mischievous. Allan Border retold the story of how, at

Derby on the 1985 Ashes tour, Phillips bet against the possibility of his captain scoring a fourth consecutive century.

Lovely, I thought, a mate betting against his skipper. And my everyday resolve to make as many runs as possible was immediately strengthened. He would suffer, I decided, for his lack of faith in his beloved captain. He would pay for it — literally. Or, if he didn't, he would sit there and squirm as his skipper made runs. Perhaps not a century, but runs nonetheless.

I was 20 not out at lunch and Flipper was still jumping up and down saying I wouldn't make it. I reminded him that I was one-fifth of the way to 100 and I'd never felt more in the mood for a ton. 'Ha,' he said, which sounded encouragingly like a man with butterflies in his stomach.

Wayne rather than the Derbyshire attack was foremost in my mind as I batted my way into the 90s. On 99 I glanced towards our dressing room and there was Flipper at the door waving a white handkerchief! I took the necessary single to complete the hundred and hit one straight in the air for a lollypop catch the next over.

I strode very quickly from the field because I wanted badly to see the expression on Flipper's face. It was sheer dejection. And it made everything worthwhile.

Allan Border (Border) pp152–3

When Geoff Lawson was convalescing from an immobilising back injury in 1986, Phillips jollied him along by correspondence.

I had been in touch with some of the guys, particularly Wayne Phillips, who wrote me a letter sloped at a 45 degree angle so I could read it easily while lying on the floor. That's the type of man 'Flipper' was ... very considerate, very funny, always looking for an angle.

Henry (Lawson) p102

A high-scoring batsman for his state, Phillips thrice passed the double-century at the Adelaide Oval. When he made 213 not out against Tasmania in 1986–87, David Hookes was his partner.

When he reached 200 in 1986–87 he wandered along the pitch and said to me: 'I'm only 34 short.' I looked at the scoreboard and said I didn't understand what he meant.

'I'm only 34 short of Bradman,' he said.

I replied: 'No, Bradman scored 369 against Tassie' (in Adelaide in 1935–36).

But Flipper had the last word: 'No, I'm 34 double hundreds short of Bradman. I've got three now. He got 37.'

Hookesy (Hookes) p189

Staying Alive in '85

Tourist Dirk Wellham was sitting with Ian Botham as England piled on the runs during the Fourth Test at Edgbaston in 1985, listening to the big all-rounder's confident expectations of how he would manhandle the attack.

Having had enough of Botham's skylarking and gibes I said as he was going to the wicket, 'I bet you can't break this window.' I nodded toward the large pane of glass we had been sitting behind all day.

Botham, full of confidence and ability, grabbed his gloves and grinned. He strode to the wicket with the crowd anticipating another onslaught in the bright sunlight. After a few warm up swipes with his 'Botham Autograph Magnum Attack' tree trunk of a bat, he took guard and settled down as McDermott charged in from his very long run.

The unprepared little red cricket ball on its very fast encounter with the big man, was sent soaring over the deflated McDermott, high into the skies. It came crashing down through a thin plastic roofing sheet and struck the window that I was nestling behind. The crowd roared its approval; Botham grinned; McDermott struggled back to his mark; and I tried to find a hole to hide in!

Solid Knocks and Second Thoughts (Wellham) p44

The Jones Boy

Dean Jones was overlooked for that 1985 tour and, when selected to tour India in September 1986, saw it as a final opportunity to prove his credentials at Test level. Craig McDermott noticed this proclivity of the Victorian.

When he is feeling fairly confident, he will have a handkerchief hanging over the top of his trousers on the left-hand side. If he is feeling even more confident, he will have part of one of the sashes that he uses to tie up his thigh pad hanging over the top of his trousers, too. Then if he also drags his bat behind him when he walks to the wicket, you can be sure he is ready to take on the world.

McDermott: Strike Bowler (McDermott) p26

All must have been in evidence when Jones joined battle in enervating heat during the First Test at Madras, and batted most of the day with extraordinary concentration to be not out 56 at the close.

I hardly slept a wink, tossing and turning and playing the innings in my mind. By 3am I was up and staring out the window at the lights of Madras wondering just what was going to happen today. If only I'd known.

I couldn't eat or drink anything at breakfast, I was just too bloody nervous. I remember wishing the innings could just have kept going without the overnight fears and tensions, but I suppose that's the way cricket is: the better you do the harder the game becomes. It was already hot by the time we set off for the ground and a lot hotter when the nightwatchman Ray Bright and I walked into bat. The humidity was even higher than the previous day and the stench from the Buckingham Canal hung on the brickworks of the stadium. It was going to be hard work. Bright did a great job, hanging in there for another 80 minutes or so despite suffering some sort of respiratory problem; breathing out there is difficult enough when your body wants to do it. He made 30 before getting out — and then collapsed in the dressing room so distraught he was actually in tears …

AB came in and was dropped on nought. He told me later the previous time he'd played in Madras he was dropped before he'd scored and he went on to make a century so the signs were obviously good for him. Not bad for me either, at least not yet. I remember pulling Ravi Shastri into the crowd for six then driving him for four through mid-on to record my first Test century and can't really describe what a thrill it was. AB was out there to shake my hand which is just how I wanted it to be.

We were doing it tough and my body was already sending out a couple of warning signs when I vomited and felt the first twinges of cramp. But the runs masked the pain all the time; I can remember thinking that I wished the old man had been there to see it, and Keith Stackpole and a close friend like Doug Patrick. That memory is still more vivid than most; funny how your mind switches in and out.

Errol Alcott tried to get some fluids into me during lunch and Simmo backed up with advice: pace yourself a bit more, don't back up as hard or run as fast between wickets, just wait for the bad ball and punish it. I felt very drained and I don't think I've ever been as glad just to get the weight off my feet, but I don't remember feeling deeply distressed at that stage. The disorientation set in after I'd scored 150 in 425 minutes (I've looked it up) and I must have been in some sort of trance; I really don't remember things in sequence. Incidents come back with reasonable clarity but then someone tells me I said such and such and I can't remember a word of it.

Deano — My Call (Jones) pp71–2

THE CAPTAIN COMBUSTS

Jones made 210 and, in a palpitating finish, the Test was tied. The tour was the first on which Allan Border, with the aid of new coach Bob Simpson, led the Australians with authority. Paceman Dave Gilbert recalled from a one-day international at Ahmedabad just how intense Border became in the heat of the moment.

Kris Srikkanth was batting and things were getting a bit tight when I came on in the 20th over or so. Srikkanth dabbed a ball to cover and took off. AB swooped, turned and threw at my end. I tried to reposition myself for the throw but it struck me in the middle of the back at top pace. You won't believe this but the same thing happened next ball ... the same shot, the same throw and then 'whack' in the back.

I was in agony and AB burst out with 'For God's sake Lizard, get out of the ^&*@$ way.'

Some players might have sympathised with the bowler but AB was just so focussed on what he was doing ... as always.

David Gilbert, *Inside Edge*, June 1994 p47

PETER WHO?

One of cricket's most celebrated cases of mistaken identity occurred at the end of the 1986–87 Ashes series. The unfortunate victim of the confusion over the composition of Australia's side for the Fifth Test of the Ashes series, Mark Taylor, recounted the tale.

The day before the announcement I was up in Newcastle playing against Tasmania and I'd had a good first year for NSW and was having a reasonable second year so there was a bit of chat about me being picked. Someone from Channel Nine came up to me and said: 'Look if you get into the Australian team tomorrow morning would you mind coming up for an interview on the Today show?'

I said that would be all right and the game finished that day so we were back in Sydney the next morning and I get a phone call at 5 past 6 saying: 'This is the Today show. You're in the Test team. Can you come in?'

And I thought: 'Fantastic.' So I raced to the shower and I'm thinking about all the things I should say on TV, but I got another phone call about 15 minutes later and they said: 'Oh Mark, is there a P. Taylor who plays for NSW?'

I said: 'Oh yes, there's Peter our off-spinner.'

And they said: 'Has he played his year?'

And I said: 'Well he played the last game against Tassie. That was the only game he played.'

They asked: 'Could it be him that's picked?'

And I said: 'It quite possibly could be.'

Then they said: 'Will you still come in?'

'No,' I said. 'I'm not coming in.'

I knew Dirk [Wellham] had been picked and they told me that David Boon was out, so I said: 'Who else have they picked?' And they said: 'Dirk Wellham and Peter Taylor.'

I thought: 'They haven't picked another opener, well maybe it is me.'

But I wasn't going to go on TV if I wasn't sure. I didn't actually know until Dirk rang me at about 9 a.m.

Extra Cover (Egan) pp347–8

Waugh's Outbreak

When Australia won the 1987 World Cup, the underwriter of its success was twenty-two-year-old all-rounder Steve Waugh. His first sustained success at international level was then validated by two high scoring summers for the English county of Somerset. That's where umpire David Lloyd found him, playing against Surrey and its fearsome fast bowler Sylvester Clarke, and recorded the following dialogue.

'Lovely day ump.'

'Yes, lovely day,' I replied.

Clarke was still bowling.

'You play in our league don't you?' he asked.

'Yes,' I said, 'at Accrington.'

'Good league.'

'Yes,' I said.

Clarke was still bowling.

Then he turned to the cricket.

'Quick wicket, ump,' Steve said.

'Pacey, very pacey,' I replied.

Clarke was still bowling.

'The black guy's sharp,' he said.

'Very,' I replied.

I thought to myself: 'He's very affable and polite for an Aussie, they don't usually pass the time of day with anyone while they're batting.'

At that very point Ian Greig, the Surrey captain, took Silvers off after a very hostile spell lasting about one and a half hours. Steve noticed this and said: 'The black guy is off. He bowled well.'

'Yes,' I said, 'Impressive spell.'

After three overs, Ian Greig had a rethink and shouted to Clarke: 'Silvers, just give me another three from this end.'

On hearing this the true Aussie surfaced in Steve Waugh.

'Jeez, they're bringing that big black bastard back again!' he shouted down the wicket to his partner.

'Now that is more like an Aussie,' I thought.

G'day Ya Pommie B......! (Lloyd) pp111–2

Psychos XI

One of Sydney's most idiosyncratic district clubs, University of NSW, celebrated a recent tradition of eccentric servicemen in 1988 by picking its Psychos XI. Cricket writer Greg Growden profiled a few contenders for selection.

It appears that the club attracts wild pacemen, including one who was infamous for the double appeal. He once hit a batsman's pad plumb in front of the stumps. The bowler gave a full-blooded appeal: 'How's that Umpy?' The appeal was turned down. He turned to the umpire and said: 'Look I'm going to give you one more chance!' He then gave an even louder appeal, only to be turned down again.

Or how about his teammate Fitzy, who used to wear a red T-shirt under his cricket shirt and when bowling undo his buttons to provide an unnerving red background for the ball. Fitz was also renowned for pitching the ball from 26 yards so neither umpire could see if he was chucking or not. There is also a confirmed rumour that another member of the side used to put the ball in the freezer overnight. His theory was that a frozen ball would bounce higher.

There also appears to be a violent streak in UNSW players, with Ratty a leading offender. During a semi-final Ratty once kicked down all three stumps after being given out. During a stormy career where he was regularly reported by umpires all over Sydney, Ratty once flattened the bowler with one punch. He claimed in self-defence that he was just holding up his hand to signal 'no run' to the other batsman.

Then there was Chad Everett who threw his bat at the tea ladies at Bankstown Oval after being dismissed. When asked why, Chad replied: 'Because they were there.'

Despite this rough streak the club atracts a fair share of law abiders including policemen. This includes Starky who came to watch a club game last season and drove his police wagon with sirens blaring onto the ground. Starky is best renowned for being given out to a dubious lbw appeal. Starky looked at the umpire and asked: 'Any particular reason?'

Wisden Cricket Monthly, October 1988 p22

BABS AND SWAMP

Allan Border's Australians played Vivian Richards' world champion West Indian side in the 1988–89 summer and — with its pace arsenal of Curtly Ambrose, Courtney Walsh, Ian Bishop and Patrick Patterson — the First Test at the Gabba proved a stern test of resolve for openers David 'Babs' Boon and Geoff 'Swamp' Marsh.

The night before at the team discussion, Swamp had opened up for one of his terse but stirring speeches: 'We know we're going to get hit, but when we do, we can't let them know we're hurt. We've got to tough it out!'

The next day I opened with Geoff Marsh to Curtly pounding in, bowling at the body, Gus Logie less than a metre away at bat-pad and Roger Harper was around the corner at leg-slip. It was either duck if you could, get caught if you nicked one or get hit.

With Swamp's speech in mind and having to regularly shoulder arms as the ball whistled past my left ear, I copped one high on the ribcage under the left armpit. Luckily the ball didn't drive me back onto my stumps, but it did knock all the air out of my lungs. I stood there with stars in my eyes, trying to remember Marsh's words.

Looking up I saw Swamp walking down the wicket, doing a bit of gardening with his bat and wearing a wry smile.

'What?!' I hissed between clenched teeth.

'It's all right Boonie,' answered my trusty companion. 'You can give it a rub.'

Boon: In the Firing Line (Boon) pp87–8

Before the First Test at Headingley in 1989 — where Australia had been defeated in 1972, 1977, 1981 and 1985 — nerves preyed upon even senior players like Marsh. Boon gave this glimpse of his partner/roommate on the morning before play.

'It was the weirdest thing,' Boonie said. 'It was still early, only about six in the morning I think, and I had this sort of sixth sense about something. I opened an eye and there was Swampy, in his helmet and gloves, with his bat, in the bollocky, and he's practising his forward defence in front of the mirror.'

Ashes Glory (Border) p66

POLISH AND SPIT

Mark Taylor made his maiden Test century, then so did Steve Waugh. For the latter, playing his 27th Test, cracking three figures was a rare ordeal.

Underneath that unflappable demeanour was a turbulent whirlpool of emotions as Waugh crept closer to shaking the monkey off his back. 'I had no saliva. I thought if I don't get it now I'm going to collapse.'

When the moment of truth arrived, the climax was more Python than Hollywood. Waugh said he tried to smack his chewing gum away with his bat in celebration but when it came to the big moment the man who had just flayed the best bowlers in England was not up to the task. 'I spat the chewie out and went to hit it and missed,' he recalled sheepishly. 'It was about the only thing I'd missed after the first couple of balls.'

Waugh Declared (Gateley) p116

THE COST OF VICTORY

Australia won the First Test with surprising ease on the last day but — with the after-effects of celebration still hanging next morning — made heavy weather of a county match against Lancashire at Old Trafford. Stand-in skipper Marsh recalled how slow was the tourists' start.

In the game's second over on a bright crisp English morning, Boonie's fellow Tasmanian Greg Campbell got a hot delivery to lift on the Lancashire opener, the ball taking the top edge of his face-protecting blade. It lobbed gently towards the unsuspecting tired-looking Aussie bat-pad specialist.

Panic set in immediately. All Babs wanted was a good 12 hours sleep and not to be responsible for ending this poor Lancastrian's innings. Boonie tumbled his way forward to at least make an attempt at completing the catch. But when a fielder fails to even make contact with the ball, the batsman is a pretty good chance to survive. He did.

Boon: In the Firing Line (Boon) pp112–3

CHINS OUT

Australia quickly seized the whip hand in the Second Test at Lord's, where they'd not been beaten since 1934, and held a winning position by the fourth day when fast bowlers Terry Alderman, Merv Hughes and Geoff Lawson were presented to the Queen and Duke of Edinburgh. Lawson recalled …

Merv, Clem [Terry Alderman] and I were standing together chatting away as usual when the Duke came up, shook hands with Clem, got to Merv and looked across at me: 'So that's why you chaps bowl so well,' he said.

We all looked at each other wondering what he was talking about. 'You never shave,' he explained. Following a long tradition, we don't shave during a Test and by now were looking fairly untidy, though Merv would look untidy in a dinner suit.

Geoff Lawson's Diary of the Ashes (Lawson) p90

SITTING IN

An early-order batting collapse sent a tremor through the Australian camp on the last day, which condemned the superstitious Border to dwelling in the shower for most of the proceedings.

I stayed in a fair while because I thought, 'I won't go back in the room until we get a bit closer; while I'm out here nobody's getting out.' When I finally dried off and went back into the room Terry Alderman and the blokes ordered me back into the shower. 'Don't change a winning situation,' Terry shouted.

So back into the shower I went. Every now and again Swampy Marsh would stick his head around the door … and say nothing, just look at me deadpan, and I'd think, 'We've lost another wicket.' Then he'd say, 'Twenty to go, skip,' and give me a bit of a cheeky grin.

When I couldn't stand the water any longer I had a shave. Finally they let me back into the room when we needed ten to win.

Ashes Glory (Border) p94

A Ring Of Confidence

A rain-affected draw at Edgbaston was illuminated by a brilliant 157 from Dean Jones, whose pitch patter was as electric as his stroke play.

At one stage, Jones surprised Angus Fraser by yelling at him as another four raced toward the mid-wicket boundary: 'Didn't you go to the team meeting? They would have told you you can't bowl on middle-and-leg to me.' Confidence is a wonderful thing.

Border & Beyond (Ray) p116

'Hit It, Boonie!'

As Australia reclaimed the Ashes by taking an unassailable 3–0 lead in the Fourth Test at Old Trafford, Boon kept his teammates waiting.

Of course Boonie just had to have his bit of fun at our expense! There we were on 77, just one short of the momentous victory, but Boon was playing Nick Cook's slow, flighty spin as if the ball was a hand grenade. I can tell you there were plenty of fidgeting feet, sweaty palms and wringing of hands up on the balcony. We all thought, 'For Christ's sake, Boonie, hit it!'

So when he and 'Tails' Taylor came back in through the dressing room door and the cheering and yahooing died down someone chipped Boonie for taking so long about it. With a sort of half-smile curling round that sergeant-major moustache of his he said, 'I only wanted to make sure I got "red inks"', which is cricket-speak for a batter who likes to see not out against his name in the scorebook.

Ashes Glory (Border) pp12–3

Merv Serves

Merv Hughes' spirited fast bowling was a key component in the Australian triumph, while his volubility became a by-word in cricket circles. Geoff Lawson noted this exchange during Australia's match against Nottinghamshire.

Merv was bowling a fiery spell and followed each delivery with a few comments: 'What sort of fucking shot was that?' and 'The next one will take your fucking head off'.

Just the normal sort of verbal intercourse between intelligent, sensitive cricketers.

This went on for a few overs until, at the end of one over, the umpire went to hand Merv his jumper and with a smile said: 'And that, gentlemen, is the end of another fucking over.'

Geoff Lawson's Diary of the Ashes (Lawson) p146

Hughes didn't get the last word in with Dickie Bird during the Sixth Test at the Oval either where, after bowling three bouncers at Robin Smith, the umpire no-balled him for the last.

AB came flying in from mid-wicket and as I walked past I heard:

AB: 'What's going on, Harold?'

Dickie: 'That's three in a row!'

AB: 'Why didn't you say something to Merv last ball instead of just no-balling him?'

Dickie: 'I did.'

Then I copped the blast from AB.

Steve Waugh's South African Tour Diary (Waugh) p159

Don's Party

The opening of the Bradman Museum was the occasion for a rare public appearance by Sir Donald Bradman, who ruminated on the continuous flood of correspondence he received.

There was one from a lad who said: 'My name is Terry White and I'm 10 years of age and I've admired you ever since I was young.' The next one wasn't quite so pleasant. It said: 'I know this request comes rather late, but I should always regret if it became too late!'

And I also referred to some letters indicating what the future calling of a boy might be. There was a potential insurance agent because the letter said: 'Don't be surprised if you get two letters from me. I posted two in case this one goes astray.'

Then there was the potential PM who finished up: 'PS — Keep this signature, it will be valuable one day.' But somebody must have heard that on air because not so very long afterwards I received a sequel when a chap wrote in similar fashion and said 'PS Don't bother to keep this signature, it will never be worth anything.' That has me stumped, I don't know what his occupation is going to be.

Speech at opening of Bradman Museum, 14 October 1989

SECOND WORLD WAUGH

Steve Waugh's twin brother Mark was by the 1990–91 season already a cricketer of some experience. When only twenty-one, he had acted as a pro for Egerton in the Lancashire leagues.

Waugh's incentive 'payment' was most unusual. His skipper, a dentist, offered to crown two teeth Waugh had knocked out in his teens. Waugh dutifully topped the 1000 run–50 wicket target to score the costly dental work for nothing.

Jim Tucker, *Inside Edge*, July 1993 p67

He had then had two prosperous summers at Essex, being captained by Graham Gooch, but when he was picked to play in the Fourth Test of the 1990–91 Ashes series was mildly perturbed at who he was replacing.

'Congratulations,' he said. 'You're in.'

Finally I asked: 'Who's out?'

Steve replied: 'Me. But I'm just another player.' We sat there stunned for about three minutes. Obviously I'd rather have taken someone else's place but I thought my turn could come in a Test if I kept scoring runs.

Of all the wickets in the world to make your debut on, you'd have to pick Adelaide. I'd played two previous first-class innings there and got 70-odd and 172. I roomed with Merv Hughes and if I had any tension he relieved it and I had a good night's sleep before the Test. Merv is a great fun sort of fellow.

Nobody had time to wish me luck when I went out to bat because everything happened in such a rush. Everyone sits up front in Adelaide with the changing room being low down below. One minute I'm putting on my pads, then Jonesy got out and I was on my way to the crease.

I'll always remember my first scoring shot — a three straight down the ground — second ball from Phil De Freitas. I wasn't nervous to start with. It was one of those days where everything hits the middle of the bat, one of those one-in-a-hundred digs.

Once I got a few runs I forgot what sort of game I was playing in. I just wanted to stabilise the innings and was concentrating so hard I forgot about everything else around me. If there was any niggling I didn't hear it. I just tried to play my shots, play naturally ...

The other stroke I remember was the one with which I reached my hundred. I was 97 and hit Tufnell through the covers for four. Graham Gooch, my captain at Essex, was over like a shot. 'Well done boy,' he said. I felt that deep down he had wanted me to do well, even though he was desperate for a win over Australia.

Bedside Book of Cricket Centuries (Smith) pp158–9

'I Love It When You Talk Dirty'

Mark Waugh's partner when he scored his century was Greg Matthews, who played a string of feisty innings in 1990–91. Craig McDermott, Matthews' partner in a long stand during the Fifth Test at the WACA, provided this account of Matthews' unquenchable spirit.

I remember batting with Greg Matthews in Perth and he and Tufnell got into a bit of a slanging match — they were both pretty good at annoying each other. And Greg had annoyed the shit out of the Poms that year because he had batted really well all that series. Anyway both of us got runs together in Adelaide and we were going well again in Perth and Tufnell was getting more and more frustrated and having a few words with Greg. Telling him he couldn't play and was just blocking — that sort of stuff.

So he's giving Greg plenty of lip and Greg handled it really well. He was going: 'Oh I love it when you talk dirty to me, Phil' and 'You're a fantastic player Phil — I can see why you're in the English team'. Greg just never got upset and I'm cracking myself up at the other end and the England guys were also pissing themselves having a good giggle. Meanwhile the steam's coming out of Tufnell's ears and he's getting tackier and tackier as he tries to tear the shit out of Greg — and Greg would just keep coming back with things like: 'I think you're a great bloke Phil and you're really bowling well.'

Ross Stapleton, *Inside Sport*, June 1993 pp80–2

Bourda Crossing

After retaining the Ashes, Allan Border's side nursed hopes of wresting the Frank Worrell Trophy when it visited the West Indies in 1991. Instead it was beaten 2–1 in one of Test cricket's most violent series, characterised by the dismissal of Dean Jones against Laws 38 (2) and 27 (5) as Australia was defeated at Bourda.

Jones ... had faced six balls in 10 minutes when he was bowled by Walsh for three. A frenetic soul, in one abrupt movement he left his crease, tucked his bat under his arm and, crestfallen, headed for the pavilion. He had not heard Clyde Duncan's call of no-ball nor seen the umpire's arm held wide to signal the illegal delivery.

By the time he had responded to Border's anguished cries to regain his ground, Carl Hooper had emerged with the ball from the gully region, ceremoniously uprooted the stump and led a robust appeal. At square leg Cumberbatch, standing in his eleventh Test in as many seasons, was unaware of the relevant laws or suffered a black-out for he unhesitatingly agreed to the demand ...

It was not until he reached the pavilion for the tea adjournment and examined the laws of the game in a *Wisden Cricketers' Almanack* hurriedly borrowed from the press enclosure, that Border realised Cumberbatch had made a grave error. With cap and *Wisden* in hand, Australian manager Lawrie Sawle approached the acutely-embarrassed officials, but in their hearts the Australians realised the dismissal could not be rescinded.

Caribbean Odyssey (Coward) p96

CAUGHT IN THE CROSSHAIRS

McDermott frequently found himself the subject of target practice for the Caribbean quicks and, by the Fifth Test at Antigua, even partners were chary of his company.

My appearance at the crease was like a red rag to a bull to the West Indian fast bowlers. There had been a few bouncers bowled in the previous period of play, but now bouncers flew thick and fast, not only at me but at Waugh too. If I counted correctly, Curtly Ambrose bowled 15 bouncers in a row over three overs. Mark Waugh came down the wicket and said to me 'Can you please do something to get out so these bastards will stop bowling bumpers'. I think he was only half-joking.

McDermott: Strike Bowler (McDermott) p16

A TEAM PLAYER

Allan Border was always admired as the quintessential 'team player'. When within sight of his first century for three and a half years during the Fourth Test against India at the Adelaide Oval in 1991–92, for instance, he demonstrated to partner Mike Whitney that the collective goals were more material to him than personal ones.

He was on 90 when their spinner, Venkatapathy Raju, came on. In mid-pitch AB said to me: 'We've got this over, and then we're declaring.'

The ensuing conversation went something like this:

Whitney: 'What? You're on 90.'

Border: 'I couldn't give a shit about that.'

Whitney: 'Mate, why not be selfish for just once in your career?'

Border: 'We've got this over, then we're declaring.'

With that, he turned and walked back to his end.

He took a single off the first ball, which left me with the strike. And do you think I could get the bloody thing off the square? In the end I just had a slog, last ball, and holed out to mid-on. And didn't I cop a bagging?

Everyone reckoned I'd just thrown it away when AB was in sight of his first Test century in three seasons. They thought I'd just had an indiscriminate slog. When we reached the dressing-room the sarcasm was dripping. At least half the blokes in the side were making comments along the lines of: 'Oh, nice batting, Whit.'

AB cut the thing dead, silenced the room. 'We were coming off at the end of that over,' he explained. 'Full stop. Get off his back.'

Thank God he said that.

Quick Whit (Whitney) p91

Further demonstration of Border's priorities was provided on the last morning of that Test, when Australia's selectors decided to omit his out-of-form but deeply-admired vice-captain Geoff Marsh. Reacting quickly and explosively, the captain turned first to 12th man Paul Reiffel.

'You'd better get your whites on quickly,' Border called across to Reiffel.

'What?'

'You'd better get your whites on quickly.'

'Why?' asked Reiffel.

'Because I fuckin' said so,' snapped the skipper. 'I'm stayin' in here for a while.'

Border was furious at the dropping of his old mate Marsh and he had decided to ring chairman of selectors Lawrie Sawle to speak his mind. Simpson came over to Border to suggest he lead his team onto the field.

'Fuck off,' Border said.

As Marsh led the team out to start the day's play, Border found Sawle's number and rang him from the dressing-room phone. Sawle was at home in Perth, settling to watch the play on television. He had noticed Border was not on the field and had assumed, like thousands around the country, that the captain was ill.

'As soon as I answered the phone I knew he wasn't crook,' Sawle recalled. 'He gave me a real rocket. I had to be conciliatory, but I had to be firm. He thought I could get the panel to reconsider, which I wasn't prepared to do. I told him it had been a unanimous decision. Eventually, he accepted it but I wouldn't say he burst into laughter.'

Border & Beyond (Ray) pp151–2

FOUR OF A KIND

Mark Waugh had the misfortune to register four consecutive Test match ducks touring Sri Lanka in September 1992. After he had completed the set, Michael Whitney endeavoured to cheer the batsman up by appealing to his punting instincts.

All I could say was: 'Gee I wish I could have got a bit of money on Mark Waugh getting four globes in a row in Test cricket.'

And he looked up, and just the barest grin formed on the corner of his mouth.

'Hell Roy,' he said. 'We could have made a fortune!'

Whiticisms (Whitney) p64

THE GREAT RACE

The other tour misadventure — when the Australians travelled in four motorised rickshaws from the Taj Sumatra to the Hilton for dinner — almost cost the team its captain Allan Border and its new vice-captain Mark Taylor. The latter related.

AB offered our driver an extra 50 rupees if we reached the Hilton first … We'd just taken the lead when we were cut off at the roundabout by a large official car. The driver of our rickshaw swerved to miss the car, locked up the steering, and we flipped over onto our side, before sliding for about 30 metres as sparks flew and our petrol tank ruptured. I ended up as a sandwich between the road and my captain, and we clambered out shaken but none the worse for the experience.

But we hadn't won, and AB refused to pay the fare on the grounds that the driver was unable to complete the journey.

Quite rightly so!

Steve Waugh's South African Tour Diary (Waugh) p158

MAY FLOWERS

Australia held a 1–0 lead against the West Indies at home in their 1992–93 series by the time the teams played the Fourth Test at the Adelaide Oval, and looked favourites for the Worrell Trophy after a brilliant contribution by South Australian Tim May. Renowned for his accidents and his off-spin, he reaffirmed his reputation for the former in the West Indian second innings by contriving to step on his bowling hand at mid-on. But this didn't stop him, as Allan Border recalled, reaffirming his reputation for the latter.

It took a big gash out of the thumb and damaged the bottom joint; as I watched him head off the field for treatment I thought: 'Oh well, that's that. Great!' But he came back. Every now and again I'd give him the ball and ask 'How's it feel?' and after a few spins he said, 'Yeah yeah, they're coming out well.'

He came on and bowled his best-ever spell, 5–9 off about six overs. In the middle of it all he said, 'This is scary AB, they're just coming out so good.'

I looked at him for a couple of seconds, then said, 'Well just keep stepping on your hand'.

Beyond Ten Thousand (Border) p254

May then showed his pluck with the bat, by sharing a last-wicket stand with McDermott that took Australia within two runs of victory. As Allan Border rolled his talismanic 'worry ball' from hand-to-hand, McDermott flicked a ball to leg that seemed certain to clinch the Worrell Trophy.

In the instant it left the bat, it looked like the winning runs. McDermott's teammates, like people all over the country, moved to the edge of their seats until a hand came down and knocked the ball to the ground.

Desmond Haynes, the great opening batsman, had had a wretched summer, his feet and reflexes looking like those of a man well past his prime ... But this time Haynes was in the right spot and he reacted quickly enough to stop McDermott's shot.

Two balls later, McDermott tried to avoid a short ball from Walsh which clipped his helmet and, in [Umpire Darrell] Hair's opinion, his bat on the way past. West Indies had won. In the viewing room, Border jumped to his feet, turned his back on the field and hurled the worry ball into the wooden floor with so much force that it rebounded high enough to hit the ceiling.

Border & Beyond (Ray) p7

EARLY WARNEING

Australia was then defeated at the WACA in the Fifth Test, and again had been thwarted by the West Indies. But Allan Border's team touring England to defend the Ashes in 1993 would be one of the best Australia has sent abroad, enhanced by an astonishingly gifted leg-spinner called Shane Warne.

Warne's route to stardom was circuitous. Grabbed from the obscurity of a brief and insubstantial first-class career, he had made an indifferent start to his Test career in two outings against India. And when in 1992 he had gone to lick his wounds at the AIS Cricket Academy, Warne was counselled by the retired leg-spinner Terry Jenner in no uncertain terms.

'What sacrifices have you made for cricket?' he asked. Warne thought about it, gave an honest answer: none.

'Have you ever had a job?' asked Jenner. Again the answer was no.

'And you've been picked twice to play for your country, basically from your club side,' said Jenner. 'That gets me. Some of us have had to take 150 wickets before we played our first game. It doesn't happen to anyone else but it's happened to you ... cricket's given you the chance to play for Australia and you don't do anything — you still go out and get pissed. You reckon you can still rock up and bowl. How about getting fair dinkum?'

Something sank in.

Warne replaced jugs of beer with jugs of water — even at Merv Hughes' wedding (no mean feat). Though he hated running he'd rise at 7am and hit the streets, working his way to 5km daily every time a little quicker. He'd then move into push-ups, sits-ups and skipping. Then he'd head for the gym for a swim and weight training.

Breakfast was of cereal, no toast. For lunch he'd eat a wholemeal salad sandwich. Dinner was pasta. In three months, Warne shed 14 kilos, going down from 95kgs to 81kgs.

He'd reinvented himself.

Graeme Sims, Inside Sport, July 1993 p 92

HOME THOUGHTS FROM ABROAD

So strong was Border's side that it could omit Dean Jones. Not that he wasn't missed.

On the last Ashes tour, Simmo was hitting fly balls, calling out a player's name and usually thumping the ball well away from him. One of the team's normal practice drills. Up goes the ball. 'Deano,' shouts Simmo. Nobody moves. Up goes the ball again. 'Deano.' And again it plops to the ground. Simmo is looking a bit annoyed when Merv shouts: 'He's not here Simmo. You didn't pick him ... ' Old habits die hard.

Deano — My Call (Jones) p59

THE WAUGH CORE

The series marked the first time that twins Steve and Mark Waugh had imposed themselves on the same series. Their match-winning stand during the Fourth Test at Leeds provided an indication of the subtleties of their simpatico.

The only problem that arose in our partnership was our running between the wickets. We were involved in two mid-wicket collisions — so much for the theory we have ESP!

Having said that, I couldn't believe it when Mark was caught behind square, off Ilott, with 15 minutes to go before stumps. I had a premonition the ball before that he was going to get out that way, which ended a superb innings and a 153-run partnership, our first century stand in Test cricket.

Steve Waugh's Ashes Diary (Waugh) p149

Generally, Michael Whitney has written, the Waughs are renowned for how little they have to do with each other.

One day, after Steve had headed off in one direction and Mark was about to go in another, I said to Mark: 'How come you and Stephen don't hang around together?'

He turned to me and said: 'I lived with him in the same room for 20 years, Big Roy. Why do I want to hang around with him now?'

Whiticisms (Whitney) p20

Where Mark Waugh is an avid punter and disco-goer, Steve seems to prefer more cerebral pursuits. Like the spontaneous game of Trivial Pursuit to which he submitted teammate Brendon Julian when Australia played Warwickshire.

I decided to quiz Brendon Julian about the history of Australian cricket. It proved a topic he would be foolish to choose if ever he was a contestant on Mastermind.

My first question was pretty simple. When I asked him who Stan McCabe was, he replied: 'Isn't he the guy out of Jake and the Fatman?' End of quiz!!

Steve Waugh's Ashes Diary (Waugh) p67

ALLAN BORDER, SUPERSTAR

After a successful Ashes defence, the 1993–94 summer was declared a testimonial season for Border. One incident early in the season, when the Irish rock band U2 held a concert at Brisbane ANZ stadium, bears out the pop star status the veteran enjoyed at the end of his career.

In front of 50 000 fans no less, [U2's lead singer] Bono dialled his oversized telephone just after 10pm to check with AB whether the Brits were indeed responsible for inventing cricket as well as punk rock.

'Who's this?' was Border's chirpy yet bemused answer on the other end.

Bono revealed only that he was his mischievous alter ego Mr MacPhisto and continued the ruse to roars of laughter from the crowd.

'Yeah it was the Poms who invented the game but they've come a gutsa since,' Border added. He puzzled further of the background noise: 'What? You're in a bar somewhere...'

The crowd lapped up every second and Bono needed no second request of the audience when he ordered a song to congratulate Border on his career. With Bono as choirmaster, a crowd big enough to fill the SCG belted out the Stevie Wonder hit 'I Just Called To Say I Love You'.

Inside Edge, January 1994 p42

When a celebratory dinner was held at the Sydney Regent, TV jester Andrew Denton paid moving tribute to the Australian captain.

'Perhaps only a seam in the hands of Sarfraz Nawaz has been picked more often.' And if Border follows the parting advice of Denton, he will be gracing cricket grounds for a while yet. 'Play until you need a runner with a walking frame,' Denton urged. 'AB ... you keep playing until Queensland win the Sheffield Shield. Then, you'll never have to retire.'

Jim Tucker, *Inside Edge*, March 1994 p79

A FEW DAYS WITH MERV

Merv Hughes returned to the Australian side after a back injury when it toured South Africa in February–March 1994. Eyes were on him as he endeavoured to prove his fitness against Orange Free State, and he did not disappoint.

A reporter wanted to know why Merv had bowled 18 overs in three separate spells of six overs (6,6,6), and Merv replied: 'Because Mark Taylor worships the devil.'

Steve Waugh's South African Tour Diary (Waugh) p57

Hughes was padded up and leaning into the press box while a journalist wrote a checklist of grounds around the world at which he had hit a six.

'Chelmsford ... yep. Christchurch ... yep. All the Test grounds in Oz. Southampton ... seven there,' Hughes went on until 25 grounds had been ticked. No guessing what was on Hughes' mind when he went out to bat two minutes later. Even then who would have dreamed of him putting the first ball he faced into orbit beyond long-on as he duly did.

'Make that 26 grounds,' Hughes spruiked with a satisfied grin as he walked off Springbok Park.

Jim Tucker, *Inside Edge*, April 1994 p17

He bowled quite well in the first innings and during the second innings bowled the second ball after lunch to Hansie Cronje. Hansie let it go but Merv keeled over on the wicket — crouching over with this awful look on his face like he's in real pain.

My first reaction was: 'Oh he's done the back in ... he's gone for the tour.' So, as we all ran up to Merv, he straightened up and did a 'bottom explosion' I suppose you'd call it. Then he went: 'Aggh, that's better.' And walked back towards his bowling mark.

Unfortunately it didn't break Hansie's concentration because he was 150 at the time and ended up with 250. So if Merv had planned it, you might say the move backfired.

Ross Stapleton, *Inside Sport*, January 1995 p87

DON, NOT

As the Australians played a tough 1–1 drawn series with South Africa, they approached the tour matches in a more relaxed frame of mind. Their game against Boland elicited a few memorable exchanges.

One of their batsmen was a big fat bloke who blocked absolutely everything. Warnie was throwing them over the moon trying to get him to play a shot, but no way would he be tempted.

Healy finally sings out: 'How about we put a Mars bar on a length? He might come out for that.'

And the batsmen fires back, 'No chance. Boonie would eat it before I had a chance to get down there.'

The players were rolling round laughing and of course the crowd had no idea what was going on.

One of the Boland players broke a finger and when the captain asked if the 12th man could bat we agreed; it was that kind of match. So this kid came in and he was a shocker: hit on the thigh, the fingers, playing and missing by a foot. Afer one particularly gruesome over Paul Reiffel shook his head and said: 'Mate you'd have been better off staying 12th man.'

And the kid walked down the pitch, looked Reiffel straight in the eye and said: 'Who were you expecting, Don Bradman?'

Deano — My Call (Jones) p19

CAPTAIN WHO?

When Mark Taylor succeeded to the captaincy, he was far from the most recognisable Australian cricketer.

A day later when he called into a pub in Glen Innes to meet some of his wife's family, the publican studied him as he ordered two beers.

'Jeez, you look like Mark Taylor,' the publican mused.

Taylor smiled: 'People say that, but I'm better looking aren't I?'
'Yeah, yeah,' smiled the publican and shuffled off.

Jim Tucker, *Inside Edge*, August 1994 p16

The preliminary sabre-rattling before the 1994–95 Ashes series was of statements attributed to England's captain Mike Atherton that Steve Waugh was fearful of fast bowling. Waugh decided to accost the Englishmen to clear the air before the First Test in Brisbane.

I saw him in a bar there — I was going out of my way not to speak to him and he was probably doing the same. I was pretty hurt by what was said so I went up and said: 'I think it's about time this stuff stopped. Let's just forget it and get on with the cricket.'

And he said: 'Good idea. I'm sorry I said those things in the paper and let's start from now.'

It was good that things got sorted out. We went back to square one. He's tough out in the middle; he's got lots of pride. England need more like him.

Graeme Sims, *Inside Sport*, February 1995 p71

The Not-So-Silent Assassin

When Steve Waugh excelled as Australia recaptured the Frank Worrell Trophy with a hard-fought 2–1 victory against Richie Richardson's West Indians in April 1995, he discovered that some do not take so kindly to self-assertion. Here, he describes a tete-a-tete with the West Indies' hostile paceman Curtly Ambrose during the Third Test at Port-of-Spain.

The war between Ambrose and myself almost erupted into a physical confrontation during a tense period in the game. A steepling Ambrose bumper cleared my head by more than a metre, after which he followed through to about two metres away from me and gave me the regulation Clint Eastwood stare. I thought he went on with the silent assassin style interrogation for longer than was necessary, so I came back with: 'What the ---- are you looking at?'

It was at this moment that I realised I had done the equivalent of smashing open an hornet's nest with a large brick. Ambrose began to move closer to me and mouthed the words: 'Don't cuss me man!' His eyeballs were spinning, and as he edged to within a metre of me it seemed he was about to erupt.

At this point I gave him a short but sweet reply that went down about as well as an anti-malaria tablet. Fortunately Richardson moved in swiftly to avert what could have been my death by strangulation, and the game was allowed to continue.

Steve Waugh's West Indies Tour Diary (Waugh) p103

Sources and Acknowledgments

Where my own resources fell short, the Melbourne Cricket Club Library was a boon for this project. Ross Peacock and David Studham ran themselves ragged on my behalf, and showed patience and amusement at all the right stages when I either read them stories or jammed the photocopier.

That fantastic servant of cricket, Pat Mullins, proffered scrapbooks of Tom Horan for my amusement and edification, while the encouragement of David Frith and Malcolm Schmidtke has been critical in whatever I've turned my hand to. My mother, as ever, turned a blind and benign eye to my circumstances as I put the squalor back into scholarship. George Thomas, the best editor a cricket writer could hope for, gave it all his expert treatment.

The editor and publisher thank copyright holders for granting permission to reproduce copyright material.

Allen, David Rayvern, *Arlott: The Authorised Biography*, Harper Collins, London, 1994
Bannister, Jack, *The Innings of My Life*, Headline, London, 1993
Bassano, Brian & Smith, Rick, *Vic's Boys: Australia in South Africa 1935-36*, Apple Books, Tasmania, 1993
Benaud, Richie, *A Tale of Two Tests*, Hodder & Stoughton, London, 1962
Benaud, Richie, *Willow Patterns*, Hodder & Stoughton, London, 1969
Benaud, Richie, *Benaud On Reflection*, Collins, Sydney, 1984
Bird, Dickie, *Not Out*, Arthur Baker Limited, London, 1978
Boon, David, *Boon: In the Firing Line, An Autobiography with A. Mark Thomas*, Pan Macmillan, Sydney, 1993
Booth, Brian C., *Booth to Bat*, Anzea Publishers, Homebush West NSW, 1983
Border, Allan, *Ashes Glory: Allan Border's Own Story*, Swan Publishing, Byron Bay, 1989
Border, Allan, *Allan Border, an Autobiography*, Methuen, Sydney, 1986
Border, Allan, *Beyond Ten Thousand: My Life Story*, Swan Publishing, Nedlands, 1993
Bose, Mihir, *Keith Miller: A Cricketing Biography*, George Allen & Unwin, Sydney, 1979
Bowes, Bill, *Express Deliveries*, The Sportsmans Book Club, London, 1958

Bradman, Don, *Farewell to Cricket*, Theodore Brun Limited, London, 1950

Brayshaw, Ian, *Round the Wicket: A Selection of Cricket Stories*, Methuen Australia, Sydney, 1979

Brayshaw, Ian, *Over the Wicket: Another Selection of Cricket Stories*, Methuen Australia, Sydney, 1980

Brayshaw, Ian, *The Wit of Cricket*, The Currawong Press, Milson's Point, 1981

Brearley, Mike, *Phoenix from the Ashes*, Hodder & Stoughton, London, 1982

Brodribb, Gerald, *Maurice Tate, A Biography*, London Magazine Editions Ltd, London, 1976

Brown, Lionel H., *Victor Trumper and the 1902 Australians*, Secker & Warburg, London, 1981

Butler, Keith, *Howzat!: Sixteen Australian Cricketers talk to Keith Butler*, Collins, Sydney, 1979

Caffyn, William, *Seventy-one Not Out*, William Blackwood and Sons, Edinburgh and London, 1899

Catton, J.A.H., *Wickets and Goals: Stories of Play*, Chapman and Hall, London, 1926

Chappell, Ian & Rigby, Paul, *Long Hops & Larrikins*, Lansdowne, Sydney 1983

Chappell, Ian, *Passing Tests*, Lynton, Coromandel Valley SA, 1973

Chappell, Ian, *Tigers Among the Lions*, Investigator Press, Leabrook SA, 1972

Chappell, Ian, *Chappelli: Ian Chappell's Life Story*, Hutchinson of Australia, Melbourne, 1976

Cheetham, Jack, *Caught by the Springboks*, Hodder & Stoughton, London

Chester, Frank, *How's That!*, Hutchinson, London, 1956

Coleman, Robert, *Seasons in the Sun*, Hargreen, North Melbourne, 1993

Coward, Mike, *Caribbean Odyssey*, Simon & Schuster, Sydney, 1991

Darling, D.K., *Test Tussles On and Off the Field*, published by the author, 482 Sandy Bay Road, Hobart, Tasmania, 1970

Davidson, Alan, *Fifteen Paces*, Souvenir Press, London, 1963

Denness, Mike, *I Declare*, Arthur Baker Limited, London, 1977

Derriman, Philip, *True to the Blue*, Richard Smart Publishing, NSW, 1985

Douglas, Christopher, *Douglas Jardine: Spartan Cricketer*, George Allen & Unwin, London, 1984

Egan, Jack, *Extra Cover*, Pan Books, Sydney, 1989

Favell, Les, *By Hook or By Cut*, Investigator Press, Adelaide, 1970

Ferguson BEM, W.H., *Mr Cricket*, Nicholas Kaye, London, 1957

Fiddian, Marc, *A Life-Long Innings*, Pakenham Gazette, Pakenham, 1995

Fingleton, Jack, *Four Chukkas to Australia*, Heinemann, Melbourne, 1959

Fingleton, Jack, *Masters of Cricket, from Trumper to May*, Heinemann, London, 1958

Fingleton, J.H., *Brown and Company, The Tour in Australia*, Collins, London, 1951

Fingleton, J.H., *Cricket Crisis*, Cassell and Company Ltd, Melbourne, 1946

Fingleton, J.H., *The Greatest Test of All*, Collins, London, 1961

Fingleton, J.H., *The Ashes Crown the Year*, Collins, Sydney, 1954

Fingleton, J.H., *Brightly Fades the Don*, Collins, Sydney, 1949

Foster, Frank R., *Cricketing Memories*, The London Publishing Co. Incorp., London, 1930

Frith, David, *By His Own Hand*, ABC, Sydney, 1990

Frith, David, *My Dear Victorious Stod, a biography of A.E. Stoddart*, David Frith, 1970

Frith, David, *The Fast Men*, Richard Smart Publishing, Kirribilli NSW, 1981

Frith, David, *The Slow Men*, Richard Smart Publishing, Kirribilli NSW, 1984

Frith, David, *Great Test Series 1894-1895*, Richard Smart Publishing, Kirribilli NSW,

Frith, David, *Thommo*, Angus & Robertson, Australia, 1980

Fry, C.B., *Life Worth Living*, Eyre & Spottiswoode, London, 1947

Gately, Mark, *Waugh Declared*, Ironbark Press, Randwick NSW, 1992

Gatting, Mike, *Triumph in Australia*, (Macdonald) Queen Anne Press, London, 1987

Giffen, George, *With Bat and Ball*, Ward, Lock and Co., Melbourne, 1898

Goldman, Arthur, *Cricket Capers*, Afrikaanse Pers-Boekhandel, Johannesburg, 1964

Green, Brigadier M.A., *Sporting Campaigner*, Stanley Paul and Co. Ltd., London, 1956

Grout, Wally, *My Country's 'Keeper*, Pelham Books, London, 1965

Growden, Greg, *A Wayward Genius*, ABC, Sydney, 1991

Hadlee, Walter, *The Innings of a Lifetime*, David Bateman, Auckland, 1993

Haigh, Gideon, *The Border Years*, The Text Publishing Company, Melbourne, 1994

Haigh, Gideon, *The Cricket War*, The Text Publishing Company, Melbourne, 1993

Haigh, Gideon, *One Summer, Every Summer: An Ashes Journal*, The Text Publishing Company, Melbourne, 1995

Hall, Wes, *Pace Like Fire*, Pelham Books, London, 1965

Hammond, Walter R., *Cricket My Destiny*, Stanley Paul & Co. Ltd., London

Hammond, Walter R., *Cricket My World*, Stanley Paul & Co. Ltd., London

Harvey, Neil, *My World of Cricket*, Hodder & Stoughton, London, 1963

Hawke, Neil, *Bowled Over*, Rigby, Australia, 1982

Hookes, David, with Shiell, Alan, *Hookesy*, ABC, Sydney, 1993

Hordern, H.V. *Googlies*, Angus & Robertson, Sydney, 1932

Hutton, Len & Bannister, Alex, *Fifty Years in Cricket*, Stanley Paul (an imprint of the Hutchinson Publishing Group), London, 1984

Jaggard, Ed, *Garth, The Story of Graham McKenzie*, Fremantle Arts Centre Press, Fremantle, 1993

Johnson, Ian, *Cricket at the Crossroads*, Cassell & Company, London, 1957

Jones, Dean, *Deano, My Call*, Swan Publishing, Nedlands, 1994

Larwood, Harold, with Perkins, Kevin, *The Larwood Story*, Penguin Books, Melbourne, 1984

Laver, Frank, *An Australian Cricketer On Tour*, George Bell & Sons, London, 1905

Lawry, Bill, *Run-Digger*, Souvenir Press, London, 1966

Lawson, Geoff, *Henry, The Geoff Lawson Story*, Ironbark Press, Sydney, 1993

Lawson, Geoff, *Diary of the Ashes*, Angus & Robertson Publishers, Sydney, 1990

Lemmon, David, *Johnny Won't Hit Today*, George Allen & Unwin, London, 1983

Lillee, Dennis, *My Life in Cricket*, Methuen, Australia, 1982

Lilley, A.A., *Twenty-Four Years of Cricket*, Mills & Boon, London, 1914

Lindwall, Ray, *Flying Stumps*, Arrow Books, Great Britain, 1957

Lloyd, David, *G'day ya pommie b......! and other cricketing memories*, Weidenfeld & Nicolson, London, 1992

Macartney, C.G., *My Cricketing Days*, William Heinemann Ltd., London, 1930

McCool, Colin, *Cricket is a Game*, Stanley Paul, London, 1961

McDermott, Craig, *McDermott: Strike Bowler*, ABC, Sydney, 1992

McGilvray, Alan, *McGilvray, the game is not the same...*, ABC, Sydney, 1986

McGregor, Adrian, *Greg Chappell: cricket's incomparable artist*, UQP, St Lucia, 1990

McHarg, Jack, *Stan McCabe: the man and his cricket*, Collins, Sydney, 1987

McHarg, Jack, *Arthur Morris: an elegant genius*, ABC, Sydney, 1995

McHarg, Jack, *Bill O'Reilly: a cricketing life*, Millennium, Sydney, 1990

Mackay, Ken, *Slasher Opens Up*, Pelham Books, London, 1964

Mailey, Arthur, *10 for 66 and all that*, Shakespeare Head, London, 1958

Mallett, Ashley, *Clarrie Grimmett: the Bradman of Spin*, UQP, St Lucia, 1993

Mallett, Ashley, *Rowdy*, Lynton, Blackwood SA, 1973

Marsh, Rod, *You'll Keep*, Hutchinson of Australia, Melbourne, 1975

Marsh, Rod, *The Gloves of Irony*, Lansdowne Press, Sydney, 1982

Mason, Ronald, *Warwick Armstrong's Australians*, Epworth Press, London, 1971

Meredith, Anthony, *Summers in Winter*, The Kingswood Press, London, 1990

Meyer, John, *From the Outer*, John Meyer, 75 Daglish Street, Wembley, WA, 1979

Midwinter, Eric, *His Life and Times*, George Allen & Unwin, London, 1981

Miller, Keith & Whitington, R.S., *Catch!*, Latimer House, London, 1951

Miller, Keith & Whitington, R.S., *Keith Miller Companion*, The Sportmans Book Club, London, 1955

Miller, Keith & Whitington, R.S., *Straight Hit*, Latimer House Limited, London, 1952

Miller, Keith & Whitington, R.S., *Gods or Flannelled Fools?*, Macdonald, London, 1954

Miller, Keith & Whitington, R.S., *Cricket Caravan*, Latimer House, London, 1950

Miller, Keith, *Cricket Crossfire*, Oldbourne Press, London, 1956

Monfries I.S.O., J. Elliott, *Not Test Cricket*, Gillingham & Co. Ltd, Adelaide, 1950

Moyes, A.G. ("Johnnie"), *The Changing Face of Cricket*, Angus & Robertson, Sydney, 1963

Moyes, A.G., *Australian Bowlers*, Angus & Robertson, Sydney, 1953

Moyes, A.G., *Bradman*, Angus & Robertson, Sydney, 1948

Mulvaney, D.J., *Cricket Walkabout*, Melbourne University Press, Carlton, 1967

Noble, M.A., *The Game's the Thing*, Cassell and Company, London, 1926

Noble, M.A., *Those "Ashes": The Australian Tour of 1926*, Cassell and Company, London

Oldfield, W.A. 'Bert', *Behind the Wicket*, Hutchinson & Co., London, 1938

Oldfield, W.A., *The Rattle of the Stumps*, George Newnes Limited, London, 1954

O'Neill, Norman, *Ins and Outs*, Pelham Books, London, 1964

O'Reilly, Bill, *'Tiger'*, Collins, Sydney, 1985

O'Reilly, W.J., *Cricket Conquest*, Werner Laurie, London, 1949

Page, Michael, *Bradman: A Biography*, Macmillan, Melbourne, 1988

Philpott, Peter, *A Spinner's Yarn*, ABC, Sydney, 1990

Ray, Mark, *Border and Beyond*, ABC, Sydney, 1995

Redpath, Ian, *Always Reddy*, Garry Sparke & Associates, Toorak, 1976

Richardson, V.Y. & Whitington, R.S., *The Vic Richardson Story*, Rigby Limited, Australia, 1967

Ringwood, John, *Ray Lindwall, Cricket Legend*, Kangaroo Press, Kenthurst NSW, 1995

Robinson, Ray, *On Top Down Under*, Cassell Australia, Sydney, 1981

Robinson, Ray, *Cricket's Fun*, Building Publishing Company, Chippendale,

Robinson, Ray, *From the Boundary*, Collins, Sydney, 1950

Robinson, Ray, *The Wildest Tests*, Cassell Australia, Sydney, 1979

Rosenwater, Irving, *Sir Donald Bradman: A Biography*, B T Batsford Ltd, London, 1978

Simpson, Bobby, *Captain's Story*, Stanley Paul, London, 1966

Sissons, Ric, *The Don Meets the Babe*, J.W. McKenzie, Cambridge, 1995

Smith, E.J., *'Tiger' Smith of Warwickshire and England*, Lutterworth Press, Guildford (Surrey, England), 1981

Smith, Rick & Williams, Ron, *W.G. Down Under: Grace in Australia 1873–74 and 1891–92*, Apple Books, Tasmania, 1994

Smith, Terry, *Bedside Book of Cricket Centuries*, Angus & Robertson, Sydney, 1991

Stackpole, Keith with Trengrove, Alan, *Not Just for Openers*, Stockwell Press, Abbotsford, 1974

Strudwick, Herbert, *Twenty-Five Years Behind the Stumps*, Hutchinson & Co, London, (1958?)

Thomson, A.A., *Odd Men In: A Gallery of Cricket Eccentrics*, Museum Press, London, 1958

Travers, Ben, *94 Declared*, Elm Tree Books, London, 1981

Trumble, Robert, *The Golden Age of Cricket: A Memorial Book of Hugh Trumble*, Robert Trumble, Melbourne, 1968

Turner, C.T.B., *The Quest for Bowlers*, Cornstalk Publishing Company, Sydney, 1926

Valentine, Barry, *Cricket's Dawn that Died: the Australians in England, 1938*, Breedon Books Sport, Derby, 1991

Walker, Max with Phillipson, Neil, *Cricketer at the Crossroads*, Garry Sparke & Associates, Toorak, 1978

Walker, Max with Phillipson, Neil, *Tangles*, Garry Sparke & Associates, Toorak, 1976

Walters, Doug, *One for the Road*, Swan Publishing, Sydney, 1988

Walters, Doug, *The Doug Walters Story*, Rigby, Australia, 1981

Warner, P.F., *My Cricketing Life*, Hodder & Stoughton, London,

Waugh, Steve, *Steve Waugh's West Indies Tour Diary*, Harper Sports, Australia, 1995

Waugh, Steve, *Steve Waugh's South African Tour Diary*, Pan Macmillan, Chippendale, 1994

Wellham, Dirk, *Solid Knocks and Second Thoughts*, Reed, Frenchs Forest NSW, 1988

Whimpress, Bernard & Hart, Nigel, *Test Eleven, Great Ashes Battles*, Wakefield Press, Kent Town SA, 1994

Whimpress, Bernard & Hart, Nigel, *Adelaide Oval Test Cricket 1884-1984*, Wakefield Press and the South Australian Cricket Association, Adelaide, 1984

Whitington, R.S., *Keith Miller, the Golden Nugget*, Rigby, Australia, 1981

Whitington, R.S., *Captains Outrageous? Cricket in the Seventies*, Hutchinson of Australia, Melbourne, 1972

Whitington, R.S., *Fours Galore*, Cassell Australia, Melbourne, 1969

Whitington, R.S. & Hele, George, *Bodyline Umpire*, Rigby, Australia, 1974

Whitington, R.S., *The Quiet Australian: The Lindsay Hassett Story*, Heinemann, Melbourne, 1969

Whitney, Mike, *Quick Whit: The Mike Whitney Story*, Pan Macmillan, Sydney, 1993

Whitney, Mike, *Whiticisms* [etc], Ironbark Press, Sydney

Wright, John, *Christmas in Rarotonga: The John Wright Story*, Moa Publications, Auckland, 1990

Writer, Larry, *Winning, Face to Face with Australian Sporting Legends*, Ironbark Press, Sydney, 1990

Yardley, Norman, *Cricket Campaigns*, Stanley Paul and Co., London

INDEX

A

Adcock, Neil 180
Alcott, Errol 240
Alderman, Terry (Clem) 229, 246–247
Alexander, Gerry 170, 173–174
Alexander, Harry (Bull) 92
Allen, David 176
Allen, George (Gubby) 110
Alston, Rex 132–133
Ambrose, Curtly 244, 251, 260–261
Ames, Les 110
Amiss, Dennis 120, 208
Anderson, Jock 180
Andrews, Tommy 80
Archer, Ken 140, 166
Arlott, John 132–133
Armitage, Tom 6
Armstrong, Warwick 33–34, 43, 45–46, 48, 52, 56, 58, 66–67, 68, 70–71
Arnold, Geoff 210
Arnold, Ted 43
Atherton, Mike 260
Atkinson, Denis 152

B

Badcock, Clayvel (Jack) 97, 111, 114
Bailey, Trevor 128, 163, 227
Bailhache, Robin 225
Baker, Charles 43
Bannerman, Alick 7, 13, 20–21
Bannerman, Charles 5–6, 7–8, 10, 21
Barassi, Ron 205
Bardsley, Warren 44, 50, 68, 69, 77, 78–79
Barnes, Sidney 111–112, 121, 122, 124, 126, 129–130, 133, 139–140, 144–145
Barnes, Sydney 48–9, 53
Barrington, Ken 200
Bates, Barry 166
Beal, Charles 12–13, 16
Bell, Sandy 92
Benaud, John 201–203
Benaud, Richie 143, 147, 154, 155, 160–163, 164, 167, 168–169, 171, 174–175, 177–178, 196
Bennett, Fred 194, 229, 232
Berry, Les 108–109

Bird, Harold (Dickie)   211–212,
    218–219, 248
Birks, Frank   24
Bishop, Ian   244
Black, John   24
Blackham, John   13, 14–16, 17,
    19–20, 23–24, 25–26
Blenkiron, Bill   120
Blundell, Rex   186
Bonnor, George   12–13, 21
Boon, David   235, 242, 244,
    245–246, 259
Booth, Brian   157–158, 178,
    186–187, 189
Border, Allan (AB)   232–233,
    234, 235, 238, 240, 241, 244,
    246–247, 248, 250–251,
    252–253, 253–254, 255, 257,
    258
Borwick, George   97, 123
Bosanquet, Bernard   43, 50
Botham, Ian   228, 230, 239
Bourne, Bill   120
Bowes, Bill   98–99
Boyce, Keith   212
Boycott, Geoff   181, 194,
    218–219, 225
Boyle, Henry   8, 9, 15, 18
Bradman, Donald   72–75, 84–85,
    86, 87, 89, 90, 91, 92, 93, 94,
    95, 98–99, 102, 104–105, 110,
    111, 112–113, 114–115, 116,
    118–119, 123, 124, 125–126,
    127, 128, 132–133, 158, 164,
    168, 170, 238–239, 248–249
Braund, Len   34, 38, 42
Bray, Charles   139
Brearley, Mike   228
Brearley, Walter   68
Briggs, John   18, 25
Bright, Ray   240
Brown, Bill   114, 121, 128,
    137–138

Brown, Edgar   63
Brown, Freddie   138, 148
Burge, Peter   181–182
Burke, Jim   162, 164–165
Burn, Kenny   19, 35
Bush, James   5, 8
Butler, Keith   197, 213

C

Caffyn, William   1, 5
Campbell, Greg   245
Campbell, James   81
Cardus, Neville   104, 113,
    139–140
Carr, Arthur   78–79
Carter, Hanson (Sammy)   53, 58,
    67, 68, 98
Casellas, Ken   230
Chambers, Haddon   11–12
Chapman, Percy   82
Chappell, Ian   184, 192, 194,
    195, 197, 199–200, 203, 206,
    207–208, 213–214, 215,
    216–217, 222
Chappell, Greg   185–186, 196,
    197, 198–199, 208, 212–213,
    214–215, 218–219, 221, 224,
    225, 226–227
Chappell, Trevor   226–227
Charlwood, Henry   6
Cheetham, Jack   142–143
Chester, Frank   102, 115,
    129–130
Chipperfield, Arthur   102
Christy, James   93
Clark, Wayne (Dunny)   222
Clarke, Sylvester   242–243
Clarke, Tom   104
Close, Brian   176
Coetzee, Carl   194
Cole, King   4
Collins, Herbert   60–62, 69, 71,
    77, 97, 126

Compton, Denis   116, 139
Coningham, Arthur   23
Contractor, Nari   168
Conway, John   9
Cook, Nick   247
Cooper, William   17
Corbett, Claude   94, 100
Corling, Grahame   181
Cornell, John   217
Cosgrave, Bryan   71
Cosier, Gary (Jaffa)   222
Cotter, Albert (Tibby)   44,
    45–46, 59–60, 55, 58, 97
Cowper, Bob   189–190
Crafter, Tony   231
Craig, Ian   145, 160–161
Crawford, John   53
Crawford, Pat   156
Crockett, Bob   34, 42–43, 77
Cronin, Peter   226–227
Cronje, Hansie   258
Cumberbatch, Clyde   251
Cussen, Sir Leo   77
Cuzens, Johnny   3

D

Daniel, Wayne   221–222
Darling, Joe   28–29, 30, 32, 36,
    37, 38, 40, 45–46
Davidson, Alan   134–135,
    144–145, 152, 156, 160–161,
    163, 168–169, 176–177, 178
Davies, George   147
De Courcy, Jim   149
De Freitas, Phil   249
Denness, Mike   208–209
Denton, Andrew   258
Depeiza, Clairmonte   152, 154
Desai, Avinish   133–134
Dexter, Ted   163, 177, 179, 182
Dick-a-Dick   2–3
Docker, Cyril   62
Douglas, Johnny   53, 65

Duckworth, George   163
Duff, Reginald   33–4, 36, 40, 45
Dumas, Charley   2
Duncan, Clyde   251
Duperouzel, Gary   221
Dwyer, Edmund (Chappie)   93,
    97
Dyson, John (Dice)   222
Dyson, Will   104

E

Eady, Charles   35–6
Easterbrook, Basil   147–148
Eden, Anthony   145
Edinburgh, Duke of   176,
    200–201, 246
Edrich, Bill   115, 122, 125
Edwards, Bert   147
Egar, Col   165, 173–174,
    179–180
Ejaz Faqih   230
Elizabeth II   200–201, 246
Ellis, Jack   80, 82–83
Eltham, Keith   35
Emery, Sid   59
Evans, Godfrey   151
Evatt, Herbert (Doc)   77

F

Farnes, Ken   110
Favell, Les   154, 156–157, 165,
    184
Ferris, John   18, 20
Fielder, Arthur   48–49
Fingleton, Jack   101, 109, 113,
    115–116, 146
Fitzsimmons, Bob   53
Flavell, Jack   176
Fleetwood-Smith, Leslie (Chuck)
    103–104, 106, 108, 111,
    112–113, 114
Fletcher, Keith   194, 206,
    209–210

Flynn, Pat 237
Forster, Lord 77
Foster, Frank 54–55, 58
Francis, Bruce 200, 206
Frank, Joseph 10–11
Fraser, Angus 247
Fredericks, Roy 211
French, Dick 225
Fry, Charles 46, 58
Fry, Herbert 43

G

Gannon, John (Sam) 222
Garner, Joel 220, 221–222,
    236–237
Gascoigne, Stephen Harold
    (Yabba) 97–98
George V 69, 104
Giffen, George 13–14, 16, 21,
    25–26
Gifford, Norman 181, 200
Gilbert, Dave (Lizard) 241
Gilligan, Arthur 75
Gleeson, John (Cho) 192–193,
    200
Goddard, Tom 88
Gooch, Graham 250
Goodman, Tom 175
Goss, Dick 63
Grace, Dr E. M. 8
Grace, Dr W. G. 4–5, 8–9, 11,
    14–16, 17, 20, 22, 28, 32
Gray, Bob 189–190
Gregory, Dave 6, 8–9
Gregory, Jack 60, 61, 62, 63, 64,
    65, 68–69, 71, 76
Gregory, Syd 25, 27–28, 58
Greig, Ian 243
Greig, Tony 202, 206, 209, 218
Grieve, Bob 63
Grimmett, Clarrie 71–72, 76–77,
    85, 87
Griffith, Charlie 186–187, 191

Grout, Wally 161–162, 169–170,
    173–174, 176, 177, 179–180,
    181, 182, 183, 185
Growden, Greg 243–244
Guha, Subroto 193
Gunn, George 69–70
Gunn, William 28

H

Hair, Darrell 255
Hall, Wesley 169–171, 173
Hammond, Jeff (Bomber) 200,
    204
Hammond, Walter 88, 96, 112,
    122–123
Hampshire, John 196
Hardie, Brian 120
Harper, Roger 244
Harris, David 156–157
Harris, Lord 9
Harry, John 19
Hartigan, Roger 49, 110
Harvey, Neil (Ninna) 131, 137,
    149, 159, 161, 167, 168,
    170–171, 175
Hassett, Lindsay 109, 111, 112,
    114–115, 117, 130–131, 140,
    141, 143–144, 146, 147, 149,
    150
Hawke, Neil (Ghoul) 181, 188,
    189–190
Haynes, Desmond 255
Hayward, Tom 28
Hazlitt, Gerry 48
Healy, Ian 259
Hearne, Jack 53
Hele, George 65, 93
Hendren, Elias (Patsy) 69
Hendry, Hunter (Stork) 70–71,
    80
Hennessy, Frank 223
Higgs, Jim (Glad) 219
Hill, Allen 6

Hill, Clem   34, 38–39, 41, 42–43, 45–46, 49, 55–57, 58
Hill, Eric   141
Hirst, George   42
Hobbs, Jack   53, 64, 76
Hodgetts, Harry   110
Hogg, Rodney   223, 224, 229, 233–234, 236–237
Hole, Graeme   149
Hollies, Eric   132–133
Hooker, Hal   82–84
Hookes, David   218, 220, 226, 236–237, 238
Hooper, Carl   251
Hopkins, Albert   34
Horan, Tom (Felix)   13, 14, 16–17, 27
Hordern, Herbert (Ranji)   49–50, 51, 53, 55
Hornby, Albert (Monkey)   15, 17
Hornibrook, Percy   88
Howarth, Geoff   226
Howell, Harry   65
Howell, William   31, 36–37, 41
Hoy, Col   152, 172
Hubble, Jim   184
Hughes, Kim (Claggie)   217, 227, 228, 229, 233–234
Hughes, Merv   246, 248, 249, 255, 258–259
Hutchings, Ken   49
Hutton, Len   115–116, 128, 132, 138, 150, 151, 152

I

Ikin, Jack   123
Illingworth, Ray   194, 196–197
Inverarity, John   184–186
Iredale, Frank (Nossy)   33, 51, 55–57
Iverson, Jack   137–138, 140

J

Jackson, Archie   84–85, 91
Jackson, Stanley   38
James, Arthur   176
Jardine, Douglas   94, 97, 99, 100, 191
Jarman, Barry   161
Javed Miandad   230, 231
Jeanes, Bill   91
Jeffrey, Selby   73–74
Jenner, Terry   184, 196–197, 214, 255
Jessop, Gilbert   40
Johns, Alf   33
Johnson, Ian   65–66, 109, 121, 124, 136, 140–141, 150, 152, 154, 160
Johnston, Bill   136, 141–142, 151
Jones, Arthur   48
Jones, Barney   236
Jones, Dean   233, 236, 239–241, 247, 249, 256
Jones, Ernie   25, 31–32
Jones, Sammy   14
Jordon, Ray (Slug)   195
Julian, Brendon   257

K

Kallicharran, Alvin   204, 205
Kanhai, Rohan   170
Kelleway, Charles   55, 66
Kelly, Joe   34
Kelsey, Len   73
Killick, Ern   102
King, Frank   154
Kippax, Alan   81, 82–84, 86, 89
Kippins, Cec   188
Kline, Lindsay   165, 167, 169–170
Knight, Donald   68

L

Laird, Bruce 221
Laker, Jim 132, 149, 160
Lamb, Allan 233
Lampard, Allie 79
Lane, William 24
Langton, Chud 107
Lapsley, John 222
Larwood, Harold 82, 85, 91, 98, 99–100, 100–101
Lauder, Harry 108
Laver, Frank 43, 46–7, 53, 55–7
Lawrence, Charles 1, 3–4
Lawry, Bill 165, 175–176, 187, 191, 192, 194, 195
Lawson, Geoff (Henry) 229, 231–232, 233, 238, 246
Lillee, Dennis 195, 196–197, 200–201, 202, 206, 207, 208, 209, 211–212, 213, 216, 224, 225, 226, 228, 229, 231, 237
Lilley, Arthur 34, 38–9, 42
Lillywhite, James 5
Lindsay, Denis 190
Lindwall, Ray 121, 132, 134, 147–148, 151, 163–164, 166, 195
de Lisle, Lord 175
Llewellyn, Buck 51
Lloyd, Clive 211, 220
Lloyd, David 208–210, 242–243
Loader, Peter 162
Lock, Tony 149, 185
Logie, Gus 244
Lohmann, George 22
Long, Ted 61
Loxton, Sam 109, 128, 131, 167
Lucas, Alfred 15, 46–7
Lyttelton, Alfred 15

M

McAlister, Peter 43, 55–7
Macaulay, George 78–79, 86

Macartney, Charles (The Governor-General) 49, 58, 67, 68, 78–79, 81–82, 98
McCabe, Stan 85–86, 90, 96–97, 106–107, 110, 112–113, 115, 257
McCool, Colin 121, 126, 133–134, 136
McCormick, Ern 107–109
McCosker, Rick (Bish) 219
McDermott, Craig 235, 239, 250, 251, 254–255
McDonald, Colin 149, 167, 173, 175
McDonald, Ted 65, 71
McErlane, Dave 196, 221
McFarline, Peter 210
McGilvray, Alan 63–64, 205
McHale, Jock 76
McInnes, Mel 152
Mackay, Ken 157–158, 159, 166, 170, 171–172, 179, 181
McKechnie, Brian 226–227
MacKenzie, Alec 50
McKenzie, Graham (Garth) 176, 201
MacLaren, Archie 38, 40
McLellan, Ross 225
McLeod, Charles (Lightning) 29, 43, 46–7
Maddocks, Dick 175
Mailey, Arthur 64–5, 67, 69, 80–81, 97, 104–105, 139, 158
Mallett, Ashley (Rowdy) 191, 192, 198–199
Malone, Mick 221–222
Mankad, Mulvantari (Vinoo) 118
Mann, Norman (Tufty) 137
Mann, Tony (Rocket) 222, 236
Marks, Lyn 184
Marsh, Geoff (Swampy) 244, 245–246, 252–253

Marsh, Rodney (Bacchus)   194,
   201, 202, 220–221, 224, 225,
   226–227, 228, 229, 231–232,
   233
Marshall, Malcolm   235
Martin, Austin (Bosser)   115
Martin, Johnny (Favourite)   169
Massie, Hugh   16
Matthews, Greg   237, 250
May, Peter   176
May, Tim   254
Mayne, Edgar   71–72
Meckiff, Ian (Count)   162, 163,
   167, 169–170, 179–180
Mendis, Duleep   210–211
Menzies, Robert   101, 145, 150,
   179
Midwinter, William   8–9
Miles, Bruce   187
Miller, Geoff   232
Miller, Keith (Nugget)   116, 117,
   118, 121, 125, 127, 128, 131,
   132, 135, 136, 138, 140–141,
   144, 147–48, 152–153, 153–54,
   155–57, 157–60, 195
Minnett, Roy   53, 55
Morris, Arthur   109, 111, 138,
   140–141, 143–144, 149, 150
Morris, Samuel   18
Moyes, Johnny   94
Mullagh, Johnny   2, 4
Murdoch, William   7, 9, 10–11,
   12, 14, 16, 17

N

Noble, Monty (Mary Ann)   36,
   40, 41, 45, 46–7, 56
Norfolk, Duke of   179
Noriskin, Jack   161
Nourse, Dudley   105, 135
Nupen, Ern   107

O

O'Brien, Leo   110
O'Keeffe, Kerry   203
Oldfield, William (Bert)   61–62,
   66–67, 76, 93, 100–101
O'Neill, Norm   165, 175,
   178–179, 180
O'Reilly, William (Tiger)   72–75,
   92–93, 98, 101, 102–103, 104,
   106, 107–108, 110, 111, 112,
   113, 114, 115, 116, 121, 134

P

Packer, Clyde   94
Packer, Kerry   216–217, 220–221
Palairet, Lionel   38
Palmer, George   13
Park, Dr Roy   65–66
Parker, Charlie   88
Pascoe, Len   218–219, 225, 229
Pataudi, Nawab of   95–96, 97
Paterson, A. B. (Banjo)   9
Patrick, Doug   240
Patterson, Patrick   244
Pawson, Tony (Spike)   130–131
Peacock, Caleb   12
Peate, Ted   13, 15, 21
Peel, Bobby   25
Pegler, Sid   51
Pellew, Clarence (Nip)   61, 66
Pepper, Cec   118–120
Phillips, Wayne (Flipper)
   237–238
Philpott, Peter   155–157, 189,
   227, 229
Pollard, Dick   129–130
Ponsford, Bill   75, 78, 79–80, 86,
   95
Prasanna, Erapalli   193
Price, John   182–183, 200

R

Rackemann, Carl   229, 233–234
Raju, Venkatapathy   252
Ramadhin, Sonny   142
Ranjitsinhji, Prince   29, 31
Ransford, Vernon   43, 58
Read, Maurice   15
Redpath, Ian   183, 191
Reiffel, Paul   252, 259
Renneberg, Dave   190
Rhodes, Harold   180
Rhodes, Wilfred   38, 43
Richards, Viv   211, 244
Richardson, Richie   235,
    260–261
Richardson, Tom   29
Richardson, Vic   86, 89, 91, 96,
    105
Ridings, Phil   138
Ring, Doug   141–142
Rist, Frank   127
Ritchie, Greg   234
Rixon, Steve (Stumper)   222
Roberts, Andy   220–221
Roberts, Ron   141
Robertson, Allen   110
Robertson, Austin   217
Robinson, Gordon   62–63
Robinson, Ray   95
Rorke, Gordon   162, 166
Rowan, Lou   196–197
Rowell, Ted   76
Rumsey, Fred   182
Rushfortz, Alf   105
Russell, Charles   70
Ruth, Babe   93–94
Rutherford, John (Pythagoras)
    158–159
Ryder, Jack   66–67, 75–76, 78,
    80–81

S

Saggers, Ron   128

Santall, Syd   113
Saunders, Jack   39, 48
Sawle, Lawrie   251, 253
Scott, Jack   119
Scott, William   43
Scotton, Bill   19
Seccombe, Don   163
Serjeant, Craig (Bilko)   222
Shaw, Alfred   5–6, 19
Sheahan, Paul (Timbers)   185,
    200, 201
Shepherd, Barry   184–185
Shepherd, William   2
Sheppard, Rev. David   178
Sherwell, Percy   51
Shuja-ud-Din   216
Simpson, Bob (Simmo)   180,
    182–183, 186–188, 190, 222,
    240, 241, 256
Sismey, Stan   116
Slater, Keith   162
Smith, Collie   152
Smith, Edward (Tiger)   52–53,
    55
Smith, Ian   226
Smith, Robin   248
Smith, Syd   55–57
Snow, John   194, 196–197, 213
Sobers, Garry   169, 197
Solomon, Joe   168, 170–171
Spencer, Tom   212
Spofforth, Fred (The Demon)   7,
    8, 11–12, 14–17
Srikkanth, Kris   241
Stackpole, Keith   193, 200, 240
Statham, Brian   151
Steel, Allan   15
Steele, Ray   199, 200–201
Stephenson, Heathfield   1
Stoddart, Andrew   22, 25–7, 29
Stollmeyer, Jeff   142
Storer, Bill   29
Strudwick, Herbert   66
Studd, Charles   15

Sutcliffe, Herbert   78, 87–88, 95, 102

T

Taber, Brian   193
Tallon, Don   132
Tate, Fred   38–39
Tate, Maurice   75, 78, 84, 98
Tavare, Chris   229, 232
Taylor, Johnny   61, 69–70
Taylor, Mark (Tubby)   241–242, 245, 247, 253–254, 258–259, 259–260
Taylor, Peter   241–242
Tennekoon, Anura   210
Tennyson, Hon. Lionel   70
Thomson, Alan (Froggy)   195
Thomson, Jeff (Two-Up)   206, 207, 208, 210, 211–212, 212–213, 215–216, 218–219, 229, 232–233,
Thomson, Nat   7
Titmus, Fred   109, 181
Toohey, Peter (Rats)   222
Toshack, Ern   166
Townsend, Charles   32
Travers, Ben   89
Trimble, Sam   227
Trott, Harry   23, 27–28, 43
Trueman, Fred   148, 179, 182
Trumble, Hugh (Little Eva)   20, 23–24, 26, 30–31, 36–37, 38–39, 46–47
Trumper, Victor   33, 37–38, 42, 45, 50–53, 57, 58
Tufnell, Phil   250
Turner, Alan   212, 215
Turner, Charles (Terror)   18, 20, 23
Twopenny   4
Tyldesley, Ernest   68
Tyson, Frank (Typhoon)   148–149, 151

U

Ulyett, George (Happy Jack)   6–7, 9, 14
Underwood, Derek   196, 206

V

Valentine, Alf   142
Veivers, Tom   182–83
Vincent, Brian   237
Vincent, Cyril   137
Voce, Bill   124
Vox, Bono   257

W

Wade, Herbert   106
Waite, John   161
Waite, Merv   113
Walcott, Clyde   153
Wales, Prince of (Edward VIII)   104–105
Walker, Charlie   88, 91–92
Walker, Max (Tangles)   204–205, 219
Wall, Thomas (Tim)   87–88, 91–92, 102
Walsh, Courtney   244, 251, 254–255
Walters, Cyril   102
Walters, Doug   194, 199, 203, 207–208, 210, 217–218
Wardill, Ben   36–7, 39
Warne, Shane   255–256, 259
Warner, Pelham   43–44, 58, 100
Warr, John   139
Washbrook, Cyril   130
Watkins, John (Wok)   203
Watson, Graeme (Beatle)   189, 200
Waugh, Mark   249–250, 251, 253, 256–257
Waugh, Steve   242–243, 245, 249–250, 257, 260–261
Webb, Syd   174–175

Webster, Rudi   221
Webster, Tom   89
Weekes, Everton   152
Weitemeyer, Ron   165
Wellham, Dirk   230, 239, 242
Weser, Don   226–227
Wettimuny, Sunil   211
Whatmore, Dav   223
White, Stud   44
White, Terry   248
Whitelaw, Arthur   90
Whitington, Richard (Dick)
   127, 195
Whitney, Mike (Big Roy)   229,
   252, 253, 257
Wilkins, Phil   230
Willis, Bob   196, 232–233
Winning, Charles 79

Wood, Graeme   235
Wood, Harry   119
Woodfull, Bill   78, 80, 90, 99,
   100, 105, 191
Worrell, Frank   142, 170, 189
Wren, John   76, 126
Wright, Doug   122
Wright, John   120
Wyatt, Bob   102

Y

Yallop, Graham (Wal)   223,
   236–237
Yardley, Norman   122, 123, 124

Z

Zulch, Jack   71